POLITICAL AND CONSTITUTIONAL IDEAS
OF THE COURT WHIGS

Political and Constitutional Ideas
of the Court Whigs

REED BROWNING

Louisiana State University Press
BATON ROUGE AND LONDON

Designer: Marcy Johnston
Typeface: Goudy
Typesetter: Graphic Composition, Inc.
Printer and binder: Thomson-Shore, Inc.

Library of Congress Cataloging in Publication Data

Browning, Reed.
Political and constitutional ideas of the court Whigs.

Bibliography: p.
Includes index.
1. Whig Party (Great Britain)   2. Great Britain—
Politics and government—1714–1760.   3. Political
science—Great Britain—History.   I. Title.
JN1129.W62B76   324.241'02   81–19372
ISBN 0–8071–0980–0   AACR2

To Susan and Stephen

Contents

Preface

≈

Several years ago John Brewer lamented that the political and constitutional ideas of the office-holding Whigs of the pre-Pitt generation had been "largely neglected by historians in favour of the opposition ideas of Bolingbroke and his compatriots."[1] It must therefore be a source of satisfaction to Professor Brewer that the era of neglect has recently ended. Within the past four years two important studies have begun the exploration of the *terra paene incognita* of Court Whig thought.[2] J. P. Kenyon's tightly focused work illuminated the difficulties the first generation of postrevolutionary Whigs (and Tories) experienced in arriving at an adequate interpretation of the events of 1688. H. T. Dickinson's more extended canvass of the eighteenth century follows Whig (and Tory and radical) thought from the exuberant era of William III to the challenging years of the French Revolution. From an examination of these splendid works we now know far more than we once did of Court Whiggery. And yet we do not know enough—nor do we have the subject quite right. Kenyon argues that the "Modern Whigs"—the precursors of the Court Whigs of Walpole's day—had by 1720 deliberately abandoned all but one of the varied interpretations of the Glorious Revolution that had emerged in the decade after William's and Mary's accession. Dickinson describes a Court Whiggery that in the 1730s and 1740s was astringently monolithic in its argumentation. Nowhere in either study can we discover the richness and diversity of Court Whig constitutional philosophy in the era of Walpole and the Pelhams—nowhere the variegated character

1. John Brewer, *Party Ideology and Popular Politics at the Accession of George III* (Cambridge, 1976), 24.
2. J. P. Kenyon, *Revolution Principles: The Politics of Party 1689–1720* (Cambridge, 1977); H. T. Dickinson, *Liberty and Property: Political Ideology in Eighteenth-Century Britain* (London, 1977).

of the polemical stances adopted by Court Whig advocates. And nowhere do we get even an inkling of the importance that the figure of
Cicero exercised in Court Whig apologetics. For these two reasons
then—their sacrificing of awkward diversity to misleading simplicity
and their neglect of the Ciceronian impact—I judge the recent works
less than adequate for our understanding of office-holding Whiggery in
the years between 1720 and 1755. I thus offer the present study as a
more accurate analysis of the nature of Court Whig thought.

In the first chapter I provide the context within which Court Whig
thought must be understood. Much of the chapter recapitulates material that will be familiar to anyone who regularly attends to the literature on eighteenth-century political and constitutional thought. The
chapter contains, however, several assertions that may strike some
readers as startling. I believe that by the end of the book those readers
will understand that substantial grounds exist for making such assertions. The next five chapters examine in turn the relevant ideas of five
representative Court Whigs—Lord Hervey, Benjamin Hoadly, Thomas
Herring, Samuel Squire, and Lord Hardwicke.[3] What is most striking
about these men is that they chose five different ways to defend the
Walpole and Pelham ministries, and a consideration of the diversity of
their ideas should lay to rest all monolithic interpretations of Court
Whiggery. I may seem in some instances to be seeking to restore repu-
tations. I regard that opinion as accurate: among other tasks I hope
through this study to wipe off a bit of the mud that hostile historians
have rather indiscriminately thrown at these figures. The seventh
chapter examines the writings of a large band of Court Whig pamphleteers and is intended to present a structured synthesis of Court Whiggery. It aims, in fact, at providing a kind of model of Court Whig
orthodoxy as it pertains to the constitution and politics. The last chapter—the capstone of the study—presents a new interpretation of political debate in the era of Walpole and the Pelhams. It argues for the
controlling importance of Roman models, suggests the inadequacies of

---

3. Lest any reader suspect that I harbor some peculiar affection for the eighth letter
of the alphabet, I must immediately note that the suspicion will only be reinforced by
the frequent appearances in the text of the names of James Harrington, Thomas Hobbes,
Richard Hooker, and David Hume.

recently published views of Court Whiggery, gives new rationale for the choice of the five figures treated in Chapters II through VI, and, by the final page, shows Court Whiggery to be a political-constitutional doctrine that is accurately denominated "Ciceronian."

My research in the United Kingdom was made possible by a grant from the American Council of Learned Societies and assistance from my mother, Mrs. Arthur M. Browning. Research in this country was aided by support from Kenyon College. Mr. and Mrs. W. L. Lampley typed much of the manuscript. I am grateful to all of these benefactors. I also wish publicly to thank two friends, Daniel Clift and Harry Clor, for reading and advising on parts of the manuscript. The endnotes suggest how wide-ranging my intellectual indebtedness is.

POLITICAL AND CONSTITUTIONAL IDEAS
OF THE COURT WHIGS

Chapter I

The Catonic Perspective

I

In 1713, with party conflict between Whigs and Tories at its most intense, Joseph Addison's tragedy *Cato* opened at Drury Lane. Most of the work had been written a decade earlier, and it is therefore unlikely that the author composed it as a deliberately partisan statement.[1] But whatever his intent—which may indeed have changed—his drama became an immediate political sensation, arousing an outpouring of comment that was not to be rivaled until *The Beggar's Opera* delighted or enraged partisan spectators in 1728.

Britain in the final years of Anne's reign was politically riven. Tories commanded the government and worked steadily, albeit discordantly, to undo much that governments of the previous decade had enacted or allowed. Above all, the Tories moved to end the war with France. It was expensive, and in light of the death of the Emperor Leopold it seemed pointless as well. They struck out at the Protestant dissenters of the kingdom, who usually supported the Whigs, by prohibiting the practice of occasional conformity and preparing to pass a measure that would close dissenting academies. They struck against rootless parliamentarians—most commonly commercial in calling and Whiggish in politics—by enacting stiff property qualifications for membership in the Commons. In all this the Tories were energized by a deep fear that

1. For the case that Addison's purpose was moral (not political) and his concerns dramatic, see Malcolm Kelsall, "The Meaning of Addison's *Cato*," *Review of English Studies*, n.s., XVII (1966), 149–62.

Britain was becoming pluralistic and fragmented—that it was sacrificing the cohesion of a traditional society for an atomicity that could
only be ruinous to both the kingdom and its inhabitants.

The Whig opposition resisted many of these actions. Whigs contended that Britain would not be safe until Bourbon power had been
totally humbled, and they were inclined not merely to tolerate dissenters but even to allow easing of naturalization procedures to promote
Protestant diversity, and consequently Protestant strength. Above all,
with Anne's reign manifestly drawing to a close, the Whigs feared that
the Tories—or at least a sizable segment of them—were prepared to
support a restoration of the house of Stuart in preference to the legally
prescribed accession of the foreign house of Hanover. Each party believed the kingdom to be in an hour of crisis and saw itself as the only
defender of national liberty. Into this highly charged atmosphere Addison introduced a stirring and fervent personification of patriotism
and love of freedom.

Cato of Utica, about whose final days Addison wrote his drama, was
one of the most fascinating and inspiring figures of late-republican
Rome.[2] The great grandson of Cato the Censor and related to the Livii
Drusi, he was of a family long distinguished for its devotion to Roman
independence and the old constitution. This family tradition he took
deeply to heart. He read the Stoics, adopted their views, and tried to
put into practice their belief that only by virtue could one know happiness. And he was remarkably successful in his effort to make virtue
the guide of his life. He became a byword for self-control, for bravery,
for absolute integrity, and for a steadfast devotion to the liberties and
greatness of Rome. He aligned himself with the *optimates*, the party
that advocated the restoration of full senatorial authority within the
balanced republican form of government; therefore he favored either a
restoration of the pre-Gracchan constitution or a revitalization of the
Sullan constitution. On the occasion of the Catilinarian plot Cato

2. Cato of Utica (95–46 B.C.) is not to be confused with Cato the Censor (234–149
B.C.). Both were patriots, and it was the Censor who transfixed the Roman Senate with
his chilling reiteration of "Carthago delenda est." The two men, each a celebrated exemplar of traditional virtue, were often confused or merged in the mind of the eighteenth
century, and the compound was potent. It suggested a mighty and virtuous patriot, as
fervently opposed to Carthaginian threats abroad as to Caesarian ambitions at home.

urged stern and swift punishment for the conspirators. He acquired further celebrity as one who resisted the authoritarian schemes of Julius Caesar. He resisted also the efforts of any who would have extended the role and influence of the popular elements within the state. Ultimately, after Caesar's triumph at Pharsalus gave the victor a free hand in dealing with Rome, Cato withdrew to Utica in North Africa and established among the exiles there a "true" Roman senate. But when he realized that his comrades in opposition did not share his readiness to remain forever as a standing rebuke to Caesar's pretensions—when he saw that he was steel whereas they were brass—he accepted this hard truth with Stoic self-command. He recommended that they make their peace with the usurper, and then, in full awareness of what he was doing, he took his own life. A long line of Roman writers thereafter hailed him as the quintessential Stoic. The Cato drawn by such diverse authors as Horace, Virgil, Livy, Sallust, Lucan, and, most influentially, by Plutarch is invariably devoted to truth and his country, stern in his expectations of himself, unflinching in the face of power or death. He had become the symbol of liberty and true patriotism.

Addison's *Cato* glorified this hero in rolling pentameters.[3] The protagonist was a man of virtue, wherefore Juba urged his listeners to

> turn up thy eyes to Cato!
> There may'st thou see to what a godlike height
> The Roman virtues lift up mortal man.
>
> (I, iv, 49–51)

And Cato presented himself as a model: "Dost thou love watchings, abstinence, and toil, / Laborious virtues all? Learn them from *Cato*" (II, iv, 64–65). A dissolute era needed strict treatment, and Cato was not reluctant to declare this truth.

> Lucius, this base degenerate age requires
> Severity, and justice in its rigour;
> This awes an impious, bold, offending world,
> Commands obedience, and gives force to
>   laws.
>
> (III, v, 66–69)

Dissoluteness was particularly fearful because it portended an unwill-

---

3. Joseph Addison, *Cato, a Tragedy* (London, 1713).

ingness to contend for liberty—and yet liberty was ever in danger. "It is not now a time to talk of aught / But chains, or conquests; liberty, or death" (II, iv, 88–89).[4] And when it became clear that the spirits of his confederates were too enfeebled to allow successful resistance, he elected to die rather than submit.

> Lucius, the torrent bears too hard upon me:
> Justice gives way to force: the conquer'd world
> Is *Caesar's*: *Cato* has no business in it.
>   (IV, iv, 25–27)

But in that death there was a lesson:

> How beautiful is death, when earn'd by virtue!
> ....
> Portius, behold thy brother and remember
> Thy life is not thy own, when *Rome* demands it.
>   (IV, iv, 90, 96–97)

In the hero's life there had also been a moral; as he himself said when addressing the senate: "in *Cato's* judgment, / A day, an hour of virtuous liberty, / Is worth a whole eternity in bondage" (II, i, 99–101).

This ringing call for liberty resonated in British hearts. Although Addison was a Whig, it was not surprising that both parties staked a claim to *Cato*. Laurence Eusden explained the lesson all drew from the tragedy:

> 'Tis nobly done to thus enrich the stage,
> And raise the thoughts of a degenerate age,
> To show how endless joys from freedom spring:
> How life in bondage is a worthless thing.

With Whig and Tory each fearful that the other meant to destroy British liberty, these were heady sentiments. If the embattled Roman patriot seemed to some Whiggish viewers a Marlborough, he struck Tory spectators as an indictment of the celebrated duke and his Whig followers.[5] Sitting on opposite sides of the theatre, Whigs and Tories vied

4. Patrick Henry was Catonic in his view of the world. So were many other American leaders in the 1760s and 1770s. See Bernard Bailyn, *The Ideological Origins of the American Revolution* (Cambridge, Mass., 1967).

5. Eusden's explanation was printed with Addison's *Cato; Mr. Addison turn'd Tory: or, The Scene Inverted* (London, 1713).

with each other in bestowing applause upon heart-stirring apostrophes
to freedom. The Tory leader, Lord Bolingbroke, conferred fifty guineas
upon Barton Booth, the actor who played Cato, as a reward for his
services to liberty. The Whig managers of the theatre duplicated this
generosity. Each gift was meant to be a symbolic act of appropriation
by the respective partisan donors.[6] Pamphlets explicating the drama or
interpreting the historical personage upon whom it was based promptly
appeared. An anonymous critic commended the play, viewing Cato as
a man who, in an age of vice, conspiracy, and hypocrisy, acted upon
"the Principles of Honour and Justice, neither aw'd nor seduc'd by Parties, with the truest Notions of the ancient Republic Form, and a
hearty Zeal for it, publickly opposing both its disguis'd and open Enemies." Richard Steele drafted an essay that emphasized Cato's insistence on the reality, not just the appearance, of virtue; Steele's Roman
was a man who knew that the virtuous life was the arduous life of rigors
and self-denial. But the fullest treatment appeared from the pen of
Lewis Theobald. Avowedly designed for readers and viewers of Addison's drama, *The Life and Character of Marcus Portius Cato Uticensis*
opened with an apposite quotation—"Quid ergo Libertas sine Catone?
Non magis quàm Cato sine Libertate"—and closed with Montaigne's
translated judgment of Cato: "he was in truth the Pattern, which Nature chose out to shew to what Height Human Virtue and Constancy
could arrive." Between these encomia Theobald compressed a biography written with the intent of accentuating "the signal Probity of his
Life, and Glory of his Death."[7] Cato had become the model for every
Briton, of whatever party, who loved both freedom and his country.

   Thus it was that those who addressed the public on affairs of state in
the succeeding years sought to identify themselves with Cato. The Roman had set a pattern for the virtuous and patriotic life; his self-desig-
nated disciples wished to have themselves seen as conforming to it. He

   6. See John Loftis, *The Politics of Drama in Augustan England* (Oxford, 1963), especially 56–62, for a fuller account of the reception of the play. See too Colley Cibber, *An
Apology for the Life of Colley Cibber*, ed. B. R. S. Fone (Ann Arbor, Mich., 1965), 196.
   7. *Observations upon Cato, a Tragedy* (London, 1713); [Richard Steele], *A Comparison
between Cato and Caesar* (London, 1713); Lewis Theobald, *The Life and Character of
Marcus Portius Cato Uticensis* (London, 1713). The Latin quotation is from Valerius Max-
imus.

had been a martyr to liberty; his followers, though hoping to avoid his end, sought to share in the praise of his steadfastness. "Cato" became the nom de plume of writers who meant to suggest, through that adoption, that they too spoke from a spirit of disinterested patriotism. The most famous of these latter-day Catos was really two men, John Trenchard and Thomas Gordon. Together they wrote *Cato's Letters*, a series of weekly essays that assailed the Walpole government of the early 1720s and, by advancing "general Reasonings about public Virtue and Corruption," called upon Britons to understand "the Principles of Liberty and Power." "By Liberty," Cato explained, "I understand the power which every Man has over his own Actions, and his Right to enjoy the Fruits of his Labour, Art, and Industry, as far as by it he hurts not the Society, or any Members of it, by taking from any Member, or by hindering him from enjoying what he himself enjoys." In the powerful twenty-fifth letter Cato evaluated "the inestimable Blessing of Liberty. Can we ever over-rate it, or be too jealous of a Treasure which includes in it almost all human Felicities? Or can we encourage too much, those that contend for it, and those that promote it? It is the Parent of Virtue, Pleasure, Plenty, and Security; and 'tis innocent as well as lovely." But liberty stood in danger. "Publick Corruptions and Abuses have grown upon us." Government had fallen under the care of "common Rogues." So desperate was Britain's plight that Cato was moved to imprecation. "Oh Liberty! Stop thy Flight. Oh Virtue! be something more than a Name and empty Sound. Return, oh return!" But return was not enough. A stern task lay ahead. "We must begin by letting out some of our adulterate and corrupt Blood. . . . We must first take full Vengeance of all those whom we can discover to be guilty." Thus Cato applauded Brutus' slaying of Caesar, a deed proclaiming that Brutus "preferred the Liberty of the World, to the Empire of the World."[8] Liberty, in brief, was Cato's cause. And just as the Roman Cato had committed his life to its service, so now was the British Cato submitting to the same vocation.

A cult of Cato was meanwhile emerging among men of letters. Jon-

---

8. Thomas Gordon and John Trenchard, *Cato's Letters; or, Essays on Liberty, Civil and Religious, and other important Subjects* (2 vols.; 1733; New York, 1969), I, xxiv–xxv; II, 244; I, 191, 140–41, 142; II, 182.

athan Swift developed what one scholar has called a "Catonic fixation" and, in *Gulliver's Travels*, linked the Roman with Brutus, Junius, Socrates, Epaminondas, and Sir Thomas More as a "Sextumvirate, to which all Ages of the World cannot add a Seventh." Lucan's *Pharsalia* represented the most extravagant of classical celebrations of Cato, and Nicholas Rowe translated the work into English just before his death in 1718. It appeared in print three years later. In 1727 James Thomson published *Summer* and through its verse proclaimed:

> Yet here, even here, into these black abodes
> Of monsters, unappalled, from stooping Rome
> And guilty Caesar, Liberty retired,
> Her Cato following through Numidian wilds—

Soon thereafter Samuel Boyse found the ultimate encomium for his heroine Sophonisba by denominating her "a female Cato." Even when offstage Cato could serve as symbol of righteousness. In Colley Cibber's *Caesar in Egypt*, produced in 1725, Cato's unseen but brooding presence provided the context of moral judgment by which the man of action whom Cibber glorified was to be measured. So prominent was the Roman patriot in the dramas of the era that Dr. John Arbuthnot was moved to ask: "What is become of the Scipio's and Cato's of Rome? They sing now on the English stage." References of this sort give substance to the recent assertion that among early eighteenth-century Britons a "Cato complex" had become an "obsession."[9]

With Cato so popular—or rather, with the invocation of Cato's prestige so prominent—it was but natural that spokesmen for the government would also try to bask in his reflected glory. As early as 1716 Cato was made an advocate for the Whig ministry. With the Jacobite uprising still aflame, Jonathon Smedley, chaplain to the Whig minister Lord Sunderland, implored his auditors to fight for their liberty. Cato and

9. James William Johnson, *The Formation of English Neo-Classical Thought* (Princeton, N.J., 1967), 63, 100–102; A. D. McKillop, *The Background of Thomson's "Liberty"* (Houston, 1951), 10; James Thomson, *Summer*, lines 951–54; Colley Cibber, *Caesar in Egypt* (London, 1725), act II, sc. i, act III, sc. iii; Jonathon Swift, *Gulliver's Travels*, Pt. 3, Chap. 4; M. M. Goldsmith, "Public Virtue and Private Vices: Bernard Mandeville and English Political Ideologies in the Early Eighteenth Century," *Eighteenth-Century Studies*, IX (1976), 489.

Caesar he likened to William III and James II or to Themistocles and Alexander. They were, that is, respectively the fathers and the spoilers of their nations. The ministerial press in 1722 recalled how Cato had supported recourse to extraordinary measures when the state found itself in great peril; the author inferred from this example that the Roman would endorse the present suspension of habeas corpus. Two works in 1723 represented Cato as a supporter of Walpole's effort to implicate Bishop Atterbury, notorious for his opposition to the Hanoverian succession, in a plot against the throne. One work detailed Cato's criticisms of Atterbury's self-exculpatory speech: the address, said this Cato, had been irrelevant, slippery, and finally ineffective. The other argued that the extralegal measures taken to punish the directors of the South Sea Company would be equally appropriate against the treasonable bishop of Rochester: the first principles of justice mandated recourse to extraordinary measures where the positive law was deficient. In later years, too, proministerial writers invoked the name of the great Roman patriot. An election broadside from 1734 cited Cato as a man who, like the British ministers, knew and spoke the truth. A pamphlet from as late as 1740 compared the ministers to Cato and the opposition to Marius.[10]

It has long been realized that in the first half of the eighteenth century Britain was peculiarly enchanted with Roman motifs, usages, and models. That the British mimetic effort failed fully to simulate the style of the Romans is scarcely surprising—and also beside the point. What matters is that in such diverse fields as poetry and architecture, historical studies and letter writing, Roman models exemplified what people believed ought to be done; where exact duplication was impossible, the capture of an authentic Roman spirit still seemed attainable. Britons of that time often saw themselves as latter-day Romans: like their predecessors, they too had an expanded role in the world, they too commanded a mighty empire, they too lived in liberty, and their civiliza-

10. Jonathon Smedley, A Discourse Concerning the Love of Our Country (London, 1716); London Journal, November 10, 1722; Cato's Dream (Dublin, 1723); Cato's Letter to the Bishop of Rochester (London, 1723); A Serious Address to the Freeholders of Great Britain (London, 1734); A Letter to a Member of Parliament. Concerning the Present State of Affairs at Home and Abroad (London, 1740).

tion bid fair to sweep Europe before it. From such a perspective it was only natural that Britons should also seek guidance from the Romans in matters political. And because they had reframed their government on a more popular basis in 1688–1689—because more particularly they had created an order in which many could participate, although rank retained its deep significance—they turned to the republic rather than the empire for their exemplars.[11] Republican Rome was marked by struggles between would-be despots and defenders of liberty, by vigorous factional contention, and by a class structure that, without excessive distortion, could be made to appear like Britain's. From the republic Britons professed to learn the absolute necessity of having good men participate in public life. Direction of public affairs was neither a sordid enterprise nor an activity best avoided by sober men concerned with the fundamental human questions. On the contrary, only by entering into the public life of a nation—as Brutus, Cicero, Catullus, Cassius, and Cato had done—could the good man live a truly good life. Of these several heroes, the one who had most zealously pursued liberty, even at the deliberate cost of his life, was Cato. In this critical hour for Britain, with liberty under assault and traitors at the gates, it was therefore Cato who best represented what the good Briton should seek to be.

And just what did Britons believe Cato had taught? His heritage—the heritage that informed the Catonic[12] perspective by which many Britons in these years viewed their world—was threefold. He taught first of all that liberty was the highest good. For liberty he had given his life, and such was the value of liberty that no one could regard the decision a pointless sacrifice. He also taught that the highest calling a

11. Much of the discussion about the implications of the adjective "Augustan" as a description for the age ignores the point that, in politics at least, *no one* thought that Britain should be Augustan. Augustus had completed the destruction of the republic. See James William Johnson, "The Meaning of Augustan," *Journal of the History of Ideas*, XIX (1958), 507–22.

12. The adjective "Catonic" was known in the early eighteenth century. In *Cato's Principles of Self-Preservation and Publick Liberty* (London, 1722), 6, "the Gray Hairs of old Heresies and Seditions of *Buchanan or Hobs*, new vampt up in *Bangorian* or *Catonick* Style" were denounced. Bailyn, in *Ideological Origins*, 44, has also used it to identify a view of politics in this era.

man could obey was service to his country. The true patriot bore the heavy responsibility of ever striving to do well by his country and must, moreover, be prepared to die for it. To these two overlapping substantive purposes Cato yoked an appropriate attitude. The good citizen, he taught, ever harbored a deep suspicion of those in authority. Men in power were apt to use it for their own ends rather than the nation's; they were tempted to confine the liberties of others to make their own lives and careers easier. The notion that eternal vigilance constitutes the price of liberty is thoroughly Catonic, but in the formulation that would have won widest assent in the early eighteenth century it would have been expanded to specify that eternal vigilance was both the stance of the patriot and the price of liberty. To a people steeped in Roman lore, struggling to make government by consent work and powerfully persuaded that a crisis of liberty was at hand, Cato was the perfect symbol.[13]

II

From 1721 to 1756 administrations that may be styled "Court Whig" commanded British affairs. In so denominating them I am not using a term that was widely current in their day.[14] To their friends they were simply "Whigs." To their opponents they were the "Court." Yet the inclusive term, yoking together the two political designations that controlled much of the political thought of the era, is easily comprehensible. The use of "Whig" identifies a partisan attachment. Most politicians of the early eighteenth century were either Whigs or Tories, and although both terms lost much of their clarity of meaning as the reigns of George I and then George II progressed and political conditions

13. For a rich and informative assessment of Cato's influence that emphasizes private rather than public morality, and literary rather than political orientation, see Johnson, *Formation of English Neo-Classical Thought,* 95–105.

14. It is assuredly not a neologism. The *Craftsman* spoke of the "Court-Whigs," as cited in Paul Langford, *The Excise Crisis: Society and Politics in the Age of Walpole* (Oxford, 1975), 13. The London *Journal* employed the phrase in three consecutive issues (13, 20, and 27 October, 1733). The term has also found its way into several secondary studies: see Archibald S. Foord, *His Majesty's Opposition, 1714–1830* (Oxford, 1964), 24; J. G. A. Pocock, *The Machiavellian Moment: Florentine Political Thought and the Atlantic Republican Tradition* (Princeton, N.J., 1975), 459; Brewer, *Party Ideology,* 4, 135.

changed, they retained until midcentury the core associations that distinguished them from each other. To be a Whig was to approve wholeheartedly of the Glorious Revolution, to accept the legitimacy of Protestant dissent, and to support the house of Hanover. Tories might also adhere to these principles, but with at least traces of reserve, for their image of a unitary state with a strong government was an unstable base for such ideas. The use of "Court," on the other hand, identifies an attitude toward government rather than a partisan affiliation. The antithesis to "Court" was "Country," and those who shared the "Court" perspective were in general more inclined than those of a "Country" disposition to see convenience pure and simple as a legitimate ground for approving of certain administrative procedures, and to doubt the helpfulness of excessively abstract constitutional models. The "Country" member, of course, sought neither to obstruct the process of government nor to submit all political practice to the strangling yoke of constitutional theory. But he was quicker than a "Court" member to draw the line of marking off what was impermissible and readier to argue that constitutional theory ought to be regarded as prescriptive. It follows, then, that a "Court Whig" was a self-declared Whig who, holding power or supporting those who did, wanted government to proceed easily and smoothly, unencumbered by what he might regard as silly or wasteful or even harmful strictures.[15]

Three chief ministers superintended the Court Whig administrations of this era. Robert Walpole came to the treasury in 1721 and held his

15. The Court-Country division has been examined for earlier periods by Perez Zagorin, *The Court and the Country: The Beginning of the English Revolution* (New York, 1969), and Dennis Rubini, *Court and Country, 1688–1702* (London, 1968). In a useful article by B. W. Hill, "Executive Monarchy and the Challenge of Parties, 1689–1832: Two Concepts of Government and Two Historiographical Interpretations," *Historical Journal*, XIII (1970), 379–401, the interplay of two noncongruent antitheses—Whig vs. Tory and Court vs. Country—is explored. The relative importance of the two antitheses is much debated. Hill's recent book, for example, *The Growth of Parliamentary Parties, 1689–1742* (London, 1976), traces the parliamentary course of the Whig-Tory antithesis. J. C. D. Clark, "The Decline of Party, 1740–1760," *English Historical Review*, XCIII (1978), 499–527, maintains that Whigs and Tories were the significant entities in politics until the mid-1750s. Dickinson, *Liberty and Property*, on the other hand, asserts that in the years between 1720 and 1760 it was the Court-Country antithesis, not the Whig-Tory one, that dominated political life.

office until 1742, when mounting popular disenchantment forced his resignation. During this tenure he molded a body of followers who, as the "Old Corps," would supply the parliamentary armies deployed by his two successors, the Pelham brothers. Henry Pelham succeeded to the treasury in 1743 after a brief and confused hiatus, and he remained as first lord until his death in 1754. Less implacable than his mentor, Pelham replaced Walpole's politics of proscription with his own easier politics of comprehension. He also abandoned Walpole's insistence on determining all matters personally, preferring to work through a triumvirate composed of himself, his brother, and their friend Lord Hardwicke. It was the brother Thomas Pelham-Holles, Duke of Newcastle, who succeeded to the treasury in 1754. For the next two-and-a-half years Newcastle stumbled from crisis to crisis. He resigned late in 1756 after embroiling Britain in a war with France under conditions that made Britain at once the aggressor and the despoiled. Newcastle's fall ended the period in which either Walpole or his disciples bore undiluted responsibility for the direction of affairs.[16] It ended, that is, the quarter century of Court Whig dominance.

Four groups of ideological opponents contended against the Court Whigs during these twenty-five years.[17] Two of them spoke from a social and political perspective that distrusted pluralism and innovation.

16. On Walpole, see J. H. Plumb, *Sir Robert Walpole* (2 vols.; Boston, 1956, 1961). For Walpole's later years, see William Coxe, *Memoirs of the Life and Administration of Sir Robert Walpole, Earl of Orford* (3 vols.; London, 1798). On Henry Pelham, see William Coxe, *Memoirs of the Administration of the Right Honourable Henry Pelham* (2 vols.; London, 1829), and John Wilkes, *A Whig in Power: The Political Career of Henry Pelham* (Evanston, Ill., 1964). On Newcastle, see Reed Browning, *The Duke of Newcastle* (New Haven, 1975). On Hardwicke, see Philip C. Yorke, *The Life and Correspondence of Philip Yorke, Earl of Hardwicke, Lord High Chancellor of Great Britain* (3 vols.; Cambridge, 1913).

17. The point will be made later in the text, but it is probably useful to state it at the outset of the discussion: I am here distinguishing oppositionist ideologies, but I am not claiming that each perspective had an important following in Parliament or that oppositionists operated only from principles. All I wish to mention initially are the four types of oppositionist arguments that are found in the journals and pamphlets of the era. For discussions of the oppositionist factions in Parliament, see Foord, *His Majesty's Opposition*; Romney Sedgwick, "Introductory Survey," in *The History of Parliament: The House of Commons, 1715–1754* (2 vols.; New York, 1970), I, 1–114; and Linda J. Colley, "The Loyal Brotherhood and the Cocoa Tree: The London Organization of the Tory Party, 1727–1760," *Historical Journal*, XX (1977), 77–95.

Throughout this study these two groups shall be called, as they were in the first half of the eighteenth century, the Tories. The two groups that operated within a Whig orientation were more receptive of social diversity than the Tories and more attuned to the benefits of change. But since the government also called itself "Whig," this branch of the opposition will be designated "Opposition Whigs." The two groups comprising the Tories were the Jacobites and the Hanoverian Tories, and since these terms come directly from the era being treated and are mutually exclusive, they should be both clear and uncontentious. The two groups comprising the Opposition Whigs were the republicans and the "Country Whigs," but though both these terms were also used in the period, neither is as unexceptionable as the terms referring to the two Tory groups. "Republican" was in general a term of abuse, one the Court Whigs used to discredit many of their opponents. "Country Whig" on the other hand abounded in happy connotations, and the Court Whigs were unwilling to let the designation go by default to the opposition. The meanings of the terms, and the natures of the groups to whose ideas they are affixed, will become clearer as their characteristic political stances are set forth.

The Tories of Georgian Britain were men who idealized a simpler past. Their sympathies lay with the men of the land—the peers and gentry living upon Britain's rolling acres, natural leaders of a stratified, deferential, and unitary society. Tories harbored suspicions about the world of finance. They distrusted liquid wealth, resisted its assertions of a right to full participation in politics, and feared the capacity of money to buy souls. Tories nurtured analogous suspicions about religious toleration. They found implausible the argument that permitting Protestant diversity would eliminate various grievances of conscience and thereby increase national cohesion. They believed instead that to tolerate diversity in faith was to accept the ultimate dissolution of a once unitary society. Focusing as they did upon the imperative of unity, Tories glorified the crown. They did not in general seek a return to the type of royal authoritarianism that prevailed before 1640, and many Tories in fact approved fully of the various inhibitions that of late had been created to confine the crown. But even if the king was to be held in check, the royal office should not be demeaned. For all these reasons

Tories were unhappy with the course of recent events. They saw men of money attaining power and using their money to secure more. They saw Protestant dissenters exercising extensive influence and hailed as patriots. They saw the throne degraded by unscrupulous and greedy advisers. As a standard against which to cast all this corruption in relief they invoked a pristine past of landed dominance, royal greatness, and religious solidarity. Theirs were, in a memorable phrase, "the politics of nostalgia."[18]

But Tories were of two sorts. The Jacobites retained a loyalty to the ousted house of Stuart.[19] At the core of their program was the need to put the Pretender upon his rightful throne, and they thus sought to repudiate the central achievement of 1688–1689. For them the Glorious Revolution had been a catastrophic mistake. The larger group of Tories, however, were Hanoverian Tories. They accepted, perhaps reluctantly, the necessity of replacing James II with William III and the later parliamentary definition of the line of succession. They accepted thereafter the legitimacy of George I's and George II's claims to the throne. But for little else that 1688 had effected could they muster approval. Along with the Jacobites they decried government by peculation, religion without mystery, and the multiform campaign against social cohension. In brief, therefore, the differences between the two Tory groups are to be understood in this manner: both the Jacobites and the Hanoverian Tories set their faces against the social and economic changes that were transforming Britain, but the Jacobites additionally opposed the monarchs under whose approving eyes such changes had in recent years occurred.

Whigs of all persuasions were proud and enthusiastic heirs of the

18. A valuable study of the Tory mind is the work from which this quotation comes: Isaac Kramnick, *Bolingbroke and His Circle: The Politics of Nostalgia in the Age of Walpole* (Cambridge, Mass., 1968). See also the best biography of the Tory leader, H. T. Dickinson, *Bolingbroke* (London, 1970), and Quentin Skinner, "The Principles and Practice of Opposition: The Case of Bolingbroke versus Walpole," in Neil McKendrick, ed., *Historical Perspectives: Studies in English Thought and Society in Honour of J. H. Plumb* (London, 1974).

19. For the political role of the Jacobites, see Sedgwick's controversial "Introductory Survey," in *History of Parliament*, I; Paul S. Fritz, *The English Ministers and Jacobitism between the Rebellions of 1715 and 1745* (Toronto, 1975); and Eveline Cruickshanks, *Political Untouchables: The Tories and the '45* (New York, 1979).

Glorious Revolution. But how they interpreted the revolution, which was after all the central event in modern British history, varied in no small degree. What may be called the orthodox reading of the events of 1688–1689 received its fullest statement in 1710 from the mouths of the Whig managers presenting the case against the inflammatory Jacobite cleric, Dr. Henry Sacheverell. In essence their contention was simply that the revolution (and the settlement attendant upon it) had been a legitimate act of resistance against a monarch who was subverting liberties. What made it legitimate was sheer necessity: had resistance not been offered, James II would have succeeded in his plan to remodel the constitution. One heard from the managers little talk of contracts and consent, and less of natural rights. They made no broad claims, invoked no universalizing or abstract theories. They spoke to common sense and self-interest. They had no desire, while legitimizing the Glorious Revolution, also to legitimize ideas that might undermine the settlement built upon the revolution. And it must be regarded as more than coincidental that the rising Robert Walpole served as one of the managers, for the Whiggery of the Sacheverell trial became the Whiggery of the early Georgian court. But this somewhat restricted interpretation of the Glorious Revolution, articulated so as to minimize the revolutionary and popular implications of what had been wrought, was not its only possible exposition. The secular saint, John Locke, had suggested that only natural rights theory made intelligible the ouster of James. Britons, he was understood to say, had asserted themselves in 1688 to protect their natural rights against illegitimate encroachment. Moreover, it was not an obvious misconstruction of Locke's words to see him further as a proto-democrat, establishing civil society upon the consent of all its members and allowing for the direction of that society through decisions ratified by the majority. Thus, beneath the uniform acceptance of the Glorious Revolution by Whigs lay discrepant theories to justify that support.[20]

20. Kenyon, *Revolution Principles*, describes in detail the course of Whig thinking from the Glorious Revolution to the eve of Walpole's triumph. He discerns a variety of strands of Whig thought early in these years, but he asserts that most had been rejected by the second decade of the eighteenth century. Since I shall later argue that considerable diversity existed *within* Court Whig thinking in the 1730s and 1740s, I find myself in disagreement with the extrapolated implications of Kenyon's study. We are at one though

Whigs also uniformly approved the Act of Toleration but differed in assessing its finality. Some believed that it was enough to have carved out an enclave of limited religious freedom for Protestant dissenters while maintaining the preeminence of the Church of England as established by law. But others viewed the limited toleration as only a first step toward the lifting of civil disabilities from the shoulders of dissenters. Whigs were not democrats, still less egalitarians. Most were men of the land and confident that possession of land was a potent sign of competence to govern. But unlike Tories, Whigs were not so alarmed by the transformations progressing around them. They saw nothing pernicious in men of finance entering politics and held no deep fears of religious or social pluralism destroying social cohesion. Many even found diversity attractive.

The division of the Opposition Whigs, who contended with the Court Whigs for power, into two groups, republicans and Country Whigs, must be regarded as somewhat arbitrary—grounded in tendencies—in the absence of a touchstone of the sort that separated Jacobites from Hanoverian Tories. Republicans tended to adopt a more radical interpretation of the Glorious Revolution, Country Whigs a more conservative one. The republicans were those who in general sought to extend the achievements of 1688–1689. Specifically, they supported such changes as a widening of county representation, greater liberties for Protestant dissenters, perhaps a broader franchise, a reduction in the power of the judges, or even in some instances a more powerful House of Commons.[21] The Country Whigs, by far the more numerous of the two groups, tended to feel that the work of 1688–1689 should be frozen in perpetuity—that no further changes or establishments were needed. In this feeling the Country Whigs were at one with the

---

in seeing a clear division emerging between left-wing and right-wing Whiggery in the years after the Sacheverell trial. Kenyon, *Revolution Principles*, 156. On that trial and its Whig ideology, see Geoffrey Holmes, *The Trial of Doctor Sacheverell* (London, 1973).

21. Many of the persons examined in Bailyn, *Ideological Origins*, and Caroline Robbins, *The Eighteenth-Century Commonwealthman: Studies in the Transmission, Development, and Circumstances of English Liberal Thought from the Restoration of Charles II until the War with the Thirteen Colonies* (Cambridge, Mass., 1959) were republicans. But some of Robbins' commonwealthmen were Country Whigs and a few—e.g., Samuel Squire—were even Court Whigs.

Court Whigs, also defenders of the status quo as created by the Glorious Revolution. Why then did the Country group oppose the Court group? Their opposition, when principled, arose from their belief that the Court Whigs were betraying the Whig legacy. Many, however, who assumed the mantle of Country Whigs were not notably actuated by principles in their opposition to Walpole and later the Pelhams. They were simply politicians out of office, frustrated by Walpole's disinclination or Pelham's inability to give authority to potential rivals, and therefore looking for ways to storm into the ministry. Any grievance, any complaint might be a suitable pretext for assailing men with whom they essentially agreed. But other Country Whigs found Walpole an unworthy successor to Lord Stanhope. They believed him a power-hungry minister, duping his master while gulling or buying the Commons. Unfit for his trust, he threatened to undo the work of 1688–1689 or, more likely, to betray it by instituting one-man rule. And thus, for a variety of reasons, there existed a Country Whig opposition to a Court Whig ministry, each side avowing the same ideas of good government but with the Country denying the honesty of the Court's avowals and the Court angry at the Country's withholding of support.

Against foes whose opposition was rooted in personal frustrations, the Court Whig ministries had no tools—save appointment to office—with which to try to effect a conversion. But against oppositionists who objected to the principles or activities of the Court Whigs, the ministries might reasonably hope to make some headway. It is certain that both Walpole and Henry Pelham pursued policies they believed would be widely popular among the political classes of the kingdom. To be sure, the Jacobites on one flank and the republicans on the other placed too great a distance between themselves and the Court Whigs to allow for a reconciliation without abandonment of principle. But by choosing moderate measures and by providing effective government, Walpole and Pelham thought they could win over many from among the moderates in the Hanoverian Tory and Country Whig groups. Thus Walpole made much of his devotion to peace and chose to keep the kingdom out of the war of the Polish Succession despite the insistence of George II himself that British honor required British participation. Pelham found himself saddled with a war when he came to office, but he worked steadily to end it and to overcome the bellicose enthusiasms of his brother Newcastle. Like Walpole, Pelham knew that the expenses of war tended to disenchant and then drive off supporters of the government. Both Walpole and Pelham insisted on keeping the Land Tax as low as possible, thereby obliging the gentry. It was this desire that led Walpole to blunder into his excise difficulties of 1733, for he needed more revenue and, too clever by half, thought to secure it without either raising the Land Tax or imposing a new duty. Both men supported low interest rates, and even though Walpole retreated from a debt-reduction scheme before the cries of worried creditors in 1737, Pelham refused to lose sight of broader national advantages and pushed such a scheme through at mid-century. In a like manner both Court Whig ministers acted to foster trade, thereby keeping the commercial community satisfied, and to uphold the existing balance between the Church of England, whose remaining privileges were treated as inviolable, and the Protestant dissenters, whose legal position was not to be eroded and whose practical situation could be gently and slowly improved. With all these policies the Court Whigs intended to demonstrate their own fitness for office and in so doing to persuade the moderate doubters that Court Whiggery merited support.

But that task was not easy. And its difficulty lay in the widespread acceptance among oppositionists of a Catonic perspective for viewing politics—a perspective that bred suspicion and distrust. To the Catonic soul moderation was no recommendation in itself, and whenever it was taken to be simply a camouflage for wicked intentions it served only to intensify the opposition's dislike of the Court Whigs. Because so many among the opposition breathed the heady air of Catonism, it did not matter that from a programmatic perspective both the Hanoverian Tories and the Country Whigs stood but a slight distance from the Court Whigs. Their tone of denunciation could be as shrill as the Jacobites' and as impassioned as the republicans'. They did not take such sweeping ideological exception to the Court Whigs as Jacobites and republicans did, but they saw evil men lodged in high places and that vision was sufficient to elicit their most fervent concerns for liberty and the constitution. The Catonic perspective, in brief, placed a moral boundary between the Court Whigs and the opposition; this moral dimension in politics transcended programmatic disagreement. The shrillness of opposition rhetoric was not a function of such disagreement. It was instead a measure of the degree to which Catonism controlled the opposition's perceptions.

Why was Catonism so intense? Why did the Catonic perspective seem to so many people the most accurate lens for refracting Court Whiggery? The Catonic spirit, defensive in origin and nature, cannot endure over a long period of time without being regularly fueled by external threats to deeply held principles. Thus, to account for the power of Catonism one must identify an event that would have aroused among Britons the most deep-seated of their fears—an event that portended the destruction of all that Britons valued. That event was the South Sea bubble and the subsequent South Sea scandal. The story of the bubble and scandal needs no extensive recounting.[22] The great South Sea Company was insufficiently capitalized for its obligations, especially after it assumed the government's debt obligations. To secure capital the company issued and sold stock, maximizing its gain from these sales by manipulating the market and artificially enhancing the value of its offering. To gain governmental complaisance toward all these shenanigans the company bribed both some of the ministers advising the king and some of the women still closer to him. But finally the market collapsed, commitments to buy destroyed numerous family fortunes, people were left with stock worth far less than they had paid for it, and a nation become restive and angry turned to vituperative outrage when the involvement of ministers received publicity. Walpole came to power in the crisis and had immediately to make a decision that would stretch across the rest of his career. Many clamored for punishment for all those implicated in dealing dishonestly with the public. Many wanted powerful legal inhibitions imposed upon the activities of the business world. Many wanted the Whigs ousted. But Walpole calculated that wholesale punishments would embarrass, perhaps irreparably, the Hanoverian family and Protestant succession. He

22. The financial details are explained in P. G. M. Dickson, *The Financial Revolution in England: A Study in the Development of Public Credit 1688–1756* (London, 1967). John Carswell, *The South Sea Bubble* (Stanford, Ca., 1960), offers a vivid picture of the fevered politics of Britain in the time of the bubble.

feared for the viability of the crucial worlds of finance and commerce if draconian measures reached the statute book, and he dreaded the consequence of a Whig retreat from office. Thus, aware of what he was doing, he chose to limit punishments to the most obvious and indefensible offenders, to encourage insofar as he could the business circles in the City, and to protect the Whigs from their enemies.

Why was all this such a traumatizing event for opposition psyches? The answer is not obscure. The bubble represented all that the oppositionists had predicted would come from the new world of liquid wealth:[23] fortunes and families would be swiftly made and unmade by forces beyond anyone's control or comprehension, the instability of money would infect government and deprive it of the stability that the regime of the landed had created, and—more metaphysically—order itself would yield to chaos. Moreover, as if that were not enough, the cover-up presided over by Walpole after the bubble burst had other fearful implications. For either the Court Whigs had abandoned their integrity, having shown that they could be bought and that men of finance could purchase politicians and therefore purchase policies. Or else they had decided to sacrifice liberty to expediency and retention of power. They had shown such a lust for power that not even their involvement in the most sordid of public crimes should drive them to resign their command. By either reckoning the Court Whigs had betrayed their heritage. And on these grounds a principled Opposition Whig press quickly appeared. Insofar as the Court Whigs failed to unmake the new world of finance, they showed that they found nothing basically flawed in it—a position that pushed the Tory press to Catonic stridency. Because it was unprecedented, because it touched so many with such extensive damage, because it was taken to fulfill so many dire forecasts, and because it raised so many fundamental constitutional issues, the South Sea bubble and the government's handling of it were together the most polarizing and transforming event in post-1714 British politics until the American Revolution. Liberty, so recently won, was again in peril.

23. See, e.g., [Charles Davenant], *The True Picture of a Modern Whig set forth in a Dialogue between Mr. Whiglove and Mr. Double* (London, 1701).

III

Precisely because the Tories and Opposition Whigs differed from each other in important ways, their complaints about Court Whig governments were not identical. Tories in general had little interest in reordering the constitution or machinery of government and were exceedingly chary about fettering the executive. What they deplored in the Walpole and Pelham administrations was not the exercise of royal power per se but rather the coterie of ambitious politicians who had surrounded the king, isolated him from the true feelings of his people, and were using his power to their own advantage. Tories idealized a monarch who, ruling constitutionally but firmly and justly, would set an example of uprightness and inspire his people to civic responsibility.[24] Whigs were less disposed to this traditional, humanistic cast of mind. Many of them—especially as the Country Whigs shaded toward the republicans—applied a theory of natural rights to politics. This theory imputed various inalienable rights to man and provided, as a consequence, a powerful motive for placing inhibitions and restrictions on royal authority. Thus, although both Whigs and Tories sought good governance, Tories looked to the character of the leaders whereas Whigs, insofar as they shared in republican aspirations, were inclined to search for constitutional devices or mechanisms.

But such dissimilarities, though interesting, are not a prominent feature of the political landscape of the Court Whig era. For in most ways, despite their separate origins, Tories and Opposition Whigs viewed Court Whig politics in startlingly similar fashions. Their approaches to the science of politics may have varied, but their analyses of the inadequacies of the Court Whig regime were basically the same. Indeed, the two branches of the opposition accepted the same four starting points—four irreducible basic ideas that defined the realm within which political understanding was possible. These four may be briefly characterized as one assumption about human nature, two laws of politics, and one prescription for political order. Shared by all opponents of the Court Whigs, they made it possible for Jacobite and republican

24. Bolingbroke's *The Patriot King* is the *locus classicus* for such ideas. In Henry, Lord Bolingbroke, *The Works of Lord Bolingbroke* (4 vols.; Philadelphia, 1841), II, 372–429.

to come together in assailing wicked government. Moreover, this underlying unity in the acceptance of basic ideas gave the lie to Court Whig defenders who argued that at least one branch of the opposition was necessarily hypocritical. Hypocrisy was no less present in eighteenth-century politics than in the politics of any other era, but the cooperation of Tory and Opposition Whig to harry Court Whig administrations does not constitute proof of it. This united opposition usually called itself "Patriotic" and its members "Patriots."[25] And this adoption of a single self-designation for all wings of the opposition was not misdirected. The same basic political ideas were credible to all.

The first of these ideas asserted mankind's depravity. This assertion was not a theological statement, though the Calvinist strand in Anglican and dissenting thought doubtless contributed to the conviction. Rather it was—if one may treat the terms loosely—simultaneously empirical and a priori. Most evidence, most experience taught that man was selfish and dangerous. And any evidence or experience that suggested the contrary was disallowed as inconsistent with a known and unchallengeable truth. The manifestation of this depravity that most caught the Patriots' attention was a lusting for power. "Cato" gave a dramatic Whig summary of the lesson:

> Those who have talked most of the Dignity of human Nature, seem to have understood it but little. Men are so far from having any Views purely publick and disinterested, that Government first arose from every Man's taking care of himself; and Government is never abused and perverted, but from the same Cause. Do we not know that one Man has slaughtered a Million, and overturned Nations, for the gaining of one point to himself; and that almost all Men would follow Evil, if they found their greatest Advantage or Pleasure in it?

The Tory Bolingbroke, though less theatrical in his mode of declaration, also embraced the idea: "We are determined by self-love to seek

---

25. Foord identifies other appellations widely applied to the opposition. He also asserts that the Tories preferred not to be called "Patriots" (though he then proceeds to identify them by that term). I believe he is wrong in the assertion. Bolingbroke was certainly not reluctant to be a Patriot, nor were various Tory pamphleteers. Foord, *His Majesty's Opposition*, 37, 113, 154.

our pleasure and our utility in society."[26] As the quotation suggests—and "Cato" agreed—the opposition was not so pessimistic as to believe that this innate selfishness could defy all efforts by society to channel it usefully. Depravity did not entail anarchy or, to check anarchy, despotism. But it did mean that all men entrusted with authority deserved the most attentive scrutiny by ever-suspicious citizens.

The second basic idea, a law of politics, held that power, abstractly conceived, posed an ever-present threat to liberty. Bolingbroke asserted that "the love of power is . . . insatiable, almost constantly whetted, never cloyed by possession." He declared that because "power is a thing of the most intoxicating nature, it ought always to have some checks on it," or else liberty would be devoured. Such a belief might have been warranted simply as a consequence of the opposition's view of human nature. After all, to give authority to a power-hungry man—and all men were so characterized—would be to create a threat to liberty. But the law that power was inevitably at war with liberty had an independent existence as well. "Power" was often conceived to be an aggressive entity with a shape and momentum of its own. "Liberty" too had structure, but because it lacked the assertiveness of "power" it was ever prey to this foe. In such a manner were the concepts reified, and discussions of their relationship leapt quickly to a metaphysical plane. "Cato" analyzed this complex relationship in the following manner:

Power is naturally active, vigilant and distrustful; which Qualities in it push it upon all Means and Expedients to fortify itself, and upon destroying all Opposition, and even all Seed of Opposition, and make it restless as long as any thing stands in its Way. It would do what it pleases, and have no Check. Now, because Liberty chastises and shortens Power, therefore Power would extinguish Liberty; and consequently Liberty has too much Cause to be exceeding jealous, and always upon her Defence. Power has many advantages over her; it has generally numerous Guards, many Creatures, and much Treasure; besides, it has more Craft and Experience, less Honesty and Innocence: And whereas Power can, and for the most part does subsist where Liberty is not, Liberty cannot subsist without Power; so that she has, as it were, the Enemy always at her Gates.

26. Gordon and Trenchard, *Cato's Letters*, II, 54; quoted in Kramnick, *Bolingbroke and His Circle*, 90.

Politics was thus characterized by a never-ending struggle between two impersonal forces. It was because, though liberty was deemed desirable, power was regarded as unavoidable, that the warfare they engendered remained a constant element in political life.[27]

Another law of politics—the third basic idea—was that all political regimes were naturally subject to corruption. By "corruption" was meant not the venal peculation that is never far from political life, but something far graver—a decay of spirit and institution that would finally destroy all political orders. Plato had taught how pure regimes degenerate by and through stages, Polybius had posited three types of constitutions and asserted that all were subject to decay, and Machiavelli, the founder of modern political science, had advanced the celebrated proposition that regimes could remain healthy only if they could manage to find a way regularly to return to founding principles and thereby to undo the destructive work of corruption. All these writers, and many others given to the same theme, were known to the opposition. Thus Tories and Opposition Whigs brooded over the signs of decay they discerned in Britain—an excessive concern for self, a wallowing in luxury, an inattention to the requirements of good citizenship. They pored through the texts of Roman history to ascertain if Britain, with its liberties and prosperity, was following the pattern of the dissolution of the republic.[28] They exhorted their countrymen to undergo a change of heart and return to the virtuous days of yore. But they did more. Corruption was not simply or exclusively a consequence of the abandonment of virtue for the allures of vice and wealth. It was also in some fashion an inevitable result of shifts in the pattern of property-holding in society. In the previous century James Harrington had proclaimed the famous lesson that power followed property,[29] and

27. Quoted in Kramnick, *Bolingbroke and His Circle*, 148; Gordon and Trenchard, *Cato's Letters*, I, 261–62. The seminal discussion of this argument is found in Bailyn, *Ideological Origins*, 55–60. See also James T. Boulton, "Arbitrary Power: An Eighteenth-Century Obsession," *Studies in Burke and His Times*, IX (1968), 905–26. Boulton casts his net too wide, but when applied to the Patriots the word "obsession" seems appropriate.

28. The decline of Rome that caught the attention of readers before the time of Gibbon was the republic's, not the empire's.

29. James Harrington, *The Commonwealth of Oceana*, ed. Henry Morley (London, 1887), 19. See Charles Blitzer, *An Immortal Commonwealth: The Political Thought of James Harrington* (New Haven, Conn., 1960).

the opposition writers took Harrington deeply seriously. Corrupting transformations in society—and particularly in British society—were linked to shifts in the nature or ownership of property. The Machiavellian stress on virtue and inner resolution sat most uneasily with this Harringtonian emphasis on the controlling role of property. But though in tension, or perhaps even incompatible, the two discrete themes nevertheless gave to the opposition's concern with corruption a broader appeal than it might otherwise have had. Both the social moralist and the social scientist could find substance for pondering in this picture of a Britain sinking beneath the weight of sloth, selfishness, ambition, and wealth. And to an opposition so attuned, the administrations of the Court Whigs seemed fearful confirmations of the truth of the ancient wisdom.[30]

A prescription for political health was the opposition's fourth basic idea. If men were naturally power-hungry, if power itself lusted avariciously after liberty, and if corruption was the besetting danger to political health, what better solution than to create a regime in which men were pitted against men, power against power, and principle against principle? Such a regime would in some fashion be balanced, and "balance" was in fact the age's chief prescription for curing all political ills. The eighteenth century was the great era for the worship of constitutional equilibrium. The selfishness of man was best controlled not by praying for an eschatological change in his nature, but by setting selfish men in opposition to each other. The liberty of all was thus guarded as each man acted to protect and extend himself. Similarly, the appetite of power for liberty was best contained if power itself was divided, and competing nodes of power thereby created. From the struggle for supremacy among these nodes liberty would emerge the beneficiary, profiting from the tendency of each part to strive to keep the others in their proper places. And by the same type of reasoning even the problem of corruption was soluble. Pure regimes were subject to decay because their natural principles—the principles

30. Good discussions of corruption may be found in Kramnick, *Bolingbroke and His Circle*, 163–69, and J. G. A. Pocock, "Machiavelli, Harrington, and English Political Ideologies in the Eighteenth Century," *William and Mary Quarterly*, 3rd ser., XXII (1965), 549–83.

that gave them identity—worked inexorably to undermine them as well. But a balanced government, crafted to pit principle in equipoise against principle, promised an end to decay. The corrupting effects of pure principles were nullified by the countervailing effects of other pure principles, all embedded to work simultaneously in the same constitution. Balance thus froze a regime: it ended corruption and marmoreal-ized virtue.[31]

Using these four ideas as the foundation for their assault, the Patriots denounced Court Whig administrations for almost all they did or planned. The precise substance and focus of the criticisms varied as the issues of the day appeared, flared, and then receded from view. But these varied indictments may be treated under six headings. As with the basic ideas, the headings are interrelated, and thus the character of the Patriots' assault on the Court Whigs cannot be fully savored until all six have been examined and their cross-fertilizing potential at least sensed. The opposition excoriated the Walpole and Pelham ministries for suppressing the independence of the House of Commons. They lashed the ministries for attempting to replace rule by virtue and good example with rule by money. They contended that Court Whig admin-istrations had encouraged the development of faction with all its at-tendant evils. They asserted that Court Whigs had limited the success of national trade. They insisted that Court Whigs sought to overbear the constitution by tolerating a standing army. And above all, perhaps in summary of all, the opposition accused the Court Whigs, especially Walpole, of fostering an unconstitutional body, the cabinet, directed by an equally unconstitutional entity, a prime minister, which was usurping the legitimate powers of the crown and the Parliament. Given vigor by the compelling prose of some of the age's greatest writers, the denunciations issued by the Patriots transformed the self-proclaimed heirs of 1688 into would-be despots.

The concern for the independence of the House of Commons was

---

31. Excellent discussions of balance may be found in William B. Gwyn, *The Meaning of the Separation of Powers: An Analysis of the Doctrine from Its Origin to the Adoption of the United States Constitution* (New Orleans, 1965); Stanley Pargellis, "The Theory of Bal-anced Government," in Conyers Read, ed., *The Constitution Reconsidered* (New York, 1938); and M. J. C. Vile, *Constitutionalism and the Separation of Powers* (Oxford, 1967).

predicated upon the yoked beliefs that only a balanced constitution could assure liberty and that a ministry would naturally seek to make any Commons subservient to itself. Patriots professed to believe, against the growing weight of historical evidence, that Parliament was an institution of greater antiquity than the crown.[32] Its age lent it authority. Because it had long been the vehicle by which Englishmen had defended themselves and their liberties, it should, they averred, retain that function. But the sight of Court Whig majorities in the House of Commons did not encourage Patriots to think that the chamber was fulfilling its duty. And once persuaded that the Commons submitted too readily to ministerial direction, the opposition needed but little insight to see that a significant proportion of the members of the house held places under the crown or had close relatives who were so beneficed. These members were therefore not independent. If they voted so as to displease the ministry, chastisement in the form of deprivation of office could swiftly follow. Walpole imposed such punishments in the aftermath of his excise debacle, and the Pelhams resorted to the same tactic after humbling George II in 1746. But usually the threat alone sufficed. Placemen, in sum, were not fit to be members of Parliament. The appropriate reform, perpetually at the core of Patriots' programs, was the enactment of a "Place Bill"—a measure that would prohibit members from holding all or most places in the gift of the crown. Moreover, to assure that the Commons used its constitutional independence as the people it was supposed to represent wished, two other changes seemed essential. First, it was necessary that the Septennial Act of 1716 be repealed and replaced by a triennial measure. By this adjustment the electorate would have the opportunity to choose its representatives far more frequently and presumably keep them more firmly under control. Second, the practice of instructing rather than just informing members should be encouraged. It did not suffice to keep members *au courant* about the mood and thinking of their constituency. Too often such information was simply ignored. Therefore, the proper position was to endorse the formal instruction of members—and to

32. See Isaac Kramnick, "Augustan Politics and English Historiography: The Debate on the English Past, 1730–35," *History and Theory*, VI (1967), 33–56, for an illuminating account of how Tories used Whig historians and Whigs used Tory historians.

punish those who did not heed the instruction. By such devices the Commons could be restored to its true position within the constitution, independent of crown and Lords but responsive to the electorate.

Closely related to the Patriots' fears about a diminution in the independence of the Commons were their concerns about the power of money to subvert traditional authority. At best ambivalent toward Britain's unprecedented prosperity in the years since 1660, the Patriots increasingly saw only the forbidding aspects of expanding liquid wealth. Their root fear was that short-sighted and selfish men of the City would supplant the ancient landed class as the directors of national affairs. The holding of land, they believed, provided the only sound basis for true personal independence, and independence in turn was the prerequisite for wise leadership. Simultaneously, the holding of land conferred responsibility upon a man and made him prudent. With his wealth immovable, he was a hostage to his own decisions in Parliament. Such a situation was good for the nation: self-interest and national interest coincided. But merchants and financiers could move their wealth about—even, if they chose, to locations outside the kingdom—and thus they had no need to consult enduring national interests when voting. Or, using their wealth to secure power within the kingdom, they might insinuate themselves into positions that conferred power, and then use that power to shape national policy to their own ends. James Harrington, the most authoritative of English political writers, had taught that power gravitated to wealth, and accordingly the amassing of fortunes by new men threatened to destroy the position of the gentry and the peers as the kingdom's leaders. Energized by such beliefs, the Patriots turned their wrath particularly upon two aspects of Court Whig financial policy. They decried the consequences of meeting the cost of government by borrowing: since taxes would be imposed to raise money for paying debts, and since the chief form of taxation in Britain bore disproportionately on the landed, the effect of resorting to credit to run a government could only be to shift wealth from the landed to the moneyed interest. Collaterally, the opposition assailed any administration decision to enlarge the tax-collecting and debt-servicing bureaucracy: such expansion simply redoubled the outrage of Patriots who, already bitter that taxes were needed to meet debt obligations, would now have to endure the creation of new places in the gift of the crown. Thus the Patriots returned again and again to the themes that government finance required austere direction and that the power of money needed fettering. Otherwise, all that honor and selflessness and loyalty had procured for Britain over the centuries would crumble into dust.

The Patriots also denounced the Court Whigs for encouraging faction. It was a point of conventional wisdom in the early eighteenth century, shared by government and opposition alike, that faction was bad. When men aligned themselves with parties, they were abandoning independence. Even more distressing for the state, they were committing themselves to a program that patently—and usually avowedly—served but a portion of the state. In an era in which opposition to the king's government was still often treated as opposition to the king and hence as disloyalty, there was scant room for the argument that an opposition party might be useful to the state. It was precisely because this distrust of an opposition party was so widely held that the Patriots sought to minimize their Jacobite component and the Court Whigs to maximize it. But the notion of a royalist party that nevertheless excluded significant sections of the community was scarcely more commendable. The ancient fears that a state dared not allow internal divisions lest it court suicide remained powerful. Thus the Patriots aimed withering polemical fire at Court Whig assertions that party differences still mattered. For if it served Court Whig interests to preserve the Whig-Tory distinction and thereby to make themselves the beneficiary of popular associations between Whiggery and the revolution or Toryism and the Pretender, it served Patriot interests to obliterate the distinction. Bolingbroke's most famous political essay was intended to effect that end.[33] And indeed, his Whig colleagues in the opposition made the same argument, for Country Whigs were quite prepared to countenance almost any strategy that might serve to unmask the palpable libel that Court Whigs represented true Whiggery. Whatever the national interest might be—and the Patriots (fortunately for them) never had to define that term—it was not served by letting a swarm

33. *A Dissertation upon Parties* appeared weekly in the *Craftsman* in 1733–34.

of banditti parade themselves as the only constitutional party in the kingdom.

National trade also suffered, in the Patriots' eyes, under Court Whig auspices. The opposition espied in the readiness of Walpole and the Pelhams to rely on the great chartered companies yet another sign of Court Whig determination to help only a tight group of cronies. In the opinion of the Patriots, the monopoly rights by which the trading companies operated worked to prevent many smaller merchants from participating in trade. Injured and aggrieved, such men naturally sought help from the opposition. But the Patriots expanded their indictment to assert that the consequences for the kingdom of resorting to the great companies was to limit the total extent of national trade. If trade were open to all, they maintained, everyone would benefit from the consequent widening. Using similar reasoning the Patriots found a further basis for denouncing the government's financial policy. Recourse to borrowing, they asserted, led to a national debt, and this debt in turn made other nations reluctant to expand trade with a potentially insolvent Britain. Clearly the economic understanding of the Patriots was not very penetrating. But when one recalls what they believed about the deepest hopes of the Court Whigs, their concern about exclusionary or beggaring policies becomes comprehensible.

If the Court Whigs truly sought to destroy the constitutional balance and to rule by masked fiat, they would need some means of securing compliance to their decrees. And the means would have to be a plausible threat of resort to naked force. Thus, the opposition resisted as vigorously as rhetoric permitted the frequent Court Whig proposals to maintain, or, still worse, to expand the standing army. Harrington had followed Machiavelli in teaching that only a citizens' militia could protect a nation's freedom. To give a government a standing army was to give it a club with which to bludgeon liberty. The Patriots had no tolerance for arguments that a professional army was more skilled and national defense required such high expertise; they saw only the spectre of military control shackling the kingdom. The ministers, greedy for power and probing for flaws in the constitution, cared not a whit for liberty. They were, therefore, eminently likely to turn to force to secure their way. And thus, although the Court Whig ministries did many things that worried the opposition, no single action so alarmed the Patriots as ministerial requests for expanded military forces.

The apparatus which, in opposition eyes, allowed the Court Whigs to pose so multi-faceted a threat to the constitution was the cabinet and, within it, the emergent prime ministry. Whereas British liberties had taken on vigor as a consequence of a decentralization of the political order in the late seventeenth century and had been protected by a continued royal reliance on the various county elites, the Court Whigs sought to reconsolidate authority and weaken the local leaders. The chief principle of the constitution was its recognition of the independence of the three great forces poised in equilibrium, and now the Court Whigs worked to create an agency that both destroyed that independence and, in doing so, superseded the forces it hoped to combine. To the opposition a cabinet seemed, at best, reprehensible, a deliberate effort to subvert the guiding principle of the constitution. And to the extent that it successfully effected that subversion it was manifestly dangerous. Should the cabinet gain command of the king, Lords, and Commons, there would be no check to restrain it. It would become the directing agency of the kingdom. And if the existence of a cabinet was ominous, what could the Patriots think of a man who dominated a cabinet? He might become—in many ways he already was—the arbiter of Britain. It was because Sir Robert Walpole stood so preeminently alone that he elicited from Patriot writers a venom that the Pelhams, though assailed, never provoked. Walpole symbolized dictatorial tyranny—the worst form of one-man rule. He was the Robinarch, who required political postulants to kiss his posterior. He represented all that the opposition detested in Court Whig thinking—a cunning opportunism, an unprincipled love of command, a readiness to measure all actions by profitability, a scorn for simple virtues. Cato would have refused to accept such a leader; the Patriots believed they could do no less. And thus it was a Catonic perspective on politics that united an otherwise ideologically disparate opposition.[34]

34. The preceding analysis of the chief Patriot complaints against the Court Whigs is based chiefly upon Herbert M. Atherton, *Political Prints in the Age of Hogarth: A Study of the Ideographic Representation of Politics* (Oxford, 1974), plate 28; Bailyn, *Ideological Origins*; Foord, *His Majesty's Opposition*; Kramnick, *Bolingbroke and His Circle*; Robbins,

IV

Assailed by all these accusations of malfeasance and wickedness, the Court Whigs concluded that their defenses must be of two sorts. At the more concrete level of individual issues they needed simply to counter Patriot arguments with reasonable replies. When Patriots leveled specific charges, specific responses were in order. Thus it was that Walpole and the Pelhams recruited a stable of political polemicists whose task was to publicize the Court Whig position on such controverted matters as the independence of Parliament, the condition of trade, and the appropriateness of maintaining a standing army. But at the more abstract level of political presuppositions the Court Whigs needed something more than mere rebuttals. Before the concrete issues could be joined, the audience to whom the political argumentation of the era was addressed needed to be weaned from whatever commitment to Catonism it harbored. Court Whigs recognized the Catonic frame of reference as fundamentally antagonistic to any line of argument that rested upon convenience or recommended trust in those exercising power. It followed that only the dissolution of Catonic fervor would permit those inclined toward the opposition to give the government a hearing. Thus, even as the Court Whigs supported the production of pamphlets that defended their actions, they worked to undermine the attitude that made the opposition so unreceptive to any line of Court Whig reasoning. The two levels of defense proceeded simultaneously. The first addressed itself to those whom the Court Whigs believed were unfettered by ideological presuppositions and who hence were qualified to pass judgment upon the reasonableness of Court Whig logic. The second addressed itself to those whom the Court Whigs regarded as still confined by a commitment to the narrow creed of Cato and thus in need of a prior attitudinal transformation.

For the first task the Court Whigs could draw on the legacy bequeathed to the eighteenth century by seventeenth-century Whigs and subtly transformed by their early eighteenth-century successors. The origin of this legacy was the matrix of ideas that constituted the core

---

Eighteenth-Century Commonwealthman. Less immediately pertinent, but essential to an understanding of Patriot views, is Pocock, *Machiavellian Moment.*

of what Caroline Robbins has called the "Whig canon"—that body of writings by Locke, Harrington, Henry Neville, Algernon Sidney, Lord Somers, and others that set forth for later ages the basic positions of Whiggery.[35] The fundamental commitment of Whiggery, these older Whigs affirmed, was the cause of liberty. But all of these men, with the exception of Somers, had written when Whigs were in opposition to government. They had never been forced to deal with the difficulties that arise for one of Whiggish views when he attains a position of trust under the crown, responsible for the preservation not only of liberty but also of order. The Glorious Revolution opened the way to such opportunities for the Whigs, and they, interpreting the revolution in terms of the canon, entered in its wake into high offices of state. Under the impact of such experience the Whigs of the reigns of William and Anne moderated their views somewhat. The virtues of stability and order grew more attractive, the dangers of unbounded liberty became more visible. And so when in 1710 the Sacheverell trial imposed on Whigs the need to define their position, they were for the most part more guarded in their pronouncements than writers of the canon had been.[36] From this diverse tradition—the canon in its own richness, and the tempered but still varied Whiggery of 1710—the Court Whig apologists had a wide range of arguments to choose among. And in those situations for which their forebears had not articulated a suitable argument, the Court Whig tribe could extrapolate one from their operative assumptions. In Chapters II through VII this development, in a variety of forms, will be analyzed.

The second task posed greater difficulties. A campaign to disabuse the opposition of its Catonic inclination could not rely on any Whig traditions; the occasion was new, the need novel. As Court Whigs surveyed the situation, what they determined they needed was an alternative symbol to Cato—a symbol that, without sacrificing any of the luster attached to Cato's glorious name, would represent a calmer perspective on politics. Because Roman precedents set the secular lessons that the educated of the eighteenth century sought to live by, and

35. See Robbins, *Eighteenth-Century Commonwealthman*, chap. II, for a discussion of the "canon."
36. Holmes, *Trial of Doctor Sacheverell*, chap. VI.

because the opposition, in appropriating Cato, had already borrowed its hero from Rome, the Court Whigs turned to the same source. Within a few years they had made their decision: against Cato's fevered perspective they would pit the cooler outlook of Cato's illustrious contemporary, Marcus Tullius Cicero. Behind Cicero's banner of moderation and prudence they soon gathered to struggle for the loyalties and understanding of the political nation. If people could be persuaded that Cicero was a sounder preceptor in matters political, they would be far readier to attend to Court Whig writings. It was central to the Court Whig polemic, then, to represent Cicero as a fount and exemplar of political wisdom. In the final chapter this campaign to bring a Ciceronian perspective to British politics will be examined. To anticipate the conclusion to be reached by the time this study ends, it may be stated that Court Whiggery proves to be a Ciceronian reading of politics and that by 1750 it had triumphed over its Catonic rival to become, among the political classes of Britain, almost universal in credibility.

Chapter II

Lord Hervey (1696–1743): The Court Whig as Courtier

I

Lord Hervey spent most of his adult life courting the charge of levity. Although his intellectual interests ranged widely, they seemed scarcely to penetrate any surface. He struck most observers as a sybarite and a gossip. His facility with languages—whether his own or the Latin, Italian, and French that he mastered—served but to make him a multilingual poetaster, and he appeared to take his chief delights in amusing his friends and twitting his enemies. In matters religious he was a foe of mystification, holding most clergy to be benighted hierophants. His sexual tastes excluded neither men nor women; indeed, he conceived grand passions for both at various times in his life. As he grew older his effeminacy passed conventional bounds, and with his mincing gait, high voice, and propensity for using white powder as make-up he invited lacerating assaults from the pens of his political and literary foes. Above all, he was a courtier and hence, in hostile eyes, a sycophantic servant to an inept royal couple and an unabashed apologist for their wicked chief minister. "As to my own manner of life," he wrote irreverently in 1731, "As it was in the beginning, is now and ever shall be, Court without end, Amen."[1] But his manner aside, Hervey was an enormously useful friend for Walpole to have. In the 1730s he penned several sharp and powerful pamphlets defending the ministry; in the

1. Giles Stephen Holland Fox-Strangways, Earl of Ilchester, ed., *Lord Hervey and His Friends, 1726–38* (London, 1950), 121.

House of Lords he aided the chief ministerial spokesmen, Hardwicke and Newcastle; and in 1740 he joined the cabinet as lord privy seal. Meanwhile, as Queen Caroline's closest friend and confidant he was ideally placed to aid Sir Robert and her majesty in manipulating the often cranky George II. Walpole's successors, the Pelham brothers, Hervey loathed. But even while criticizing their administration he continued to praise Sir Robert's. Failing health and loss of office in the summer of 1742 cast a cloud over his final year that not even his enduring love of classical literature could disperse: he died in 1743 a bitter man. But he had passed most of his life happily, and however one assesses his androgyny, Hervey is striking proof that Court Whigs were not all dull.[2]

II

A study of Hervey's political and constitutional views must begin with the recognition that the ideas he entrusted to correspondence with friends or to his Memoirs were not at every point consistent with the notions he broadcast in his political pamphlets. An important part of understanding Hervey involves coming to terms with the inconsistencies between his two personae. They reveal much about the pamphleteering conventions of the day and about his perception of which structures of constitutional argumentation carried the greatest plausibility. Precisely because Hervey tailored his private views for public consumption—changing little that was fundamental but adjusting them in a variety of ways—he provides a useful introduction to the world of Court Whig polemics.

And what were his private views of government? of administration? of the king and his ministers? They found random expression in his letters and more deliberate, but still candid, expression in the Memoirs. They rested, as most postmedieval political views did, on certain conclusions about human nature that had, it was believed, been borne out

2. The fullest biography of Hervey is Robert Halsband, Lord Hervey: Eighteenth-Century Courtier (Oxford, 1974). Also illuminating, and far more interpretive, are the splendid introductory essays to the two editions of Hervey's memoirs: John, Lord Hervey, Some Materials Towards Memoirs of the Reign of King George II, ed. Romney Sedgwick (3 vols.; London, 1931); and John, Lord Hervey, Memoirs of the Reign of George the Second, from His Accession to the Death of Queen Caroline, ed. John Wilson Croker (2 vols.; Philadelphia, 1848). The Sedgwick edition will be used in all citations.

by experience. To Stephen Fox Hervey outlined his notions about the motivations behind human behavior. "People," he wrote, "may be kind, beneficent and friendly, from principle, charity and compassion. But they feel sensibly for nothing but what is conducive some way or other to their pleasure, or their interest, or their pride."[3] The expression lacks the precision we might wish for, but it is important to note immediately that Hervey was not the thoroughgoing pessimist that so many of his Patriot contemporaries were. People might be impelled largely by self-regarding concerns, but they were capable of shaping behavior to the expectations and even the needs of their fellows. Even more, such behavior could be touched by presumably autonomous sensations of affection or pity. Hervey began, in short, with a view of mankind that embraced at least a modicum of complexity.

From this interpretation there followed, in Hervey's view, certain implications about the nature of government. Since all human beings pursued pleasure, served self-interest, and catered to their own pride, their actions in the arena of the community required controlling and channeling. Only government could accomplish this end, and thus government meant, for Hervey, just one thing: the application of power to people. The purpose of any government was to employ power in such a way as to bring stability to a society. To achieve this goal it was necessary that the rawer varieties of self-seeking among the populace be suppressed, that conflicts among groups and individuals be resolved, and that obedience be imposed and enforced. Hervey was not afraid to approve the exercise of power. He admired the Romans in part precisely because for centuries they had known how to use power without letting it destroy them. It was the mark of a good constitution, he believed, that the ruler be free to respond to threats to the state with the most forceful ripostes available. Thus Hervey saw the chief duty of those who would serve their state to be the defense of the government's capacity to act determinatively as it saw fit and to mobilize its power swiftly when it wished.[4]

But if Hervey's view of human nature told him that mankind needed

---

3. Ilchester, *Hervey and His Friends*, 132.
4. This paragraph is based chiefly upon *Letters between Lord Hervey and Dr. Middleton concerning the Roman Senate* (London, 1778), 112–16, and *Memoirs*, II, 432, but distills ideas found elsewhere in Hervey's private writings.

government, it did not reveal to him what type of government was best. And the conventional authorities on such matters were no more helpful. Hervey was in fact quite skeptical about the capacity of human intelligence to gain knowledge of any matters not immediately present to the senses. He was furthermore suspicious of efforts to systematize bodies of knowledge into coherent patterns. Accordingly he rejected the claims of the historians, the philosophers, and the theologians that they possessed by virtue of their training and perspectives the requisite knowledge for organizing mankind politically. For two reasons Hervey did not share the common view of his age that history could legitimize certain institutions or ways of life. He distrusted the historian's tendency to account for the deeds of former generations by recourse to overriding principles. "No bodies of men," he remarked in criticism of Dionysius of Halicarnassus, "any more than any particular men, ever act so constantly and uniformly, as to admit of all their actions being reduced to one principle." Moreover, after reflecting on the problems of distilling the truth from discrepant accounts of events taking place in his own day, he found it implausible to credit the assertions of historians that "exactness" about events of ancient days could ever be secured. People who were so credulous he denominated "history-bigots"—a term that gains in force when one recalls Hervey's contempt for most prejudice. The philosophers were no more reliable. "How the devil can you read philosophy?" he asked Henry Fox. "No body ever wrote upon that subject that was not mad himself, or did not do all he could to make other people so." And theologians of course were equally useless. "Parsons," he explained, "talk nonsense."[5] But if the historian, the philosopher, and the theologian were all disqualified by their particular superstitions from being helpful sources of wisdom about organizing political society, where could Hervey turn?

The answer was simple, or at least unreflective. Rather than invoke the authority of scholarship or refined intellectuality to justify a particular organization for the state, he urged a simple acquiescence in that which historical accident had conferred on Britain. His belief that a government must be left free to act led him, when regarding the

5. *Letters*, 73; Ilchester, *Hervey and His Friends*, 207, 209.

matter abstractly, to declare that "the most absolute government, provided it were well administered, would always be the most beneficial
government to any society."[6] But the contingencies of the past had
given Britain in the concrete present a constitution that distributed
power among several agencies and accorded a generous measure of liberty to those subject to its authority. Any tampering with the fundamentals of this constitution could lead only to civil discontent and
disorder. Habituated to a life of regulated liberty and to at least indirect
participation in political affairs, Britons would not lightly countenance
any efforts to resettle their constitutional order. Hervey therefore never
sought the remodeling of the British constitution. Indeed, he urged all
who paid him heed to honor it, for only by respecting it could one
secure its sound operation. It was therefore the duty of the Briton who
wished to serve his state to protect the constitution under whose jurisdiction he had been born against those forces that threatened its capacity to allow the effective exercise of power.

In practice, this consideration led Hervey to envision threats of a
different nature than we might at first suppose. Despite his intense
concern that the government retain broad power, he did not see pa-
ralysis through institutional conflict or counterpoise as a pressing danger—that is, he did not dwell upon the possibility of a mixed government becoming a stalemated government. Instead he feared that the
power of the government might fall into hands that would use that
power so selfishly or capriciously as to provoke a reaction from dissat-
isfied groups. This misuse of power would lead in turn to civil conflicts
of unspecified sorts that could only immobilize the state. The potential
captors of power that Hervey so feared were polar opposites: the sole
despot and the impassioned mob.

The threat of the despot was the more easily disposed of. In an encomiastic analysis of the government of republican Rome Hervey noted
that the Romans chose not to confine power but instead to limit the
length of time any man might be authorized to command such power.
"By this manner then of making power absolute but temporary, and
making those who were entrusted with it, accountable afterward for

6. *Letters*, 112.

the use they had made of it, the Romans had all the advantages of an absolute Government, without being exposed to its inconveniencies; and enjoyed all the benefit, that arises to any society from the quick execution of prudent counsels in despotic governments, without being exposed to those disadvantages, which will, I believe, always attend the entrusting power with those, who are as little subject to future punishment, as present control."[7] The British practice varied somewhat from the Roman, but the end was the same. In Britain it was the ministers who exercised greatest power, but they could do so only so long as they retained the support of Parliament. Thus, though tenures of power were not fixed in Britain, the goal of confining the opportunities of the incumbent while freeing the potency of the office was still achieved. The minister who misused power would quickly be deprived of support, his effectiveness would thereby disappear, and the king would thereupon dismiss him. As long as Parliament continued to exist, the sovereign power of the British state could not be abused by the single individual.[8]

The danger of the "rabble" securing power was more worrisome for Hervey. It might do so, he feared, by making the monarch submit to its will. "The clamour of the people and the insolence of a mob" were poor guides for a king to resort to when naming a minister. If once the monarch heeded their outcry, he would thereby delegate "for the future all his authority and all his privilege of choosing his own servants into the hands of a riotous multitude." Nor, Hervey warned the king, could he later retrieve his loss. Thereafter, every man selected as a minister "would look upon himself as the Minister of the people, not of Your Majesty." Power thus relinquished to an irrational mob lay beyond reclamation and under the sway of caprice and folly. Predictably then, Hervey viewed the advent of the Gracchi as the age in which "confusion" and "slavery" first became characteristic of republican Rome. He knew full well that, to a superficial glance, Britain scarcely seemed in

7. Ibid., 115.
8. The extension of Hervey's argument to England—i.e., the substance of the last four sentences—represents a structure of inferred views. In his published writings Hervey does not advert to how Britain wards off the potential despot, but his Memoirs provide ample evidence that he thought much as this account suggests.

danger of falling prey to a democratic regime: the crown commanded both money and troops, conventionally regarded as the "nerves and sinews of royal power." But a more penetrating view produced the "paradoxical" conclusion—"I know not how to account for it"—that the crown had never been less powerful in its role as counterpoise to popular feeling. And then, despite his disclaimer, Hervey even proposed a tentative explanation for the paradox. Borrowing from Bolingbroke's rhetorical armory, he cited the "spirit of liberty" that permeated British society as the source of the crown's weakness and therefore as the basis of the popular threat.[9]

What might all these reflections mean at the concrete level of policy? What should Walpole's administration do to protect its power? What should its friends do? To Hervey these were the most pressing of political issues. Given the institutional arrangement that had been inherited in Britain—given too the fortunate truth that monarchs were usually inept and hence not in themselves dangerous—Hervey focused attention on the need to keep the populace quiet. His fundamental maxim was essentially Walpole's famous *quieta non movere*. "Things are very well as they are," he wrote to the prime minister's brother Horace in 1735. "Why stir them? It is with many parts of policy, both in Government and Religion, as it is with some liquors. They will neither of them bear being shaken. . . . It is very ill-judged to run the risk of spoiling all that is clear and good only, to squeeze a little more out of what is bad." But Hervey did not therefore oppose all change, for obdurance could itself sometimes arouse a people who felt aggrieved on an isolated issue. Thus when he assigned to Sir Robert the description Tacitus gave to Tiberius—"Nihil aequè Tiberium anxium habebat quàm ne composita turbarentur"—he did so as a criticism. "How right soever this policy might be in general, it exposed him to severe censures in particular cases."[10] All of this was of course truistic. And Hervey provided no clue for the key problem that confronts politicians: how to discriminate what ought to be reformed from what ought to be left alone.

Most of the rest of his privately offered advice was of a similarly

9. *Memoirs*, I, 167, 223, 281; *Letters*, 94.
10. *Memoirs*, I, 45, II, 365; Ilchester, *Hervey and His Friends*, 227.

prudential nature. He warned against excessive explicitness in governmental pronouncements. "Modern kings," he pontificated to Henry Fox on the occasion of a speech from the throne, "like the ancient Oracles, should never deliver their meanings too plain, that the ambiguity of their sense may leave a possibility of different expositions according as future events develop." He warned too that a government should never court the appearance of corruption. Specifically, he indicted Walpole's reflexive aversion to permitting parliamentary inquiries into administration activities. For even while granting the validity of Sir Robert's desire to keep Parliament curbed, Hervey felt that the attendant disadvantage of appearing to be covering up scandals outweighed any political advantage to be secured by keeping Parliament in its place. Hervey thought it short-sighted to refuse to use times of peace to reduce a national debt that would certainly increase in times of war. But he never made clear exactly why such a policy was disastrous or what fate awaited a Britain that behaved with such financial insouciance. His most interesting and revealing bit of advice—too sophisticated to be called a truism—was offered to the king. "The Court," he explained, in discussing preparations for the election of 1734, "have truth and money on their side. . . . Almost all mankind are either to be convinced or to be bought."[11] Here again Hervey showed his belief in a less simplistic image of man than the one the Patriots adopted. Money alone, though important, would not suffice: there were numerous people whose support could not be purchased. Truth was thus also vital to the government's political efforts, and although we may safely infer that by the term "truth" Hervey really meant the aggressive explanation of the government's policies (most of which, it must be recalled, he believed sound), the acknowledgment that many of the inhabitants of the political world were reasonable beings capable of evaluating alternative arguments showed that Hervey was less entrapped in anthropological mythologies than many critics of the government.

This then is the substance of Hervey's private views. Human nature made some type of government necessary; any government, to be effec-

11. Ilchester, *Hervey and His Friends*, 186; *Memoirs*, I, 186, 222–23, II, 447.

tive, needed access to unrestrained power; historical accident had conferred certain discrete governmental institutions on Britain; therefore the public-spirited politicians of the kingdom should work to assure that the accidental inheritance did not hamper the administration's capacity to mobilize power. The reader may have noted that several concepts which played central roles in the political debates of the era scarcely figure at all in Hervey's private views. He had, in fact, little to say about either the nature of the British constitution or the protection of British liberties, although in the public arena no other issues matched these two in prominence. Of the historical mode of justification—the most prevalent type of constitutional exegesis in the era—he at least spoke. But his views, as we have seen, were skeptical. Indeed, Hervey was finally scornful of those who thought that the past had lessons to teach the present. He thus simultaneously ignored the key issues of the public forum and scorned the mode within which they were usually debated. There was one other important way in which his private views contrasted with the assumptions governing public debate—or, more accurately, with the assumptions of the proministerial writers in that debate. Hervey thought conventional party distinctions almost useless and conventional designations spurious. The parties of Anne's day, he believed, had dissolved. The Whigs now in power behaved much as the Tories formerly had, not only in the sense that the Whigs acted high-handedly but even in the sense that they had become defenders of the prerogative and the established church. Jacobitism and a belief in a hereditary right to rule had meanwhile virtually disappeared. "The chief struggle," Hervey concluded, "now lay not between Jacobites and Hanoverians, or Tories and Whigs, but between Whigs and Whigs."[12] Most assuredly this was not the type of language Walpole used.

Hervey was a man of wide reading. He was not therefore speaking from ignorance when he declared Tacitus and Machiavelli to be the most valuable of the political writers. His selection is interesting because it reveals something about his biases and reinforces the interpretation of his private views just presented. There are many similarities

12. *Memoirs*, I, 5–6.

between the Roman and the Florentine.[13] Both were realists in analysis, both viewed human nature as multi-faceted, both granted a major role in human affairs to chance or accident. Moreover, both were widely viewed as teachers of political techniques rather than political values, and though we today would regard that view as imperfect, it is undeniable that from the Renaissance forward men had culled the works of Tacitus and Machiavelli to extract from them aphoristic dicta about politics. Hervey approved of all these attitudes and assumptions. He shared the two writers' interest in intrigues at court and their equivocal stance toward princely power. He recorded his opinion that "the fortuitous influence of chance" was "so much more decisive of the success or miscarriage of statesmen's schemes, than the skill or dexterity of the most able and most artful of them." He approved of their disinclination to invoke the supernatural. Above all, he rejoiced in their presupposition—for it was his too—that complexity and ambiguity were the keynotes of everything human. A man, Hervey once mused, who wanted always to make "practice tally with theory" would be "seldom pleased" with the world.[14] Tacitus and Machiavelli were not so foolish. As the Roman once noted in a discussion of Cicero, it was easier to praise a mixed constitution than to create one. But if Tacitus and Machiavelli were wise enough to see the fatuity of reducing man and society to abstractions, Bolingbroke and William Pulteney—at least in Hervey's eyes—were not. And therefore the contemplation of having such misguided men with their unfulfillable principles achieve power brought fear to Hervey and led him into the public arena.

III

The public Hervey was in a number of ways a different man from the private Hervey. Whether one consults his most famous tract, *Ancient and Modern Liberty Stated and Compared*, or his most effective work, *The Conduct of the Opposition*, or his most introspective essay, *Miscel-*

13. The linking was a commonplace of the age. John Oldmixon, for example, called Machiavelli "the modern Tacitus." *The Critical History of England, Ecclesiastical and Civil* (2 vols.; London, 1724–30), II, xxv.

14. *Memoirs*, I, 46, II, 450. Important elements of this discussion are drawn from P. Burke, "Tacitism," in T. A. Dorey, ed., *Tacitus* (New York, 1969), 149–71.

laneous Thoughts, or any of his more ephemeral publications, one can only conclude that Hervey was a conforming member of the guild of eighteenth-century pamphleteers. He turned his attention again and again to the glories of the constitution, and what his examinations lacked in analytical consistency they made up for in enthusiasm. He composed eulogies to liberty, all the while espying the familiar Court Whig bogies of a levelling republicanism on one flank and a papistically servile Jacobitism on the other. He careened about through the pages of English history, and when he was not dressing out several of the more nefarious personages of the past as prefigurations of Walpole's enemies, he was neatly standing on its head Bolingbroke's vision of the kingdom's history. Above all, he was a partisan. The Court Whigs were guardians of political truths vouchsafed them by the giants of the revolution. The opposition was a pack of unscrupulous, frustrated, disappointed, perhaps treasonable and certainly petty men who, unable to prevail in any fair political contest, were thoroughly prepared to employ deceit to sweep to power. Here was Court Whiggery in its effulgence.

All public commentators in the years between 1720 and 1756, whatever side they fought for, praised the British constitution. Hervey was no exception. He described it as "our most excellent Constitution" and later in the same tract as "the only Form of Government left at present, that I know of in the World, worth living under." These expressions were commonplaces. No less derivative were his efforts to account for the success of the constitution. Britain had, he explained, a "mixed Government." By this term he simply meant that the government was constituted of different parts, each with its appointed role. The gravest threat to such a constitution—and here he invoked Machiavelli's authority—was that the "Districts of the chief parts of that Government" would be "so indistinctly known" that those men entrusted with administering the parts would find themselves compelled to struggle with one another for the simple power to administer. But in England, and by extension Britain, this threat had dissolved through the wisdom of the Whigs. "As therefore no Government can be free but a mix'd Government," he instructed his readers, "and no mixed Government peaceable, but where particular Jurisdictions are allotted, and the

Bounds of each Part fully known and settled; so I think one may with great Truth and Justice affirm, this Government was never on so free and so desirable a Foot, as after the *Bill of Rights* was pass'd, and when the farther Limitations on the Crown by the Act of Settlement took place." The British constitution was thus characterized by a "wise structure," the product of Whig statesmanship.[15]

At this point in the reconstruction of Hervey's public analysis of the constitution one must simply admit that vapidness gives way to incoherence. What he said in one place is often irreconcilable with what he said elsewhere. The notion of a constitution being mixed suggests a frame of government within which several different elements contend. But the nature and even the number of these elements was elusive for Hervey. Within *Conduct of the Opposition* alone he hinted at four different ways in which one might view the constitution as balanced. In his first scheme it consisted of two "scales," the crown and the security of the people, between which a balance should be kept. That formulation was, to put it gently, obscure. Immediately thereafter he clouded his imagery even more by alluding to three "powers" in the constitution, presumably crown, Lords, and Commons. Further on, while continuing to employ the term "powers" he returned to his initial dualism, pitting the crown against a united Parliament. But he promptly reverted to the triadic view, seeing in the "rights" of the crown, the "privileges" of Parliament, and the "liberties" of the people the "three great assistant Springs on which this Government moves." And by introducing a separate tract, *An Answer to a Country Parson's Plea*, one can find Hervey employing "Parliament" in the older sense of the sovereign legislature incorporating Commons, Lords, and crown.[16] From among these various allusions to springs and scales and powers, from his two different definitions of Parliament, and from the tendency of his constitutional image to modulate capriciously between duality and triality, no coherence is to be found. But perhaps none should be expected. Hervey was a propagandist. The concrete situation of the de-

15. [John, Lord Hervey], *Miscellaneous Thoughts on the Present Posture both of Our Foreign and Domestic Affairs* (London, 1742), 72.

16. [John, Lord Hervey], *The Conduct of the Opposition and the Tendency of Modern Patriotism* (London, 1734), 18–19, 34, 39–40; [John, Lord Hervey], *An Answer to the Country Parson's Plea against the Quakers Tythe-Bill* (London, 1736?) 21–22.

bate he was engaged in did far more to determine the images he chose than any drive for overriding consistency. The only point he needed to insist on was that the constitution was "balanced." Still, it must be acknowledged that when he spoke of the "structure" of the constitution, he used that term in a rather cavalier fashion.

The constitution conferred several important and interlocked benefits. It promoted prosperity, it allowed for the fair administration of justice, and it fostered peace.[17] But it did not accomplish these praiseworthy ends by being some disembodied spirit brooding over and thereby regulating the British nation. Hervey's instincts as a primitive political scientist were reductionist. He brought the constitution down to earth. In the last analysis the constitution was well-nigh indistinguishable from the government—or, still more precisely, from Walpole's Court Whig government. Thus, for Hervey it was illegitimate to maintain that criticism of the government was not criticism of the constitution or that one might be an enemy of the government but a friend of the constitution. Through this virtual conflation of what are usually regarded as two radically distinct concepts Hervey was denying Bolingbroke's important counterargument that the government was different from and subordinate to the constitution.[18] It very much served Bolingbroke's purposes to insist on such a distinction. If it were accepted, it would spare the Patriot critics of the Walpole government from the imputation of disloyalty to the regime. It would thereby immensely widen their field of possible combat and simultaneously secure them against the type of counteroffensive from Walpole's friends that was most damaging to the Patriots—namely, the charge that they opposed the Protestant succession. Understandably then, every reason that impelled the Patriots to plead for a disjunction moved Hervey to resist it. He wanted the critics to be viewed as no less than traitors.

17. [Hervey], *Miscellaneous Thoughts*, 9; [John, Lord Hervey], *Ancient and Modern Liberty Stated and Compared* (London, 1734), 61–64; and many other places. The defense of property is notably missing from this list. Aside from passing references in *Answer* I found no indication that Hervey's Court Whiggery placed any notable emphasis on the protection of property.

18. [Hervey], *Conduct*, 58. See Harvey C. Mansfield, Jr., *Statesmanship and Party Government: A Study of Burke and Bolingbroke* (Chicago, 1965), though Bolingbroke himself is less consistent on this issue than Mansfield suggests. See also J. H. Burns, "Bolingbroke and the Concept of Constitutional Government," *Political Studies*, X (1962), 264–76.

The single most important benefit provided by the British constitution was the guarantee of liberty. Indeed, liberty constituted the chief
glory of Britain's frame of government. Liberty, Hervey wrote, was essential "both to our Grandeur as a Nation, and our Happiness as a
People." "The Freedom of this Country," he declared elsewhere, in explicit agreement with the opposition, "is the Basis of its Prosperity." If
happiness, prosperity, and grandeur were the fruits of liberty, the protection of that liberty thereby became a fundamental responsibility of
any man claiming to be a friend to his country. Hervey accepted the
notion that liberty was not the same as license—that it could exist
only within a framework of laws. At the opening of *Ancient and Modern
Liberty* he staked out a Whig claim to the middle ground between the
antinomians and the authoritarians. "And as it must be granted, that
all Peace, all Order in Society is maintain'd by some Restrictions on
natural Liberty, and that the Anarchy of natural Liberty wholly unrestrain'd, would be as great an Evil as the Slavery of no Liberty at all
allow'd; so the best regulated and best concerted Form of Government
must be that which avoids the Inconveniencies of both Extremes, and
at once preserves Mankind from the Oppressions consequent to an absolute Submission to the Will of another, and from the Confusion that
would result from an unlimited Indulgence of their Own."[19] But if the
rhetoric suggested that Hervey was heroically holding the pass for common sense against the weapons of despots and raving anarchists, the
reality was far staider. Hervey, as usual, was voicing commonplaces; the
political nation was at one in its adherence to the conventional notion
of regulated liberty.

Why then, with all this agreement, was liberty a prominent issue in
pamphlet warfare? Its centrality followed from the truth that, though
all Britons thought it worth preserving, they were divided about what
it was and whom they were preserving it from. The Patriot opposition
viewed liberty as the condition of any nation in which the legislature
was independent of the executive. They painted Walpole and his band
of toadies as the villains who sought to destroy this independence in
Britain. They drew lurid verbal pictures of a British people bravely

19. [Hervey], *Ancient and Modern Liberty*, 1, 3; [Hervey], *Conduct*, 7.

struggling to fight free of the tentacles of Court Whig money. They assailed placemen and, more fundamentally, the numerous mechanisms by which the ministry sought to inform itself about the mood of the Commons and secure its compliance. They argued that corruption was destroying liberty. Hervey sweepingly rejected these charges. "I believe I may venture to say," he boldly exclaimed, "this is almost the only Court, the only Reign, in which no single Instance was ever pretended to be given, of Solicitation made, or Favour shown, by the force of Money."[20] This was, we may judge, a rather brazen declaration. But for Hervey the opposition argument was also beside the point. In his view liberty was a condition pertaining to individuals—the condition of being able to act according to uncoerced volition rather than by the dictates of constraining authority.[21] Liberty had enemies aplenty, he acknowledged, but Sir Robert was not among them. The prime minister sought to extend the range of private liberty, not to circumscribe it. He favored a broader religious toleration and supported commercial participation in politics. Indeed, Hervey concluded, if Britain wished to remain free it needed to retain Walpole. Rather than being the enemy of liberty, he was its palladium.

Who then were its enemies? One candidate—but not the most dangerous—was the Church of England. It is easy to imagine that a man of Hervey's anticlerical inclination enjoyed savaging the nest of the parsons. Ecclesiastical power was growing, he warned, especially the power that land conferred, and "if it be unchesk'd in its Progress" it would "extend its Sway over all the Property of the Kingdom . . . tending to the Destruction of this free Government."[22] But two other forces constituted far more serious threats. One was the mob, variously called

20. [John, Lord Hervey], *Observations on the Writings of the Craftsman* (London, 1730), 22–23.

21. I have discovered only one context in which his use of "liberty" manifestly does not conform to this definition. Hervey called Elizabeth's reign unfree because the queen did not seek the "consent" of her subjects. Clearly he is thinking of something more here than merely the capacity of her subjects to act volitionally. But Hervey's difficulties with making Elizabeth's reign fit his historical dogmatism will soon be noted in the text; this is, I suspect, simply another example of them. [Hervey], *Ancient and Modern Liberty*, 23.

22. [Hervey], *Answer*, 42. In this same pamphlet Hervey voiced guarded approval of wider religious toleration: "to define *Duties to God*, is beyond the Bounds of Human Authority," 83.

a "riotous Multitude" and a "Mad Dog." Incapable of rational thought, prey to passions, and vulnerable to demagoguery, the mob was a ruler to be dreaded. Nothing, it was presumed, would be proof against the uncontrollable whims of a democracy. And therefore those who urged the king to heed the cry out-of-doors, as the Patriots were doing, were undermining the very liberty they pretended to venerate. The other formidable enemy, the Tory party, endangered the Protestant succession. Hervey asserted that in the final years of Anne's reign the Oxford ministry had intended to replace her with James, a claim that was far from incredible. If such had been Tory policy toward a Stuart, he asked, what would the party wish to do with a Hanoverian? His answer borrowed imagery from the days of the Civil War. "No body can doubt"— though many did—"but they would be glad not only to lop a Branch, but to cut up the very Root, destroy all its fair and flourishing Fruits, and extirpate the very Seed out of the Land." A Catholic monarch would bring in his train all the despotism that the British attached to popery. Between the flanking threats of Jacobitism and democracy the "present Government must steer." The dangers could be compactly symbolized by pregnant dates. A "Republican" ascendancy would return the nation to 1641: it would use royal power to destroy royal power. A "Jacobite" ascendance would return it to 1660: it would bring in a new and unfettered monarch.[23] Only through the fidelity of the Court Whigs to the constitution and the people's support for the Court Whigs could the nation retain its freedom in the face of these menaces.

There was, however, a final and still greater enemy to liberty. Hervey's most bitter denunciations, and his shrewdest use of political argumentation, were reserved for the army. Being a sincere advocate of the power of peace to promote welfare, and being therefore a most reluctant warrior, Hervey harbored no private reservations about the truth of his campaign against the army. The issue that gave focus to the debate was the opposition demand that the crown be deprived of its capacity to cashier officers at will. The Patriots resented the punitive sackings of Lords Cobham and Bolton in 1734. But Hervey, in defending the prerogative, did not confine himself to the narrow issue. An

23. [Hervey], *Conduct*, 40–49; [John, Lord Hervey], A *Letter to the Craftsman on the Game of Chess, &c.* (London, 1733), 17.

"Army," he declared, "is in its Nature a Body, that must obey, or will command." If it commanded, he warned, it would establish "the worst sort of Slavery, which is that of a *Stratocracy*, a military Synod, arbitrarily dictating and cruelly executing their own Laws, without Controul, Redress, or Appeal." To place an officer beyond the punitive hand of the king—worse, to leave his fate, when accused, up to a court of his peers—was to repose all powers of disciplining an army within that army itself. This would only serve to remove all checks on its authority. Officers would become "the Masters of the State instead of the Servants of the State." And the army would become—"in the modern Style," as he put his parody of Patriot patter—"the most *All-governing, All-dictating, All-directing, All-grasping, Power-ingrossing* Body of Men, that can be supposed to exist in any Nation." Alluding to the rule of the major generals in Oliver Cromwell's day, Hervey described a military ascendancy as "a Power known but once in this Kingdom, then felt with Calamity, Anarchy, and Confusion; and ever since remember'd with Horror and Deprecation." The dispute, he finally insisted, rested on one point: since either the military or the civil power must be superior, which type of dominance would be more "consistent with a free Government?" In one stroke Hervey had the pleasure of lashing two of his most despised enemies: the army of which he was always suspicious, and the "Patriot-Parents of a Tyrant-Child" who spoke in its behalf.[24] It is no wonder that *The Conduct of the Opposition* was his most powerful essay.

Hervey never claimed to be an historian. But he knew that to engage in pamphleteering he had to accept its conventions—and one of these was the appropriation of history for partisan advantage. So he romped through the relations of English and Roman history, ransacking the texts for illustrative incidents and jumbling events into politically useful molds. He gloated over his success at borrowing useful examples from the work of Paul de Rapin-Thoyras, the "*Craftsman's* own political Evangelist." He ignored most forms of crucial historical distinctions, with results that were scarcely enlightening and might even be taken to bear out the notorious maxim about the danger of a little knowledge.

24. [Hervey], *Conduct*, 8, 19–21, 26–27.

But unquestionably they were entertaining. Hervey's gifts as a writer were not great. All too often his cadences wavered, and he squandered both forcefulness and precision to excess verbiage. When inspired, however, he could become a passable aphorist, and his most readable tracts were those that gave him occasion to limn a figure with a few quick strokes. Historical essays fell most readily into this category, and it is from them that we cull a few memorable etchings: Richard I as a "Royal Don Quixote" or Henry VIII as the "Butcher of his Wives."[25] Thus, while skeptical of the validity of historical knowledge, Hervey enjoyed playing with it, and twentieth-century readers can still enjoy perusing his games.

Ancient and Modern Liberty was his major foray into English history, although in the various tracts entitled *Observations* he explored the reign of Edward IV in some detail.[26] The argument in *Ancient and Modern Liberty* was the one that rang from the pages of Walpole's press:[27] England before 1688 had not been free, the freedom of the present was the product of Whig wisdom as embodied in the Bill of Rights and the Act of Settlement, and the protection of that freedom was best entrusted to the Court Whig heirs of the Whigs of the revolution. This entire line of argument was designed to confute the Patriot contentions, most dramatically expressed in Bolingbroke's *Remarks on the History of England*, that old England had been free but that Whig domination in the modern era was sapping the hard-won liberties of old.[28] Where Bolingbroke had focused attention on a "spirit of liberty," alive even under the oppressions of James I, Hervey turned his more mundane eye to institutionalized liberty and located it, sustained by certain forms of administration, only in the generations since the Glorious Revolution. Thus Hervey was determined to demonstrate that all of England's history before 1688 was characterized by monarchs who, usually ruling despotically, invariably reigned over an unfree people.

25. [Hervey], *Ancient and Modern Liberty*, 9, 18, 51.

26. These were responses to the eighth letter in Bolingbroke's *Remarks on the History of England*, a series of twenty-three weekly letters published in the *Craftsman* in 1730–31. Hervey's tracts constituted a defense of Queen Caroline against the *Craftsman's* attack through proxy.

27. See Kramnick, *Bolingbroke and His Circle*, 127–36.

28. Samuel Squire would later adapt the Bolingbrokian view to ministerial purposes, but in Hervey's day it remained a weapon in the Patriots' armory. See Chapter V herein.

In some instances it was an easy task. From the Conquest down to Henry I's day "It was *Force* only prevail'd." Thereafter the church and the barons began to encroach on royal power, but the people received no relief. Richard I, for example, "exhausted the Treasure of his Kingdom to raise his Fame upon Earth; and spilt the Blood of his Subjects, to purchase Glory in Heaven." The barons who humbled John were simply men "who had long tyrannised in their particular districts." Edward I, though a "great Man, and a great King," brought no liberty with his conquests. Henry IV was "as able a Tyrant, as ever sat on this Throne," and the War of the Roses simply allowed people, through armed struggle, to exchange one master for another. Henry VII's reign was "odious and oppressive." But it was Henry VIII's reign of "rapaciousness and cruelty" that provoked Hervey's most withering fulminations. The king's religious pronouncements were so opaque that "many miserable Wretches were put to Death for saying they believed, and many for saying they disbelieved, the same thing," and the king himself ruled as the "Terror of his Nobility," the "Scourge to all Mankind," and a "Dupe abroad, and Tyrant at home."[29]

Neither the religious somersaults of the next two reigns nor the triumphs of Elizabeth's introduced any freedom to England. The young Edward VI was "one of the worst Kings" to rule in the kingdom and Somerset "one of the weakest Ministers that ever govern'd." Mary was "devout but execrable," and in league with her popish advisers she sacrificed "whole Hecatombs of Victims, to their *edible* God, and his *infallible* Ambassador." Elizabeth posed interpretative difficulties, for Hervey could not deny that she had served England well. But, *pace* Bolingbroke, she did so as an absolute ruler. Although she had given many benefits to her kingdom, she had granted them without conferring freedom. Her subjects prospered—but by virtue of her insight, not their liberties. "Never were the Reins of *Prerogative* held with a stricter Hand, or the Yoke of Slavery faster bound upon the People's Necks than at this Period of Time." A useful comparison then offered itself, designed to show that the glories of Gloriana herself paled beside the still richer glories of Georgius. Both reigns were characterized by great ministers: Walpole was Lord Burghley reincarnated. But the Hanover-

29. [Hervey], *Ancient and Modern Liberty*, 8–19.

ian secured more for his people than the Tudor. "We now," Hervey instructed, "reap all the public Benefits that accrued to the Nation from her Counsels, without the latent Evil of their being forced upon us, and consequently rather inflicted than bestowed." And for the sottish reader who might miss the point of that remark Hervey had a still simpler formulation: "every Good which Queen *Elizabeth* compell'd her Subjects to receive, without the least Show of Freedom, the *present King* has procured for them, without the least Infringement of it."[30]

If Hervey found no liberty under Elizabeth it can scarcely surprise that he adjudged the early Stuart and Puritan states unfree. He moved through them quite quickly, dismissing the reigns of James I and Charles I as "one continued Series of Folly and Injustice." Cromwell then imposed a "Stratocracy." Some relief came with the Restoration, owing not to the "silly" Charles II but to "that true Patriot and real Benefactor to an unthankful People," the earl of Clarendon. But James II, by failing to draw the proper lessons from his father's unhappy reign, recklessly attacked both the civil and religious liberties of his subjects. The people thereupon drove him out. "From King *James* the Second's Banishment, Abdication, Deposition, or whatever People please to call it"—so much for the constitutional niceties of 1689!—"I date the Birth of real Liberty in this Kingdom, or at least the Establishment, if not the Commencement, of every valuable Privilege we now enjoy."[31] It was true, Hervey noted, that liberties were thereafter often endangered: William III relied too much on Tories, and Anne made her chief contribution to the cause of liberty by contriving a timely death. But now, under the wise guidance of Sir Robert Walpole, liberties were secure. What the revolution generation of Whigs had wrought, the Hanoverian generation of Whigs would sustain.

Hervey was more knowledgeable about Roman history than his own nation's.[32] And although he had no polemical opportunities to set forth the course of Roman development in a manner analogous to his pre-

---

30. *Ibid.*, 21–27.

31. *Ibid.*, 29, 39, 40. The historical method of this pamphlet is discussed in Duncan Forbes, *Hume's Philosophical Politics* (Cambridge, 1975), 247–49.

32. In letters Hervey cites Livy, Cicero, Eutropius, Velleius Paterculus, Plutarch, Aurelius Victor, Dionysius, Suetonius, Don Cassius, and Sallust.

sentation of English history, he found many occasions for making important comparisons. The Patriots, he asserted, wanted to create "English Decemviri"; the army should not be given the leverage acquired by the Pretorian Cohorts; customs and excise men were not modern *publicani*. Sometimes comparisons were expanded into elaborate parallels. Hostile to the administration after Walpole's fall, he likened the ruling trio to the second triumvirate. He named no contemporaries, but his meaning was unmistakable. All knew who Lepidus was, he asserted, and then to make the task of identification still easier he drew a biting picture of the weak and unskilled Newcastle. Antony was Lord Bath (William Pulteney), a man of "great natural Talents" who once in office behaved as if he found power and reputation incompatible. Octavius was Lord Carteret, a man who knew that the key to success lay in securing Rome (George II).[33] The same sort of insensitivity to nuance and willful dismissal of the inconvenient that marked his rendering of English history is to be found in his rummagings among Roman analogues.[34] Hervey once asked what the writers of the *Craftsman* did and answered himself by declaring that they "pervert the Characters of the Dead, and . . . torture the *English* history, to furnish out new Parallels, and new Invectives." He was right. But it was a classic case of the pot calling the kettle black.

As much of the previous discussion demonstrates, the public Hervey wore his partisanship proudly and clearly. The point of seizing the middle ground in his discussion of liberty was to enable him to designate the opposition as extremists. It was the favorite Court Whig conception of politics: Walpole and his friends defended the proper bal-

33. [Hervey], *Conduct*, 24, 60; [John, Lord Hervey], *A Letter to the Author of Common Sense; or The Englishman's Journal, of Saturday, April 16* (London, 1737), 15–17; [Hervey], *Miscellaneous Thoughts*, 28–30.

34. His true view of the worth of drawing on the past for examples for the present was expressed to Henry Fox. He was sick, he said, of hearing Patriots rant about the "wisdom of our ancestors and the virtues of the Romans. I would be glad to know for which age of our ancestors they would like to change the circumstances of the present? Or if they would choose to have England resemble Rome in the time of what they must call that of its great virtue—that is, when it was miserably poor, without any trade, involved in perpetual wars abroad, and torn by conflicting factions of the nobility and commonalty at home. For my own part I like extremely to read of those times, but to live in these." Ilchester, *Hervey and His Friends*, 242.

ance between liberty and order that the Tories and republicans wished to undo. Hervey sought to make "Tory" virtually synonymous with "Jacobite." He was, it is true, not always consistent, and even in his most Tory-baiting moods he was ready to allow that a man might become a Tory from folly rather than wickedness. But he had little sympathy for those who would spin subtle distinctions to set themselves apart, within the opposition, from the Jacobites. They were, he remarked, like Socinians to Arians or Pironists to Skeptics—that is, they avowed different names but preached the same doctrines. Hervey generally affected a bluff contempt for "sublimated superfine Distinctions" and portrayed himself as a rugged empiricist who let "Things and Facts speak for themselves." It was a shrewd position for him to assume. In an age in which the legitimacy of opposition was manifestly suspect and the proponents of opposition were therefore trying to educate the public about the difference between opposition to an administration and disloyalty to a regime, Hervey was adopting a most satisfactory stance by expressing scorn for such sophistic analysis. When it was useful, he was even prepared to minimize the distinction he drew between Jacobites and republicans. In his *Observations on the Writings of the Craftsman* the spirit of 1641 and the spirit of 1660 became strangely interfused, and it was this sort of coalescence among opponents that Hervey had in mind when he called the Patriots a "motley amphibious faction." Nor was he at a loss to explain how the disciples of a popishly authoritarian Pretender might find common ground with latter-day levellers. They were, in a word, unprincipled. They were men "who whilst they have nothing but the Preservation of the Constitution and the Liberties of the People in their Mouths; have nothing in View, or at Heart, but the Gratification of long disappointed Rage, private Piques, and particular Resentments; and which rather than not gratify, they would gratify at the Expence both of our Liberties and our Constitution."[35] So professing, Hervey was naturally a Court Whig. Only the party of wisdom and moderation could save the kingdom from the faction of disappointed and frustrated office seekers.

35. [Hervey], *Observations*, 14–18; [Hervey], *Conduct*, 33, 58, 60; [Hervey], *Ancient and Modern Liberty*, 59.

IV

It seems indisputable that the public Hervey spoke with a different voice than the private Hervey. The bemusedly annoyed private man became a pugnaciously aroused public man; the somewhat idiosyncratic topics of private discourse yielded to the conventional topics of public debate. But it would, I believe, be wrong to conclude that the two persons were disjoined—that Hervey the pamphleteer was simply Hervey the hypocrite. Above all, it must be recalled that his polemical task was defensive. Although he might find occasional opportunity to counterattack Walpole's antagonists, he was in general compelled to fight the struggle on grounds chosen by the Patriots. This alone might account for any discrepancy between his personal evaluation of which issues were important and his patent public concern with a different set of problems. The opposition selected the target; Hervey then had to defend it. Thus *The Conduct of the Opposition* was a brief on behalf of the challenged royal prerogative in matters of military discipline, *Ancient and Modern Liberty* was a modernist rejoinder to Bolingbroke's Saxonist view of English history, and *Miscellaneous Observations* was a vigorous defense of the Walpole ministry against charges of corruption, selfishness, and mismanagement. Whatever attention he managed under such confining circumstances to give to matters he believed truly important was obscured in the overview by the major defensive thrust of the pamphlets. Hervey himself noted in the opening of *Observations on the Writings of the Craftsman* that it was more difficult to defend than attack in a "Paper-War."[36] And though he was in fact alluding to what he believed to be an irrational popular inclination to side with those who sneered at government and against those who defended it, his remark was perhaps truer when interpreted as a tactical judgment.

Since the opposition chose the grounds on which the battles were to be fought, it cannot be expected that Hervey's selection of pamphlet themes will coincide with his private notions of what was important. The more interesting test is whether his public view of politics contradicts his private one. Clearly it does—but only at two points. Despite his stirring vindication of Walpole's abstinence from corruption, he

36. [Hervey], *Observations*, 5.

knew full well—he had told the king as much—that money was vital to success in elections. Hervey did not believe that the direct or indirect purchase of votes was as destructive of spirit and liberty as the opposition did, and he was thus not frightened that a cash nexus accounted for some of the government's power. But he nevertheless avowed in public what he denied in private. Similarly, despite his most minatory rhetoric to the contrary, Hervey in truth did not see Jacobitism as a threat. Followers of the Pretender were few in number and weak in political understanding. It was useful in public to depict an opposition that had sold its soul to popery and absolutism, but in private Hervey saw Walpole's opponents as something far less profoundly sinister: a band of place-hungry, ambitious men employing very dangerous, half-digested ideas. It would appear that with these two exceptions the worst that might be said of the public Hervey was that he employed arguments he personally thought unsound—that he did not believe in the persuasiveness of some of what he said. With respect to the political use of history he even admitted as much, noting at the conclusion of *Sequel of a Pamphlet intitled Observations on the Writings of the Craftsman* that what he had just done with Edward IV's reign was neither fair nor honest, but that he believed it effectively showed how easy it was for any partisan to find "Historical Masks and Daggers."[37] We must recall that Tacitus and Machiavelli were Hervey's tutors; both taught dissimulation to be a necessary aspect of politics, and Hervey found it sensible to act on their lesson.

Underlying any surface discrepancies between the public writings and the private thoughts there lay the same basic vision of human nature and the same prescription for political life. In *The Conduct of the Opposition* Hervey alluded to the frailty of man and to his propensity to aggrandize. In his *Miscellaneous Thoughts* he was more explicit. "By the universal Laws and Principles of Nature," he declaimed, "Selfishness is the fundamental primary Ingredient in the Composition of every Being throughout the whole animal Creation, and in human Kind, as well as the rest." And though this remark sounds far more perversely single-minded than his private view, he immediately qualified the pes-

37. [John, Lord Hervey], *Sequel of a Pamphlet intitled Observations on the Writings of the Craftsman* (London, 1730), 29.

simism with a distinction that brought the whole published image of mankind into congruence with earlier private formulations. A man might be either a "good" or a "bad" citizen. The former allowed his "Disposition, Principles, and Judgment to direct his Selfishness to take a convenient Turn for the Rest of Mankind, and the Society he lives in." The latter permitted his "Passions and Inclinations to lead him into Ways inconvenient and prejudicial to the Community."[38] By both public and private reckoning man was egoistic; but in both accounts he was capable of restraining and channeling *amour propre* and of heeding a natural inclination to consider others. This view of mankind was essential to Hervey's Court Whig position, for it allowed him to make his chief constitutional point—namely, that power within the state should not be so feared that it was consequently fragmented.

The private Hervey thought power best placed when entrusted to a monarch who accepted ministerial guidance. This was precisely the view of the public Hervey. He had his moments, it is true, when he seemed bent upon amplifying the authority of Parliament—*An Answer to the Country Parson's Plea* comes to mind—but he never became incautious in his pronouncements. "The noblest Prerogative" of the House of Commons, he declared, is "the Redress of Grievances." "The proper and essential Care of Parliament," he later stated, is "to protect People from Injustice." These were scarcely extravagant claims. Even when he described Parliament's responsibility as being to serve as a "check" on royal advisers, he seemed to have nothing more restrictive in mind than a Hanoverian version of the old Roman practice whereby the Senate could try consuls after their retirement for crimes committed while in office. Thus he never suggested that kings exercised too much power in Britain. His clearest statement of his considered views appeared in *The Conduct of the Opposition.* Therein he took the Patriots to task for "descanting on the Nature of all Power" rather than "adapting their Reasoning to the present Purpose." He accepted a presupposition that the opposition often advanced: "Wherever Power is, no doubt it is liable to abuse." But it was mindless to argue—and here he broke with the Patriots—that because power was dangerous it should

38. [Hervey], *Conduct*, 11–12, 21; [Hervey], *Miscellaneous Thoughts*, 6–7.

therefore be lodged nowhere. Society cannot exist without a "Superior Power," nor is every man unfit to exercise it. Therefore the question that should be addressed is not how power can be eliminated but rather where it can with the least danger be reposed. For Hervey the answer was transparently obvious. The crown, for a variety of reasons, was the institution that could exercise "Superior Power" with the least threat, and it would be best for postrevolutionary Britain if the remaining powers of the crown were not forced to submit to precise definition. Limited though he was, the monarch needed a kind of residual discretionary authority which would allow him, in emergencies and with the concurrence of his ministers, to take vigorous action. After all, as Hervey noted elsewhere in what was surely the most frequently cited if substantively impoverished classical dictum of the era, *Salus populi suprema lex.*[39] Necessity, in short, could justify any action. It was wiser to leave the power to make such decisions with the king than to transfer it to any other constitutional agency.

Why was the crown the safest repository for power? What were the variety of reasons that moved Hervey to devote considerable energy to the cause of eighteenth-century monarchy? The answers to these questions emerge from both his public and his private writings, and, though sometimes vague, are cut of the same cloth, whether privately pronounced or publicly declaimed. One can best get at them by examining the constitutional implications of Hervey's view of liberty and by analyzing the reasons for his detestation of "confusion" within the state. A bonus attendant upon this inquiry will be an explanation of why Hervey called himself a Whig.

Hervey, it will be recalled, defined liberty as that condition in which a person acts volitionally rather than under compulsion from an external authority. He assumed that everyone would find liberty so defined attractive, since acting volitionally is acting pleasurably. The definition has some implications of importance. However much liberty might be spoken of as a benefit possessed by groups, it was in the last analysis exercised and hence known by individuals. Moreover, it could

39. [Hervey], *Answer,* 7, 9, 83; [John, Lord Hervey], *The Question Stated with Regard to Our Army in Flanders* (London, 1743), 26; [Hervey], *Miscellaneous Thoughts,* 10; [Hervey], *Conduct,* 11–13, 21–24.

not be absolute. Excessive liberty was license, the condition in which unfettered private wills came into dangerous conflict with each other or with the collective aims of the community. Thus liberty had to be kept bounded. It sat precariously between the antithetical threats of anarchy and tyranny. Too much liberty led to the erosion of the laws and customs that restrained selfishness. Too little liberty fostered the sensibility of being oppressed while stultifying the spontaneity and creativity that made Britain prosperous. Liberty could exist only when maintained by a balance of forces in the state. It was a product of a political order in which neither arbitrary rule—whether by crown, aristocracy, army, church, or mob—nor normlessness prevailed. We may now begin to see why Hervey was strikingly indifferent to the claims of consistency when invoking models of balance. Each of his formulations hinted at the broader truth. The constitution was more than a balance between two powers or among three springs—more than an equipoise between the crown and the people or among kings, Lords, and Commons. It was all these and simultaneously something bigger that comprehended all these. It was the settled British way of doing things, the pattern of conventional interactions to which the British submitted themselves. Those who truly understood the nature of liberty and who truly supported it were friends of the existing British constitution. They knew that that constitution, through all its richness and complexity, was the fortress of liberty. To value liberty was to honor the constitution.

If liberty was the glory of a state, confusion was its shame and, when severe, its destruction. The point, already noted, that Hervey argued for a virtual conjunction between "constitution" and "government"— that he asserted the virtual identity of the Walpole government and the constitution—can now be developed. The Walpole government was not the entire constitution but was the key part of it. The customs and conventions of the constitution existed, if it makes sense at all to attribute location to them, in the British people as a whole. But the Walpole government stood guard over the system, respecting the traditions and defending constitutional usages from their enemies. We must keep in mind this postulated virtual identity between the Walpole administration and the constitution if we are to understand Hervey's reiterated and, by our standards, not very plausible argument that those who sought to "confuse" the people were by that act subverters of the constitution. "Confusion" seems a less than imposing threat, but Hervey warned against it again and again.[40] One might think that, at worst, the Patriots' efforts to confuse people about Walpole were simply attempts to effect his ouster. But Hervey saw a more sinister meaning in the opponents' rhetoric. He was always directing his reader to look beneath the surface of the declarations of the *Craftsman*—that "political Alcoran of a false prophet"—to discern their implications. Did not the designation of the Act of Settlement as a contract, when conjoined with accusations about royal iniquity, promote the belief that the king's subjects were absolved from obedience? Did not the assertion that British liberties were secure whether a Catholic or a Protestant sat on the throne invite a resurgence of Jacobitism? Did not the demand that the king consult popular opinion in choosing his servants entail the eventual accession to the ministry of latter-day Ketts and Tylers? In each and every instance, Hervey believed, the Patriots were employing the means of "Distress and Clamour," seeking to confuse the simple and correct understanding of the constitution held by the bulk of the British. The Patriots sought with beguiling logic of this sort to dissolve the people's loyalties. Hervey accused the administration's opponents of using "guarded Treason," a term he learned from parliamentary shoptalk and found peculiarly satisfactory because it worked to obliterate the vital legal distinction between the small range of utterances that violated the treason laws and the vast range that did not. With the insight that would later play a central role in the writings of such disparate thinkers as David Hume and Edmund Burke, Hervey recognized the importance of public opinion as a foundation for stability. A well-disposed populace was the prerequisite to a successful constitutional order; a confused populace portended constitutional calamity. In sum, in

40. E.g., [Hervey], *Conduct*, 7, 58–59; [Hervey], *Letter*, 94; [Hervey], *Ancient and Modern Liberty*, 59; [John, Lord Hervey], *Farther Observations on the Writings of the Craftsman* (London, 1730), 18. Preeminently in Hervey's writings "confusion" means something like perturbation of reasoning processes or disorder in thought. But in the eighteenth century it was a richer term than it is for us, conveying overtones of overthrow, ruin, and tumult. Precisely for that reason, of course, it was a useful danger to espy when an enemy threatened.

Hervey's view, "a few mercenary *Journalists* and testy *Pamphleteers*," by seeking to confuse the people of Britain with lies, innuendoes, and suggestions, were building "Steps leading to Despoticism." Confusion inevitably begot tyranny.[41] It was an argument that becomes credible only when Hervey's conflation of government and constitution is borne in mind.

These remarks about liberty and confusion allow us to see more clearly why the crown was central for Hervey. It was neither because he was infatuated with monarchs nor because he thought the crown the most powerful institution in the state. On the contrary, he often expressed—candidly in private and guardedly in public—his fear that Parliament could overwhelm the crown. But that consideration becomes the starting point for understanding one of the grounds for Hervey's defense of the prerogative. He was a friend of royal power precisely because it was weak and because its weakness, if unremedied, might undo the balance that secured liberty. Of the nature of that balance he was, as noted, unsure; of its existence and importance he was absolutely persuaded. It must therefore be preserved. The crown was restrained by law and, in the light of Stuart history, was less likely to be that institution within the constitution that would hazard everything for an accretion of power. And the ministry provided a still more effective restraint upon the power of the crown. Hervey's understanding of Parliament's dominating power led him to believe that whereas a monarch who chose his own ministers would nevertheless be constrained by them and by Parliament, a Parliament that imposed ministers would be constrained by nothing at all. Thus—and in appearance paradoxically—the cause of liberty, which could be advanced only by the healthy confinement of both royal and parliamentary power, was eminently served by maintaining uninfringed the crown's prerogative in the selection of ministers. The second ground for Hervey's support for the crown was its mythic character. It was an institution that spoke to sentiment and elicited loyalty. It evoked the affections of many and respect from almost all. It stood above party. Because it appealed in

41. [Hervey], *Conduct*, 7, 47, 50–56; [Hervey], *Ancient and Modern Liberty*, 56–61; [Hervey], *Letter*, 94; [Hervey], *Observations*, 7; [Hervey], *Farther Observations*, 11. See also Ilchester, *Hervey and His Friends*, 46.

these ways to the heart rather than the head, it was proof against the cunningly reasonable arguments of men who sought to confuse. Senti- ment, in short, yielded less readily than untutored reason to the blan- dishments of confusion. Therefore, to foster devotion to the existing constitutional order it was appropriate to direct attention to that com- ponent of the order that commanded the stablest support for the con- stitution.

Only two difficulties remain. If Hervey was publicly so fearful of the pernicious consequences that partisanship could create for the consti- tution, why was he so fervent a Whig? And if he privately believed that the great parties of Anne's day had been transmuted into various factions of Whiggery, on what grounds could he resist the claims of the opposition? The answers emerge from a reading of the finest of his tracts, The Conduct of the Opposition. "The Family," he declared, refer- ring to the Hanoverians, "and this Government, can only be supported by Men acting on Whig-principles." He then distinguished between the principles of the Whigs of the Civil War and the Whigs of the Glorious Revolution, and he proclaimed his commitment to the latter because they were "not Anti-monarchical, Republican Whig-prin- ciples, (Principles defective in Theory, and more extravagant when thought of with a Possibility of being reduced to Practice;) not such chimerical Whig-principles as are imbibed from Eutopian Speculation, but the only honest and good Whig-principles, those of preserving a limited Monarchy in the Shape and Fashion we now enjoy it." This preserving responsibility of the Whigs accounts for Hervey's dislike of innovators—"projectors" as he called them in the Swiftian style of the day. On the title page of The Conduct of the Opposition he set forth the ancient motto revived by the northern lords who had stood with the Prince of Orange in 1688: "Nolumus Leges Angliae mutari." It was the principle of conduct Hervey applauded. He discerned danger to the state in a "Spirit of Innovation, a Propensity to Novelty, and a Thirst for Change."[42] He viewed the prophets of the unfulfillable as menaces to order and trust. The Bill of Rights and the Act of Settle-

42. [Hervey], Conduct, 13, 37.

ment had defined the existing order, and though he could approve of a few later emendations and particularly of the Septennial Act, it was with the Whigs who had created the regime that Hervey identified himself.

Two points about Hervey's thinking in this pamphlet merit consideration. The first meets the objection that he uncritically decried partisanship and yet espoused the Whig cause. Hervey in fact was not inconsistent. He conceived of the Whigs as something greater than a mere party, indeed as nothing less than the embodiment of the nation. The principles upon which the Whigs had built the new constitution were now the kingdom's principles. In short, in calling himself a Whig Hervey was boasting not of a partisan affiliation but of a constitutional commitment. To be a Whig was to be a Briton, and Whiggery—at least true Whiggery—was thus not a partisan perspective but a national faith. The small band of opponents might be attached to parties. It was only to be expected that they should, since faction was the home of those who would subvert liberty. They spread lies and sought to confuse the people. But the men who supported the government and the constitution were not a party; they were the nation itself, unconfused and unseduced, knowing themselves free and prosperous. The second point to be emphasized in reflecting upon this pamphlet deals with the objection that Hervey, by believing that virtually all politicians had become Whigs, had logically deprived himself of any principled grounds on which to oppose the Patriots. But again the charge can be met. Hervey clearly distinguished between two Whig legacies—a utopian, extravagant one, and a sober, preserving one. He stood with the latter and resisted the former. And he resisted because, in light of the success of the revolution settlement, any proponent of change was in his view an advocate of subversion. Such men were not numerous—but they were very dangerous. And for this reason the intensity of Hervey's language no longer seems jarring. In the last analysis Walpole was waging not merely a political battle but a moral war. Right was pitted against wrong. "If," Hervey declared at the conclusion of *The Conduct of the Opposition*, "in delineating Measures, Schemes, and Projects, the Colours may seem too thick, or grosly laid on, or the Lines too strong, or coarsely drawn; all I can say is, that in describing Vice, it is impossible to make it look like Virtue, or in painting Deformity, to represent it like Beauty."[43] Hervey took the constitution seriously.

Hervey is easily summed up. The foundation of his thinking about the political world was an unrefined utilitarianism. All that he praised—whether liberty, the balanced constitution, nonbelligerence, the Hanoverian succession, or Sir Robert himself—merited that acclaim because they were means for securing wider prosperity. The material happiness of the people stood for Hervey as the most relevant type of evidence for establishing the legitimacy of Court Whig administrations. As a disciple of Tacitus and Machiavelli, Hervey prided himself on his realism. He could, he believed, look cold reality in the face and thereby come to understand the true nature of the political world. He was, it is true, not without his passions. The life of the court, for example, provided him immense amusement. He grew addicted to its enchantments, and he so thoroughly mastered its intricate network of role-playing obligations that he became the most gifted courtier in the age of George II. Equally fervent was his devotion to his creature comforts. The opposition's picture of a simpler, less luxurious past appalled him. He enjoyed the amenities of material civilization and regarded challenges to them as personal assaults. But even in these passions, as the last example clearly shows, Hervey remained the realist, scorning political and social theorizing as so much cant. As a guide for his own life he chose instead the truths of the senses: he became a votary of the pleasure principle. In Hervey then, the quintessential courtier, we meet the utilitarian version of Court Whiggery. His clinching argument on behalf of the government was in effect the argument adopted by the Conservatives of a far more recent day: you never had it so good.

43. Ibid., 62.

Chapter III

Benjamin Hoadly (1676–1761): The Court Whig as Controversialist

I

In the eyes of posterity Benjamin Hoadly played but one part: unforgettably he was the redoubtable bishop of Bangor. It has not mattered that he figured prominently in the political pamphleteering of three different reigns, serving the embattled Whigs of Anne's day and their triumphant successors in the days of the first two Georges. Nor has it mattered that Bangor was only the first and lowliest of the four episcopal plums to fall his way, and that he moved steadily upward through Hereford and Salisbury to Winchester. His enduring fame rests on one short-lived furor he initiated early in the reign of George I when, with a single paradoxical sermon, he transformed himself into the most discussed—and, among his clerical brethren, most disliked—clergyman in England. From the protection of episcopal office he used the pulpit to lay waste the foundations of church authority. No other sermon of the century generated so much ecclesiastical debate. "The Bangorian controversy" stands as one of those critical moments in the history of a society when events call forth an examination of the bases of secular and religious order. It thus fully merits the attention it has been given. But Hoadly himself, aside from this brief moment, has been oddly neglected.[1] Yet he carried his crippled body through eight rich decades of

1. Brief biographies of Hoadly may be found in the *DNB*; in the opening volume of Benjamin Hoadly, *Works*, ed. John Hoadly (3 vols.; London, 1773); in H. T. Dickinson, "Benjamin Hoadly, 1676–1761: Unorthodox Bishop," *History Today*, XXV (1975), 348–

life. Witnessing the accession of George III, he could recall the deposition—for such he always affirmed it to have been—of James II.
Throughout his adult years he was a pugnacious Whig, steeped in the
thought of John Locke, and until he was almost sixty one of the party's
most energetic defenders. To some he was no less than a hero.[2] Every-
where he stepped he sparked rancor, for he was, above all else, an
enthusiastic controversialist. Sir Leslie Stephen quipped of Hoadly's
work that it "once more slays the slain," but the remark sacrifices ac-
curacy to effect.[3] Hoadly's foes were still among the quick, and it was
this vitality of the enemy that gave importance to his career. In the last
analysis Hoadly was right in seeing himself as a warrior on the ideological battlefields of the age. "If any," he declared, "think such Controversies, especially amongst the Clergy, of scandalous and pernicious
Consequence; I answer that it is not the Difference, but the manner of
handling and debating it, that is the Scandal; that I see no way left but
that, either All must agree in Judgment; or all must equally consent to
be silent; or, one side only must speak; or, there must be Debates and
Controversies."[4] Sentiments of this order will forever be the declaration
and justification of the controversialist. Sir Robert Walpole was wise to
befriend him.

II

With waves of public indigation over the South Sea scandal rolling in
upon the Whig ministry during the early 1720s, the government desperately needed defenders. In September of 1722 a forceful advocate
found voice. His nom de plume was "Britannicus," and he wrote weekly

---

55; and—the finest of all—in Norman Sykes, "Benjamin Hoadly, Bishop of Bangor," in
The Social and Political Ideas of Some English Thinkers of the Augustan Age, A.D. 1650–
1750, ed. F. J. C. Hearnshaw (London, 1928), 112–56. The biography in *Works* includes
a catalogue of Hoadly's writings.

2. As late as the 1780s Horace Walpole spoke of his "real affection for Bishop Hoadly"
and wrote to Lady Ossory that "I suppose tonight I shall dream of Bishop Hoadly—for
you see, Madam, I am an Old Whig even in my sleep, and that the powers of darkness
cannot affect my principles." W. S. Lewis et al., eds., *The Yale Edition of Horace Walpole's
Correspondence* (42 vols.; New Haven, Conn., 1937–80), XVI, 283, XXXIII, 339.

3. Sir Leslie Stephen, *History of English Thought in the Eighteenth Century* (2 vols.;
New York, 1962), II, 130.

4. Hoadly, *Works*, II, 188.

in the London *Journal*, recently bought by Walpole's government. Many knew even then that this new exponent of Court Whig prudence was none other than that experienced controversialist of the previous decade, the new bishop of Hereford, Benjamin Hoadly. From the late summer of 1722 until the opening month of 1725[5] Hoadly turned out letters for publication.[6] They addressed the reigning issues of the day and were clearly, in this sense, tracts for their times. But they were not therefore careless of consistency. Because one mind and one theory of government lay behind them, they reiterated the same views and assumptions again and again, displaying a high degree of integrity. And if one generalizes somewhat from their most concrete contexts and cuts through their often prolix prose, one can see that they spoke repeatedly to a cluster of three great questions that were pivotal for Court Whigs. What was the significance of the Glorious Revolution? What powers might the government exercise? How ought the responsible citizen to behave? From the answers advanced to these questions Britannicus constructed a defense of Court Whiggery that was at once more refined than and yet not inconsistent with Hervey's. Indeed, in his writings Court Whiggery acquired a veneer of philosophical respectability.

Everything that Britannicus wrote was a celebration of the events of 1688–1689. They were for all Whigs the Glorious Revelation, and regularly each November, to commemorate the landing of the liberator, Britannicus devoted several letters to his happy theme.[7] But even when not dealing specifically with the revolution he was assaying its importance. What, he implicitly kept asking, makes it the central event of modern history? Above all other considerations the achievement of 1688–1689 merited respect because it had created "*that Limited Form of Government* which is our only Security"; the constitution under which all the Britons of his day lived was a product of the revolution. This new constitutional order had replaced the one of absolutism under which James II had assaulted true religion and confiscated possessions.

5. January 9, 1724, by the calendar then in use.
6. Hoadly's *Works* contains 110 Britannicus letters. At least eight—numbers 89 to 96—are generally believed to be from another hand. The rest are taken to be Hoadly's, although in a few instances the attribution may be wrong.
7. Hoadly, *Works*, III, 219–26.

The purpose of the new order was no less than the preservation over many generations of *"Liberty* and *Property,"* two concepts that continually inspired the essayist. The importance he attached to liberty is revealed in numerous declarations: British society, he sweepingly wrote on one representative occasion, is formed "upon the *General Basis* of *Liberty.*" Property was to be no less revered. Even before the civil order was brought into being men had secured by their own labors a "Right to Property." The new constitution was designed to protect that right from invasion.[8] Britannicus' chief train of argument on the Glorious Revolution is thus clear (and absolutely unoriginal): the revolution was the central event of modern history because it begot the constitution; and the constitution was important because it was the bulwark of liberty and property.

More, however, may be said. Britannicus drew his readers' attention to several liberties he deemed of special moment—liberties that lent peculiar distinction to the British constitution and that, in a recoiling fashion, were as much guardians as wards of that constitution. One such liberty was that afforded to the spoken and printed word. More confidently than most Court Whigs Britannicus asserted the fundamental importance of freedom of speech and the press. He knew, as all ministerial spokesmen did, that abuses could occur. The social order was widely regarded as fragile and the emotive bond that constrained most citizens to obedience was held to be of dubious strength. Both therefore seemed vulnerable to manipulation by the words of disaffected partisans. But such a threat called for watchfulness rather than suppression. The freedom to disseminate ideas was simply too valuable to be cast aside. Besides being an end in itself, it was a defense against many other evils. Without freedom of expression, Britannicus boldly affirmed, Britons would suffer "all the *Mischiefs,* of *Darkness* in the *Intellectual* World, of *Baseness* in the *Moral* World, and of *Slavery* in the *Political* World."[9] Walpole's friends did not ordinarily speak so expansively of a liberty many thought potentially pernicious. Thus these words serve to place Hoadly among the most libertarian of the Court Whigs.

8. *Ibid.,* III, 225, 7, 215, 285–88.
9. *Ibid.,* III, 79–81.

Another prized liberty secured by the constitution was the freedom to worship God as conscience directed. The persecution of German Protestants in Thorn in 1724 provoked a series of pieces from Britannicus (or, in some instances, ostensibly *to* him), all designed to underline the value of religious toleration. The British constitution, he declared, conferred religious liberty, protecting both the established church and the Protestant dissenters. It ought, he argued on one occasion, to extend its protection more fully to Jews. To insist on all these points was to insist that the state had no right to command religious belief or understanding; Britannicus did not shrink from that conclusion. The Glorious Revolution, he wrote, was effected in part to prevent a tyrant from enforcing precisely such a command. Moreover, freedom of worship was not only worthy of constitutional protection, it was also—like freedom of expression—constitutionally useful. A stable and tranquil society was the most desirable type of social order. It existed when the people were in "*Good-temper* and *Good-humour*." Such benignity of spirit was possible only in an uncoerced society. Therefore, a constitutional order that did not impose credal points upon those subject to its dominion was far likelier than a narrowly doctrinaire one to produce happy and well-affected citizens.[10] Liberty, as always for Britannicus, was simultaneously ends and means.

The fervency of Britannicus' devotion to liberty, to the constitution that lived symbiotically with that liberty, and to the revolution which produced that constitution found its most vigorous expression in assaults on those wicked men who would destroy liberty, betray the constitution, and repudiate the revolution. Chief among them were the Pretender and Bishop Atterbury. A short series of essays on a declaration issued by the Stuart claimant revealed Britannicus at his most passionate. The Pretender, he warned, if ever given authority in Britain, would work to impose uniformity upon all. Britannicus noted gravely that even when seeking to mollify his foes, the Pretender found himself resorting to such revelatory phrases as "rooting up" and "extinguishing" opposition. What, Britannicus asked with rhetorical flourish, may thus be said of the Pretender? "Not only that he *must* destroy your

10. *Ibid.*, III, 370–73, 56–58, 223–26, 301–304, 354.

Civil and *Religious* Rights, but that he plainly before-hand has here *told* You, *to your Face*, He will do so."[11] To Atterbury, whose Jacobite scheming Walpole revealed in late 1722, Britannicus devoted less fren-zied but more extensive attention. He needed almost thirty letters to examine the government's case against the bishop and to rebut Atter-bury's defense. The churchman he found to be a hypocrite and liar, his goal to be the extirpation of liberty. In sum, both the Pretender and the bishop were opponents of the Glorious Revolution. Insofar as they sought to undo its work they conspired to return Britain to the evils of absolutism and to deny the kingdom all the benefits and blessings of liberty emanating from that triumph.

But to say that the revolution was carried out against a tyrannical government to secure liberty was not to say—as all Court Whigs knew—that government itself was evil. All political writers of the era acknowledged the indispensability of order and recognized government as the key mechanism for securing that order. Thus, if the first great question Britannicus answered sought the meaning of the Glorious Revolution, the second sought the rationale for governmental powers. What powers, he inquired, could the British government legitimately exercise? It was a question to be explored within the context of his conviction that all power ultimately lay with the people, and that gov-ernment, far from being a source of power itself, controlled only those powers "vested" in it by the people.[12] Britannicus saw the people as participants in governing. Indeed, if the "Limited Form of Govern-ment" peculiar to Britain was one vital consequence of the Glorious Revolution, two related ones were the unshackling of Parliament, that body through which the people consented to the laws they lived by, and the liberation of the administering of those laws, assuring justice to all. Thus, in Britannicus' view, the people used Parliament as the arena for their deliberations, and laws as the vehicle for their pro-nouncements. But since government, whether despotic or free, had been established to protect certain possessions deemed valuable, it

11. *Ibid.*, III, 36–52, 84–208.
12. This view is not strictly inconsistent with the argument for governmental sover-eignty attributed to "Philopatris" in the letter of May 11, 1723. But it is worth noting that the second view is not advanced by "Britannicus." *Ibid.*, III, 114–17.

needed power to actualize such protection. Thus the question could finally be neither avoided nor defined away: in a free state what power may a government legitimately exercise in behalf of the people?

The rule that Britannicus laid down by which to assess legitimacy was that of happiness: those governmental powers were right which, on balance, served to bring happiness to the citizenry. This rule would appear at first to raise few problems. It was easy and unobjectionable, and it seemed a quite appropriate rule for a government subject to popular control. What could be more simple? As Britannicus surveyed the range of activities a government might undertake, three caught his attention as particularly fruitful sources of national happiness. The first variety was the collection of activities that promoted public credit. An increase in stock prices he construed as a rise in credit, and a government could contribute to such a rise by providing the kingdom with an adequate supply of money and by behaving in such a financially responsible manner as to foster confidence in its own soundness. The second set of activities that Britannicus commended was the effort to promote foreign trade. On this point he dwelt with enthusiasm. Trade prospered in a free nation. The government's responsibility therefore was to keep its commanding hand light, to administer justice fairly, to protect property, and to encourage freedom—particularly religious freedom. In such an atmosphere commerce flourished. Moreover, when an expanding trade coincided with an ascendant stock market, the country was indeed fortunate. "The *Estate* of the *Nation*," Britannicus enthused over precisely that juxtaposition, "can never be esteemed better disposed towards *Happiness*, than when *Those Two* are seen and known undeniably to exist at the same time."[13] If Hoadly stood in the libertarian wing of the Court Whig camp, he also stood—not surprisingly—in the commercial wing. Trade and liberty went hand in hand to those of his persuasion.

But there existed a third category of actions that a government could legitimately engage in—those designed to insure a "General Tranquillity." And it is with this category that the bite of the question about governmental power first revealed itself. Tranquillity was manifestly useful. It was, Britannicus argued, the prerequisite of happiness, the

13. *Ibid.*, III, 255–62, 314–16.

foundation for healthy credit and trade. But it involved the suppression of confusion, anarchy, and violence. It necessitated a vigorous prohibition of popery and arbitrary power.[14] In sum, Britannicus was here dealing not with those governmental actions that promoted happiness by opening opportunities but with those that defended happiness by closing opportunities. And thus precisely because tranquillity presupposed the exercising of governmental power against its various enemies, the difficult problem arose of defining those occasions on which a free government might legitimately restrict the liberty of some of its citizens. It was, of course, a classic dilemma. May a free government suspend civil liberties to affirm civil liberties? May it confiscate property to protect property? May it build an army of defense indistinguishable from an army of oppression? Britannicus was prepared to answer affirmatively in every instance. But he needed a rationale for such an answer, and he was finally compelled to resort to that hoariest of justifications—necessity, robed in the guise of *salus populi*.

The contention over civil liberties arose late in 1722 when the Walpole government refused to make public the grounds upon which Bishop Atterbury and his fellow conspirators were arrested. Detention without cause was one of the aspects of Stuart government that the seventeenth century had presumably rejected. The habeas corpus law stood as British society's response to the practices of Charles I and Charles II. But in this hour of impending national peril Britannicus was prepared to tolerate its suspension. He asserted—truly, but not to the point—that the undetected accomplices of Atterbury were the ones most desirous of full disclosure: if they could force the government to reveal its case, they would discover where their own conspiratorial apparatus had been penetrated by government spies. He also argued, more abstractly, that every government must at times be granted the right to withhold information. In a crisis, he explained, a recourse to regular procedures of justice too often served the interests of a disloyal enemy. Britannicus knew he was playing with fire. He devoted one entire essay to specifying the rare conditions that would warrant abandoning the law, and essentially they reduced to the notion that the

14. *Ibid.*, III, 263–66.

danger must be real and present. But if he thereby limited the application of his doctrine, he did not repudiate it. This doctrine that a government could arrest without cause he treated under the rubric of "*Arcana imperii*," resorting to the traditional Latin in an effort to soften what, starkly considered, was a harsh precept.[15] For what Britannicus taught was this: even a constitutional order that deliberately seeks to restrict the capacity of mistrusted government to infringe on liberties will occasionally be compelled to place faith in the arbitrary actions of that government.

The same precept underlay Britannicus' apology for governmental assaults on property. The fact that the protection of property was one of the chief reasons for which government was created did not impose a prohibition upon governmental seizures of property. When the property was held by enemies of the state, and when the state was spending its wealth to secure its defenses against those enemies, it seemed only proper to raise the required money from the estates of those enemies. A free society, Britannicus suggested, could not provide sanctuary for those who would work from within to destroy its foundations. It was an attractive argument and one that, in principle, seemed impervious to challenge. But when reduced to concreteness it raised difficulties. The enemies referred to were the Roman Catholics of Britain, even though many lived peaceably and gave no support to the Pretender. Was not, critics asked, a punitive tax measure that indiscriminately touched all Catholics simply an act of religious persecution and hence an act that Britannicus' own standards condemned? Britannicus thought not. Catholics, he argued, were punished not for their religious beliefs but for the political consequences of those beliefs. This distinction sounded fair but was in fact unsustainable. It was the universality of application of the measure that Britannicus was compelled to justify. He accomplished this by asserting that all Catholics, simply by virtue of their faith and regardless of their overt behavior, nursed a "*General, Uninterrupted Design*" against the house of Hanover.[16] Therefore all merited punishment. But—though he did not add this commentary— they would appear to have harbored this "design" because they were

15. *Ibid.*, III, 23–30, 59–62.
16. *Ibid.*, III, 52–56, 62–66, 70–74.

believing Catholics, or rather, because they held to a faith that the government disapproved of. In short, despite the verbal camouflage, they were being punished for their religious convictions.

The inflammatory issue of the proper role of the army was a third area of debate in which Britannicus took the side of those who urged wider governmental powers. His arguments against a reduction of land forces even in time of peace were not novel. Indeed, no enduring dispute of this era showed less inclination to alter its terms over time than this one. Against those in the opposition who evoked an image of liberty succumbing to standing armies, Britannicus directed an equally predictable counterimage: a nation left defenseless before its foreign foes. He thought beneath contempt the opposition fear that a standing army might be turned against Britons. He reminded his readers that British soldiers were in the pay not of the king but of Parliament, that their number had been determined not by the king but by Parliament. He reminded them too that hostile nations lay across the channel—traditional enemies who were laying plans for the humbling of Britain, or Catholic enemies who were plotting the overthrow of the Protestant Hanoverians. Liberty, he concluded, was best protected by maintaining one's strength: the old case for deterrence remained for him persuasive.[17]

When drawn together this series of considerations about civil liberties, property rights, and standing armies placed Britannicus firmly among those who acknowledged that a government must retain a full range of powers. Even though the powers were only "vested," they must in the final analysis be sweeping. In time of emergency wide discretionary authority could not be withheld from those charged with leadership. Otherwise they would be denied the necessary capacity to serve the happiness of the citizens. Britannicus, with this conclusion, was not abandoning his contention that the constitution was created to protect liberty and property. But clearly he was modifying it—even if, in his own view, it was a modification designed to secure the vitality of the original contention. It was also a modification that shifted attention to the character and wisdom of those leaders to whom such discre-

17. *Ibid.*, III, 13–16, 304–307.

tionary authority was entrusted. Not surprisingly, Britannicus lauded Robert Walpole as an exemplar of the requisite statesmanship. Without tricks or deceits he had pacified the kingdom. Without endangering liberty he had detected and destroyed a conspiracy against the state. He deserved even higher commendation than a general who saves a state in time of civil war because, through prompt action, he had dealt with such a fraternal bloodletting by averting it. With public credit rising, trade prospering, and debt diminishing, he had done all that a nation could ask. "*This*," exulted Britannicus, "is the *Work* which calls for the *Whole Man*, and the *Whole Minister*."[18] The discrete sentence displays Hoadly's wonted lameness of expression, but it rises from its still more turgid context as a kind of battle cry. Walpole and the Court Whigs alone had the insight and prudence to keep a free kingdom free and a tranquil one at ease.

Britannicus thus believed Britain to be a free constitutional order that maintained itself through the dialectical juxtaposition of personal liberty and governmental power. The third great question that he addressed in his essays sought to identify the appropriate behavior for a citizen living in this constitutional order. How ought a responsible British subject to act in the political arena? Of all the topics that Britannicus surveyed this one was preeminent. He wanted, above all else, to encourage sound citizenship. And he sought to accomplish this goal by demonstrating the essential wisdom of two complementary attitudes toward government. The first was that of political realism: expectations of political success ought not to exceed the severe limits imposed by human nature. "If a Man were to sit down and frame a *Model* of a New *Commonwealth*, He might please himself by fashioning it, in the *Theory*, to all that Perfection of *Beauty* and *Usefulness*, which his own *Imagination* could invent, or his *Judgment* approve of. But"—and here the antiutopian realist intrudes, implicitly rebuking the aery proposals of Plato, More, and Harrington—"as *Government* is a matter of *Practice*, and not of *Speculation*; and as the *Administration* of it, whenever it comes to *Accident* and *Experiment*, must be deposited and trusted in the Hands of *Men*; Let the *Idea* be as perfect as it will, the *Thing Itself* will

18. *Ibid.*, III, 215.

soon partake of the Imperfections and unavoidable *Humanities* of Those, who alone are to guide and direct the *Machine*." Elsewhere Britannicus was unwontedly succinct: "*All Perfection*, and *No Mistake*, belongs to *No Administration*, but that of *Heaven*." The second attitude was that of farsighted prudence. The responsible citizen was urged always to take the long rather than the short view, to tend to the kingdom's "real and true Interest" rather than its ephemeral ones, or—since it was the same thing—to consult the enduring good of the people rather than their ill-considered clamors and unconsidered passions.[19]

A British subject imbued with both attitudes would be a valuable citizen. He would—in one of the writer's favorite antitheses—be able to distinguish love of popularity, the source of demagoguery, from true patriotism, the source of statesmanship. The leader who curried mere popularity would have no compunctions about misleading the citizenry by promising either what no government could ever deliver or what no sensible government would want to deliver. The true patriot, however, knew all government was by nature forbidden to create a utopia and that wise government was forbidden by prudence from pandering to appetites. The true patriot gave not merely—or even chiefly—his zealous heart to his country's cause. That was important, but still more so was a prudent head. "True Patriotism," Britannicus wrote, "is built upon *Equity* and observes the Measures of *That* alone." As a consequence—and here Britannicus moved to the practical conclusion he felt so necessary—a true patriot will often support the government. The target of such a conclusion was obvious to all: the self-styled Patriots who assailed the Walpole ministry at every turn. Britannicus did not enjoin invariable support. Instead he called upon responsible citizens to weigh each governmental action, assess its impact upon the long-term interests of the kingdom, determine what range of actions was available to the government, and judge the action accordingly. From one point of view all that the patriot needed to do was to refer to enlightened egoism. "*Self-interest* rightly understood," Britannicus explained, "and rightly applied, at least in its Effects and Consequences, is the same as *Publick Virtue*. . . . He who does *Good* to the *Publick*, let

19. *Ibid.*, III, 213, 13–16.

the Motive or Principle be what it will, is a *Patron* and *Benefactor* to it." But from another point of view one elaboration was still needed: the right understanding and the right application of self-interest required definition. For this task Britannicus invoked the traditional link between patriotism and nationalism. "The Love of our Country in particular, as we are *Britons*, is the Love of our Constitution, and of the Establishment of the present Royal Family; without the Safety of which, no Man in his Senses can hope for any lasting Good to his Country."[20] With this statement Britannicus identified the common focus of his three great questions. The true patriot, he declared, honored the constitution and acknowledged the need to protect its accomplishments by defending the revolutionary settlement that planted it. He would best do so, Britannicus urged, by supporting the Court Whigs.

III

Benjamin Hoadly, the man who treated these themes in the weekly Britannicus letters, had already written a celebrated and systematic discourse on the nature of the British constitutional order. Its celebrity arose not from its undistinguished exposition but from its political reception. Titled *The Original and Institution of Civil Government Discussed*, it had been issued in 1709 as a Whig defense of the Glorious Revolution. The House of Commons, at the behest of the Whigs then directing affairs, had voted a commendation for the work—an act testifying more to partisan zeal than to soundness of judgment. Derivative in substance and prolix in style, *Original and Institution* is a tedious work. Sir Leslie Stephen spoke with characteristic bluntness when he wrote of Hoadly that "his style is the style of a bore; he is slovenly, awkward, intensely pertinacious, often indistinct, and, apparently at least, evasive."[21] In the choice of words for *Original and Institution* Hoadly was exasperatingly careless, sometimes, for example, employing "right" as a synonym for "power" but often using the terms to designate two contrasting concepts. Still the work remains a formal treatment of one strand of Whig constitutional thought. A reader familiar with Hoadly's ideas as presented in *Original and Institution* and his other

20. *Ibid.*, III, 16–19, 13–16, 217–18, 7.
21. Stephen, *History of English Thought*, II, 129.

political publications would have had no difficulty fitting into that scheme the views advanced in the Britannicus letters. Whatever nom de plume the occasion suggested, Benjamin Hoadly was invariably an adherent of contract theory.

Original and Institution is an exploration of the grounds that legitimize the exercise of authority.[22] It is divided into two long chapters. In the first Hoadly sought to refute that theory of political life that derived legitimacy from descent—a theory he called "patriarchalism." In essence his characterization of patriarchalism reduced the theory to three assertions: 1) that succession by primogeniture in the male line had brought the absolute power of Adam and then Noah down to the present; 2) that in cases where it could not be demonstrated that the present possessor of a throne was directly descended from Noah, his possession itself was evidence that he ruled by right; and 3) that in cases where a true dispute between claimants arose, the subjects of the kingdom were the final judges of this right. The twentieth-century reader should be struck immediately by the diverse—even contradictory—set of elements Hoadly chose to criticize under the rubric of patriarchalism. It appears, for example, that the third assertion, by conferring on the subjects a final authority to specify which among rival claimants is a legitimate ruler, either contradicts or at least supersedes the first assertion, whereby legitimacy is measured by bloodlines and gender. Meanwhile, the second assertion established still another foundation for legitimacy, and one that seems but a rationalization of might making right. Hoadly himself noted that these views were not totally consistent, but since the immediate purpose of *Original and Institution* was to refute the patriarchal views of government he attributed to Charles Leslie, he held that he had to follow Leslie through a bramble patch of Leslie's rather than his own making.[23] Hoadly dealt with each of the three assertions in succession.

The assertion that Adamite and Noachian authority has passed by

22. It is printed in Hoadly, *Works*, II, 182–287.
23. On patriarchalism see Gordon J. Schochet, *Patriarchalism in Political Thought: The Authoritarian Family and Political Speculations and Attitudes, Especially in Seventeenth-Century England* (New York, 1975). The dispute between Hoadly and Leslie is treated on 219–24.

primogeniture in the male line down to the present Hoadly treated as absurd. Such descent was unprovable, improbable, and unscriptural—and even if verified was irrelevant, for paternal authority had no power to confer political authority. The assertion that present possession of power legitimized the exercise of power Hoadly found more interesting. Under certain conditions—namely, when the passivity of the citizens could be construed as a sign of consent—he was prepared to grant that possession appeared to legitimize authority. But a closer view of such instances indicated that it was not the possession that provided the legitimization but rather the tacit consent that lay behind it. "*Mere Possession*," Hoadly wrote, "though of never so long a continuance, gives no *Right*, properly so called." Might, in short, did not make right. But it was the final assertion that Hoadly found most irritating. How, he asked, are the people to whom patriarchalists would appeal to decide disputed cases? Should they vote? Should they fight? Hoadly derided the competence of the people—"the Tinker and the Cobbler"—to make such judgments. He assailed as "Mobb-principles" the teachings that claimed such right for the people.[24] Yet this response was inadequate and could stand only so long as Hoadly was prepared to defend a more moderate form of the same assertion. For he did not finally quarrel with the contention that authority derived from the people and hence the people could choose their rulers. He quarreled only with the broad definition of "people" he saw his opponents adopting. The "people," Hoadly believed, could mean neither everyone nor even all adult males. In a legitimate constitutional order "people"—that is, those who confer authority—must be understood to mean something like "responsible people." Hoadly, then, when dealing with the third assertion, treated it as an exaggeration rather than as a total error. But his conclusion in this instance remained what it had been for the earlier two: the patriarchal scheme did not supply a legitimization for the exercise of political authority. It was quite natural that, having dismissed three justificatory theories as false, he would then address himself to the issue of determining where the true foundations lay.

24. Hoadly, *Works*, II, 236, 237, 238.

Chapter II of *Original and Institution* was Hoadly's essay into constructive political theory. All political authority, he reiterated, rested on consent. Before civil society was formed all people had a "Right of Self-Preservation," but they discovered that life in an anarchic condition was intolerable. Too many evils threatened their very existence to make freedom pleasant. Therefore, driven by a fear of such evils, people finally consulted together and agreed, as a way to secure an easier life, to deliver their right of self-preservation into the custody of governors. These governors would then assure the lawfulness and tranquillity that the people so desperately needed. In sum, in Hoadly's view, all that was necessary to form a legitimate government was "that some Persons should meet, and deliberate, and consent, to transfer the *Right* of *Self-Defense*, formerly lodged in themselves, to a particular Person, or number of Persons." The government created by this contract remained in principle the instrument of those who formed it. In practice, however, it wielded extensive power. Those who accepted the contract conferred "Authority" over themselves to their governors. It was these governors, not the people, who judged what was useful for society, what should be legislated, what should be enforced. Since in the final analysis the safety of the civil order legitimized all actions of civil self-defense—since, that is, "there must remain in the *Governed Society* a *Right* to defend, and preserve itself from *Ruine*"—the governors were authorized to exercise a potentially unlimited power. Thus, if the theory tended to confine government, the need to give the state the capacity to deal with emergencies tended to shatter the theoretical fetters. This entire edifice rested on the doctrines of natural right, which defined the powers existing in the civil order, and consent, which explained how the government came to exercise some of them. Only the consenting conveyance of rights to government through the contract could make the authority of the state legitimate. "A Right to Civil Government," Hoadly wrote, "can result from nothing but the voluntary Consent of the people governed, or to be governed."[25]

---

25. *Ibid.*, II, 271, 265, 255, 266. In typical fashion Hoadly weakened the force of the final quotation by appending "unless God thinks fit to nominate Persons to this Office." But it is an addition without significance: Hoadly made clear that God does not in fact nominate rulers.

As the reader will doubtless have recognized, Hoadly's celebrated work is simply a massive crib from John Locke.[26] In structure, in tactics, and in substance—though not in perspicacity—*Original and Institution* was shamelessly patterned on Locke's two treatises on government. Locke's first treatise leveled an attack on patriarchal schemes of government; Hoadly's first chapter did likewise. Locke's second treatise argued for the contractual origin of legitimate political power; Hoadly's second chapter did the same. Both founded their arguments on the doctrine of natural rights. In justifying the use of contract theory Hoadly followed Locke even in his practice of invoking the prestige of Richard Hooker. Locke himself would appear to be a more obvious writer to resort to, but he was not yet a regnant authority and, as the shrewd controversialist Hoadly suggested, "there are many who will hear *that* with *Patience* from Mr. Hooker, which they will receive with *Abhorrence* from another." Hoadly noted early in the work, rather coyly, that he was dealing with themes already handled by an eminent author. He justified his rehearsal of these themes on the grounds that he would devote attention to new aspects of them.[27] But the only truly novel element in his chapters was his rebuttal of the patriarchal effort to set up the people as a judge among rival claimants. Elsewhere any deviations from Locke were well disguised. And though various differences between Locke's and Hoadly's work remain, they all reflect unfavorably on the disciple. Without exception, the bishop showed himself to be less fertile of imagination, less agile with ideas, less thoughtful in discourse, less careful with language, and less forceful in argument than the learned physician.

The exposition of contract theory presented in *Original and Institution* left a number of important issues only cursorily explained. But three of the most obvious of these were subjects of fuller analyses which Hoadly had either already written or was soon to write. These analyses thus supplemented *Original and Institution*. One such issue involved the extent of the obligation for political obedience: to what degree does

26. It also bears a resemblance to James Tyrrell's *Patriarcha Non Monarcha* (London, 1681). On Tyrrell's relationship to Locke, see Peter Laslett's introduction to his edition of John Locke, *Two Treatises of Government* (Cambridge, 1960), 73–75.

27. Hoadly, *Works*, II, 250–51, 190.

the citizen owe obedience to the government? *Original and Institution* suggested that obedience to illegitimate authority was not required. This conclusion formed the burden of a famous sermon Hoadly had already preached in 1705, when the chief threat to Whiggery appeared to be the renascent doctrine of passive obedience.[28] Explicating the opening section of Romans 13—a standard scriptural citation for those seeking to magnify the obligation to obedience—Hoadly found even in this textual citadel of his opponents adequate grounds for limiting that obligation. It was true, he acknowledged, that St. Paul had enjoined obedience—but only to rulers who did good and who promoted happiness and well-being. Toward wicked rulers no such obligation existed. In fact, in the last analysis obedience was not owed to rulers at all but to the "public Happiness." When rulers served that happiness they merited obedience; when they failed, they abdicated their responsibility and cast off their legitimacy. But another aspect of the question also needed treatment, for if it was demonstrable that obedience was owed only to legitimate authority, it was still not clear whether authority, once legitimized, could command absolute obedience on all points. Hoadly's libertarian inclinations found the latter conclusion intolerable, and contract theory afforded him a satisfactory way of rejecting it. "If *Government*," he wrote in a vigorous defense of the sermon just cited, "be founded upon voluntary Contract, and if the People never designed any thing by this Contract, but to bind themselves to such a *Submission* as carries forward, and is consistent with the Public Good," then their obligation went only as far as the contract. Four years later he amplified this position. In accepting the contract men conveyed their "Right of Self-Preservation" to the government "in all ordinary Cases." But such a transfer did not make self-defense illegitimate when one was under attack, even if the attacker was exercising legitimate authority: men retained "a *natural Right* to kill the *Attempters*, resulting from that *Right* to Self-preservation given them by God."[29] In the strictest construction then the right of self-defense was inalien-

28. "A Sermon Preached before the . . . Lord-Mayor," in *ibid.*, II, 18–25.
29. "A Defense of the Foregoing Sermon," in *ibid.*, II, 26–97 (quotation from 64); "Some Considerations Humbly Offered," in *ibid.*, II, 131.

able. On the issue of obedience Hoadly thus stood with those who emphasized the limits of this obligation.

A second issue raised in *Original and Institution* but more fully examined elsewhere was the problem of specifying how far a society might go to defend itself. Could it, for example, unseat kings and deny authority to churchmen? Unequivocally—and in both instances—Hoadly replied in the affirmative. His arguments on this issue provided the chief substance of a major and controversial tract of 1716, *A Preservative against the Principles and Practices of the Non-jurors both in Church and State*, a work written when the threat of passive obedience had waned but that of Jacobitism was in the ascendant.[30] The deposition of kings was a matter Hoadly handled easily. Since government was created for the happiness of its citizens, if a monarch failed to serve that need, he might legitimately be dismissed. The matter was of great moment, for upon its resolution, in Hoadly's view, hung the legitimacy of the Glorious Revolution.[31] He thus entered combat gladly. Seeking to rebut those who supported the house of Stuart, he noted that even the most fervent defenders of the indefeasibility of monarchic rights acknowledged that mental incapacity warranted the removal of a ruler. The bishop argued that a moral incapacity was functionally indistinguishable from a mental incapacity, "for *All Incapacity* is the same, in the Effects and Consequences of it, to the Concerns of a Nation. It is of no Importance, whether it be *Natural*, or *Moral*." He further asserted that adherence to popish doctrines constituted precisely such a moral incapacity, because devotion to a faith that the British found reprehensible would make any man "uncapable of answering the *Ends* of Government, in our Nation." The deposition of the Catholic James II was therefore proper.

30. *Ibid.*, I, 557–97.
31. Kenyon, *Revolution Principles*, becomes the standard treatment of this topic. But H. T. Dickinson, "The Eighteenth Century Debate on the 'Glorious Revolution'," *History*, LXI (1976), 28–45, remains useful. By 1716 many Whigs had shifted their ground in defending the Glorious Revolution. The Lockean camp in which Hoadly figured so prominently was a diminishing minority among Whig writers. Dickinson clearly makes this point. But precisely because he does make it I cannot understand his remark elsewhere that *Preservative* presents "the standard Whig case against Jacobitism and in justification of the Glorious Revolution." Dickinson, "Benjamin Hoadly," 350.

The legitimacy of state action that denied authority to ecclesiastics was a more difficult matter for Hoadly. And it was a very live question. Nonjuring bishops, conscientiously unable to take oaths to the successors of James II, represented themselves as the true embodiment of the Church of England and declared the state-ordered deprivations under which they suffered to be unlawful. At first it seemed possible that Hoadly might be able to build a defense of the government's actions by resorting to the traditional distinction between temporalities and spiritualities: the state conferred the former and could therefore resume possession of them. But after examining this distinction Hoadly realized that it did not cut to the core of the dilemma. What needed justification was not the denial of a specific diocese to a bishop but the enforcement of a general government prohibition on the exercise of episcopal authority by any bishop whom the government deemed unreliable. Citing the examples of both life and property, Hoadly noted that there was precedent for the state's depriving people of what it had not conferred. But his central argument was the unabashed invocation of *raison d'état*: the state could not tolerate *imperium in imperio*. "Every Civil Government," he wrote, "hath a Right to every Thing necessary for its own Defense, and Preservation."[32] With the inclusion of this justification for the exercise of state power in the *Preservative* of 1716 Hoadly took a major step toward undermining the doctrine of limited government that the sermon of 1705 was predicated upon.

The third issue suggested by *Original and Institution* but examined more extensively elsewhere was the bearing that this contractual theory of government had on one's view of the British constitution. In an assize sermon of 1708 Hoadly addressed this issue. Titled *The Happiness of the Present Establishment*, it asserted the fundamental soundness of the British constitution.[33] Happiness—one of Hoadly's favorite themes—was the end of governed society, and happiness required the protection of civil liberty, private property, and religious freedom. The British constitution provided these protections. But Hoadly was unwilling to leave the matter in this banally truistic position. Both civil liberty and private property, he argued, must be subordinate to the laws

32. Hoadly, *Works*, I, 566, 574.
33. *Ibid.*, II, 109–17.

of the governed society. He depicted both of these concepts as golden means, lying between two sets of unfortunate extremes. Civil liberty in his view stood between the licentiousness of an anarchy and the slavery of a tyranny. In the free British society this mean was defined by the law. Private property—and here Hoadly's taste for parallelism led him to strained constructions—stood between the conditions of momentary possession under an anarchy and nominal possession under a tyranny. In free Britain property too was secured by law. The operative consequence of such reasoning was patent: a constitutional order such as Britain's merited support.

IV

It is striking how closely the concerns that dominated Hoadly's pre-Walpolean writings replicate themselves in his Britannicus letters. It was not simply that the persisting reliance on contract theory and the natural rights doctrine that lay behind it assured that the theoretical justifications for government would be identical in both periods.[34] Nor was it that the repeated invocation of utilitarian psychology guaranteed that the theoretical analyses of the ends of government would also be identical. Beyond these important points it would appear that the very issues Britannicus saw as central to political understanding in the early 1720s were themselves identical to the issues Hoadly had poured out so much ink upon in the first two decades of the eighteenth century. When Britannicus assessed the importance of the Glorious Revolution he was resuming the examination of political obedience that Hoadly had treated in the sermon of 1705. The revolution showed that the obligation to obedience was not absolute, and the sermon affirmed the same conclusion. When Britannicus sought to defend the right of a government to protect itself, he was picking up the theme that Hoadly had placed at the heart of his *Preservative*. In each instance the author invoked *salus populi* or *raison d'état* to justify governmental heavy-handedness. Finally, when Britannicus reminded his readers that state building was a practical rather than a speculative enterprise and that it involved balancing various ends in some suitable and enduring fashion,

34. For Britannicus' use of this doctrine, see *ibid.*, III, 314–16.

he was reiterating what Hoadly had taught about the medial nature of liberty and property. This persistence of themes was important. It meant that what Hoadly held to be crucial for Whiggery in its heroic age retained its relevance in the age of Walpolean management. It showed that Court Whiggery need not be uncomfortable when defended with Lockean ideas. This was no small achievement.

Chapter IV

Thomas Herring (1693–1757): The Court Whig as Pastor

I

Thomas Herring was something of an anomaly among eighteenth-century archbishops.[1] In an age in which the choicest plums in the ecclesiastical orchard usually went to men of rather undisguised ambition, he evinced little taste for the highest promotion. In a century in which scholarship was a major recommendation to the archiepiscopal dignity he was, self-confessedly, ill qualified. Yet despite these deficiencies Herring ascended the ladder of preferment, became archbishop of York in 1743, and—aided by his friendship with Lord Hardwicke, his heroic behavior in 1745, and his celebrated homiletic talent—was finally in 1747 raised to the see of St. Augustine himself. His was a triumph of benignity over political innocence. But for that reason the tale of Herring's career cannot end with this lofty investiture. As he himself had

1. The fullest biographical treatment of Herring is in Aldred W. Rowden, *The Primates of the Four Georges* (London, 1916), 167–229. See also the *DNB*; William Dickinson [Rastall], *Antiquities Historical, Architectural, Chorographical, and Itinerary, in Nottinghamshire and the Adjacent Counties* (Newark, U.K., 1801), 248–53; the preface to Thomas Herring, *Seven Sermons on Public Occasions by the Most Reverend Dr. Thomas Herring, Late Lord Archbishop of Canterbury* (London, 1763); John Nichols, *Illustrations of the Literary History of the Eighteenth Century* (6 vols.; London, 1817–31), III, 451–58; S. L. Ollard and P. C. Walker, eds., *Archbishop Herring's Visitation Returns, 1743. The Yorkshire Archaeological Society. Record Series*, LXXIX (1931), 1–30; British Museum, Add. MSS 35599, fols. 346–47; University of Nottingham Library, Pw V 121 (bound at the end).

feared, he had been promoted above his abilities. Archiepiscopal duties proved too diverse and complex for Herring, and his tenure at Canterbury was marked by defeats in virtually every arena in which he chose to contend. Illness then capped this fatuity with disability, and he died repenting his reluctant acceptance of his high office. Herring is today remembered for his earlier years at York, not his final years at Canterbury. Grappling with the far less exacting responsibilities of the northern archdiocese and confronted by the advancing troops of the Pretender, he had shown himself a resolute Whig, a brave Briton, and a commanding prelate. He was a man who took his humbling faith seriously; his gifts were pastoral, not political. Yet it was his political loyalty that secured him attention. And thus we confront the final anomaly. Although he merited ecclesiastical recognition by virtue of his character, he gained it by virtue of his politics. But precisely because these politics were congruent with the rest of his character—which is to say that they were honest and a bit naive—he failed his patrons and disappointed himself in his conduct of the high station he had accepted. Still, whatever his deficiencies as an ecclesiastical administrator and national politician, Herring remained a forceful apologist for the Court Whigs. The pulpit was as important as the bookstall in the political wars of the eighteenth century.

II

The controlling center of Herring's political and social thought was his commitment to Anglican Protestantism as the reasonable middle ground between what he believed to be the absurdity of Roman Catholicism and the madness of the sectarians. With Richard Hooker before him, from whom he took many of his ideas, Herring held the Church of England to possess a truer understanding of the Gospel message than either the incanting priests or the canting ministers. Firmly grounded in reason, its teachings about the nature of man and God, the role of belief, the foundations of morality, and duty and obligations were self evidently superior to the metaphysical mumblings of its enemies. With scorn he dismissed "the mischief of popery or the stiff nonsensical & stingy [?] systems of the several sectarians." Both rival faiths, he believed, were havens of superstition.[2] And within Herring's armory of denigrating terms "superstition" was a particularly forceful one. He shared Hooker's high estimation of reason, but as a child of the Enlightenment he was able to extend its dominion further than the Elizabethan could have conceived. In Herring's eyes reason was the measure of both the right and the true. Any version of Christianity that made irrational claims for itself was a corruption of Christianity. To brand a system of ideas and beliefs as superstitious was, for Herring, to place it beyond the pale, to deny it legitimacy, and to imply that its adherents were captives of mind enslavers. And since advocates of both these pernicious faiths were using British liberty to promote their respective causes, Herring dreaded religious complacency. His public life was one long struggle against Rome and dissent.

Against the sectarians Herring raised three major objections. He found their understanding of human nature evil, their blind devotion to Scripture idolatrous, and their fervor dangerous. The pessimistic view of the nature of mankind, generally accepted by dissenting theologians, was "wicked and blasphemous."[3] To Herring it was a calumny on God to suppose that He would have made man so innately sinful that on his own he could do nothing at all meritorious and so clouded in mental capacity that unaided he could not see through to what was good. Both Scripture and history confuted this pessimistic view. God had made man in His own image, and many great men—some of whom lived before the broadcasting of the Christian dispensation—had discovered the good and tried to live by its demands. Of the sectarians' tendency to prove all religious points by reference to the Bible Herring was suspicious. Being proudly Protestant, he could not deny that Scripture possessed very great authority. But he would not countenance an unquestioning faith in the words of the Bible abstracted from all else.

2. British Museum, Add. MSS 35598, fol. 410; Herring, *Seven Sermons*, 152. Herring deliberately chose not to let most of his sermons be printed. But to the two he did authorize for publication five others were posthumously added by the editors.

3. *Letters from the Late Most Reverend Dr. Thomas Herring, Lord Archbishop of Canterbury, to William Duncombe, Esq; deceased, from the Year 1728 to 1757* (London, 1777), 174. The terms are affixed specifically to Wesley's views. They would apply *a fortiori* to more orthodox Calvinists.

Veneration of Scripture was like veneration of the magistracy, he re-marked: each must "in some measure [be] supported by outward circum-stances and ceremony."[4] The scriptural text, he averred, should be in-terpreted in light of knowledge about both present and biblical times and with due attention to the significance of traditional church views. Unlike Hoadly, Herring had great respect for the patristic writers. The biblical text thus remained the chief source of understanding, but Her-ring wanted the text glossed in accordance with certain nonscriptural considerations. Finally, Herring dreaded the "enthusiasm" of the dis-senters. This was a conventional fear of eighteenth-century Anglicans, and by "enthusiasm" they meant less an unbecoming zeal than a readi-ness to disparage the importance of reason while elevating emotional-ism, and a tendency toward antinomianism that might, if unchecked, dissolve the bonds that made society cohere. These three sectarian points to which Herring took objection were really all aspects of one central attitude in dissenting Christianity. Because sectarians held man to be so morally incompetent and deformed, they had to place great emphasis on the scriptural promise of salvation by faith alone. And because they accepted that promise they denied the final power of the law to bind them. Antinomianism—in principle, at least—was a con-sequence of a soteriological system that pitted an invincibly wicked man against an unfathomably gracious God.

Still, if Herring disliked the sectarians, he reviled the Roman Catho-lics. He regarded himself and his church, after all, as Protestant. The Church of England, like the sectarians, stood on the correct side of the great divide of the sixteenth century, true to a reformed, restored, and purified Christian tradition. Those in communion with Rome, on the contrary, had been raised "in a sort of Profession of Christianity, but in reality in heathen Ignorance and Savageness of Temper." And in ser-mon after sermon Herring railed against the errors and threats of the Roman Catholic church. Its priests were "pestilent People," bent upon "deluding silly Women" and "spiriting away the Children of the Na-tion, or tainting their first Principles." Its services were filled with "monstrous Absurdities." It withheld Scripture from its votaries, mis-

4. *Ibid.*, 22.

leading them instead with childish and useless legends. Wherever Roman Catholicism prevailed, social virtues were blighted, spirit and vigor declined, industry waned, prosperity receded, and in their place a "furious Spirit of Cruelty" came to hold sway. Moreover, Roman Catholicism was invariably linked with "tyrannical and corrupted Courts" and therefore liberty was yet another of its casualties. The generalizations based on these indictments could only be crushing: the Church of Rome was a "Medley of Wickedness and Superstition," "as base as it is absurd"; its goal was to sink the world again into "Barbarism and Idolatry."[5]

Herring devoted much of his constructive energy to the task of identifying the truths the Church of England had been called upon to defend in its struggle against both Rome and Geneva. His answers were not original. Drawing on the vigorous apologetic tradition that had its origins in Elizabethan days, he reasserted the conventional Anglican rejoinders to those who believed the *via media* to be a *via confusa*. It was a tradition that felt the impress of Hooker's moderation and employed it against the more extreme claims of both Rome and dissent. It was also a tradition that, as a consequence of the historical accidents that had given form to the Church of England, placed great emphasis on the concept of *adiaphora*—that is, on the notion that many regulative decisions in religious matters were neither scripturally enjoined nor soteriologically significant and were therefore to be shaped in accordance with custom and convenience. And although this Church of England happened to be truer to the scriptural faith than its enemies, it was not the only possible type of church. "You and I have often reason'd on the essence of religion & Xtianity," he wrote his cousin, "& never thought it to consist in this or that form of national settlement." To this adiaphoristic tradition Herring added a latitudinarian faith in the simplicity of true Christianity. Living a life in Christ did not, he believed, require great understanding; nor did grasping the core ideas of the faith call for great application. "Christianity," he asserted, "is more the Religion of the Heart, than of the Head, and the Excellence and Majesty of it consists in the Reasonableness and Simplicity

5. Herring, *Seven Sermons*, xx, 31–32, 147, 183, 222–25.

of its Doctrines, productive of an innocent, and useful, and pious Life."[6] His message was Hooker's, as mediated by Locke.

And what was that message? Herring thought Christianity to be chiefly concerned with conduct. During his fullest extant treatment of the nature of the faith he declared it to be "calculated for the *common* Use and benefit of the World" and, "though made up of the most precious and valuable Truths, yet . . . communicated with free Grace and Bounty." It was "not confined within the Studies of Philosophers, or locked up in the Cabinets of Princes; but dispersed abroad for the common Instruction, and, if they will follow it honestly, for the common Happiness of the Poor and the Rich, of the Ignorant and the Learned." With the sole exception of its teaching about the Resurrection "the Dispensation of the Gospel" had no new lessons for mankind. What Jesus taught was instead "a clear and certain and consistent Scheme of moral Duty, not itself newly discovered, but vindicated from Error and Corruption, and false Casuistry." It was a scheme that stood "in pure Agreements" with the "Dictates of Natural Reason." But Christianity had this advantage over natural reason: it made morality accessible to all, not just to the ethically lettered. Doctrinal points, though not unimportant, did not bear emphasizing; controversy over them was to be sedulously avoided, since internal bickering could be "the disgrace and ruin of Christianity." Ceremony and hierarchy had their proper place, since they inculcated respect for the church they served. But sacramentalism was somewhat more dangerous, breeding a sympathy for mystification when clarity and reason were needed.[7] In sum, Herring saw Christianity as a reasonable philosophy of ethical behavior predicated on the credible promise of reward in a life after death and vouchsafed to an established and hierarchical church.

Of commanding significance to an understanding of the connection between Herring's theology and ecclesiasticism and his political and social thought is his Christian anthropology. Since individual men and

6. University of Nottingham Library, Pw V 121, letter 84.

7. Herring, *Seven Sermons*, 6–7, 11; Nottingham University Library, Pw V 120, letter 23; *Letters from Herring*, 134. The statement about sacramentalism is an extrapolation from the views Herring expressed about Hoadly's eucharistic doctrine, but it is consonant with his general view of Christianity. *Letters from Herring*, 28.

women were the constituent parts of any political order, it was the inherent nature of these men and women that provided the boundaries of possible variation among human societies. Herring took his understanding of human nature from Anglican Christianity. Much of that understanding was simply a broadly Christian view of man's nature, but Herring's struggle to discriminate Anglicanism from both Roman Catholicism and dissent had echoes in his anthropology. His central conviction was that man was a rational being. "Before the Gospel Dispensation, and in every Age of the World, Men had their Reason to guide them," and this already powerful tool had been further elevated by the advent of Jesus, sent of God "to assist, and as it were, rekindle the Light of Reason." The mind, Herring remarked elsewhere, is "the most valuable and noble Part of us."[8] With these views he was reaffirming his rejection of the Calvinist doctrine that fallen man was blind, deaf, and muddled. On the contrary, natural reason was a powerful gift of God, sufficient to provide even those who had never heard the Word with a proper comprehension of morality.

Herring's view of man as a rational being had consequences for his implicit epistemology. One of the dominant concerns of religious thought in the eighteenth century was to establish persuasive foundations for religious knowledge. Herring concurred with many of his fellow Anglican clerics and with powerful currents of thought of the day in looking for foundations other than the conventional Christian ones of Scripture, revelation, and ecclesiastical tradition. These had proved dangerously vulnerable to rationalist assault. The strategy of Christian apologists was therefore to bring the power of rationalism into the religious camp—to use reason to buttress faith. Herring did just this. Time and again, with only minor terminological variations, he referred to three autonomous sources of understanding. They may be called reason, experience, and religion—terms that are Herring's, though he sometimes used synonyms.[9] By "reason" he seems to have meant logic, philosophy, and natural science: reason, that is, operated by public

8. Herring, *Seven Sermons*, 8, 27, 265–66.

9. The ensuing discussion is an attempt to give order to a type of tripartite distinction frequently found in Herring. It oversystematizes his thought but does not violate its spirit. And the distinctions will later be important. Such a three-fold distinction is traditional.

rules of procedure that allowed the reasoner to confirm or disconfirm various statements about reality or logical entailment. Reason was related to, yet distinct from, the source he called "experience."[10] By this term he appears to have meant political and social thought: experience was that realm in which reflection and intuition combined to derive probable truths from the pasts of either the individual or society. Whereas the product of reason might be called knowledge, the product of experience might be called wisdom.[11] Both were to be sharply distinguished from "religion," alternatively called "scripture" or "revelation," the source in which understanding came not as a product of human thought but as a declaration from God, mediated through the written word, sermons, or Christian tradition—or occasionally received directly. The existence of three autonomous sources of understanding did not entail the existence of three realities. Truths derived from one source could not conflict with truths from another—after all, something was either true or false—and when conflicts appeared they indicated that one source was being misunderstood. Herring believed that by introducing reason to support Christianity he could make the faith more credible.

This epistemological strategy had consequences for Herring's pleas in behalf of his faith. Miracles had traditionally been a powerful argument in support of religion, but Herring shared his century's uncertainty about the reliability of ancient accounts of miracles and, with many others, noticed the paucity of contemporary wonders. Thus he was sympathetic with the tendency of the theologians of his day to argue for God's existence and power from celestial order rather than from arbitrary interventions. "I think," he wrote to a friend, "the rising and setting of the sun is a far more durable argument for religion, than all the extraordinary convulsions of nature put together." Miracles he dismissed as "the Props of the Infancy of Christianity." Herring was also inclined to establish the foundations of morality in experience and reason rather than religion. Experience taught that certain activities—for

10. Herring also called it "history," "utility," "policy," and "interest."
11. I realize that I may be reading twentieth-century usages into Herring's terminology. But if the dichotomy between knowledge and wisdom does not capture all of what Herring meant by his distinction of reason from experience, it must at least suggest the nature of that distinction.

example, being merciful—were natural, and that human beings were so formed that they could be happy only in doing good. Reason taught which of man's activities were in fact virtuous. By applying reason man could discern the natural law by which God had rationally ordered His universe. It was true that, according to Scripture, Jesus instructed his followers in virtue, prescribing certain activities and proscribing others. But what he prescribed was what man was inclined by his nature to do anyway. And Jesus' directives were accessible as conclusions to any person who applied reason and experience to ethical questions. Religion thus did not contradict reason in moral matters; it did not even provide the basis for morality. It simply shortcut the method by which moral orders were derived. Jesus taught mankind the good, but the good drew its authority not from the fact that Jesus taught it but from the fact that it was the directive of natural law, illuminated by reason and experience.[12]

Man was not, however, an unflawed being. Herring avoided lapsarian language in explaining man's nature, but a vestigial notion of original sin remained. He thought man to be self-interested, and he dismissed as absurd the social theories of those who posited a disinterested and honest mankind. It was this inherent baseness in man—this inability finally to resist self-service—that made necessary God's most critical intervention in history, the gracious sending of His Son "to inform and raise human nature," to redeem mankind. But if salvation was impossible without divine assistance, improvement lay well within the capacity of unaided man. And to foster such improvement in morality, Herring believed, society should vigorously act to protect the rights of property. When a man attained "the secure Enjoyment of Property" he became infused with a "Spirit of Labour and Industry." And since people who devoted themselves to "honest Labour and useful Arts" were fine citizens as well as moral persons, Herring pointed with characteristic bourgeois pride to the happy congruence among what reason enjoined, what experience counseled, and what religion commanded.[13]

Herring was, as has several times been noted, a representative An-

12. *Letters from Herring*, 172; Herring, *Seven Sermons*, 14, 28, 36, 58–60.
13. Herring, *Seven Sermons*, 8, 11, 91, 150; British Museum, Add. MSS 11275, fols. 67–68.

glican thinker of his day; nothing in his religious thought was unusual for his century. The Church of England had long pleaded for the autonomy of reason and the value of ceremonials. It had long honored the doctrine of natural law. For at least a full generation many of its leading spokesmen had also argued that the fundamentals of Christianity were simple and that the faith was chiefly concerned with encouraging right conduct. The fiery language that had accompanied the church's struggles against Roman tyranny abroad and dissenting license at home had seared enduring brands into Anglican thought. The "whore of Babylon" and the frenzied enthusiast were stock enemies—metaphors or descriptions that came to have a life of their own for many who preached and heard Anglican sermons. Like many other Anglicans, Herring visualized the Church of England as a citadel beset from two sides. It held the middle ground in defiance of both the Roman Catholics and the sectarians, thus becoming the famous *via media*. From this vision of his church came Herring's political ideas. For if the *via media* was the soundest path in religion, it might well be the soundest in politics too. That, at any rate, came to be Herring's view.

III

Herring's political views derived from his religious views, but they were not logical extensions of them, in the sense that the Christian matrix of his thought allowed only one acceptable political order. Almost a century and a half earlier Richard Hooker had declared that Christianity did not entail any particular regime, and that a Christian society might take a number of different forms. Decisions about the nature of politics in a society rested upon prudential considerations such as the traditions and history of the people, the presumed nature of the people, and their current situation. Herring concurred, but he was not therefore indifferent to political and constitutional issues. He shared the virtually unanimous judgment of his countrymen that Britain possessed "the best Constitution in the World"; and in referring to its division into "several Powers," which were "balanced perhaps as perfectly as human Affairs will admit," he relied on conventional imagery to explain it. His list of the attendant benefits derived from the constitution was no less conventional: the happiness of the people, "a free and manly Government," a king "by Inclination and Nature the Parent of his Country," liberty under law, property, and wealth.[14] Britain's past provided fearful examples of the two errors into which a political society could fall. Charles I's reign showed how royal power, directed by insolent and wanton ministers, could eat away at liberty; the recoil from Stuart excesses into civil war and regicide demonstrated the destructiveness of liberty run riot. Britain's constitution had been crafted to ward off both dangers. Nevertheless, although one can immediately notice the parallels between this constitutional *via media* and the earlier ecclesiastical one, Herring's Court Whiggery has not been explained. It is therefore necessary to look deeper into the relationship between his religious views and his political views if the bases on which he distinguished himself from the Patriots are to be recovered.

There were three fundamental bases for Herring's support of Court Whiggery. First of all, he was a Court Whig because he believed the Protestant Succession indispensable to Britain and feared that the Patriots, however vigorously they protested his concern, might either choose to restore the Catholic Stuarts or inadvertently create a situation in which such a restoration would occur. He was also a Court Whig because he valued social tranquillity highly; he saw those who possessed power as the guardians of quiet and those who sought to wrest it from them as restless upsetters of order. Finally he supported the administrations of the 1730s and 1740s because he was obsessed with a vision of France as the military and political arm of Rome and because Walpole and his successors opposed France far less ambiguously than did the Patriots. These three bases were clearly interrelated, and separating them for purposes of analysis may have the effect of lending a bit more coherence to Herring's thought than it actually possessed— which is not to say that his thought was entirely muddled. It was natural that the three bases be interconnected, for each represented in a different sphere of social-political thought the appropriate conclusion that Herring drew from a single fabric of religious conviction. For because he believed as he did about God, man, the Bible, and the church, he found himself impelled to support a Protestant monarch as the foundation of the British constitution, a tranquil public order as

14. Herring, *Seven Sermons*, 99, xxii, 13, 210.

the environment that gave vitality to the constitution, and an opposition to France as the only foreign policy stance that promised to defend
that constitution.

Herring was one of the staunchest upholders of the Protestant
Succession as embodied in the house of Hanover. In public exhorta-
tions and private musings he turned again and again to the need for
Britons to focus their attention, trust, devotion, and commitment
upon the throne of George II. "Let us remember," he intoned from the
pulpit in 1748, "that, next under God, Union at Home, and Loyalty
and Affection to the King and his Royal Family, are our great and sure
Defence." To those who questioned George's right to occupy the throne
he had a multi-faceted reply. The king, he declared, "enjoys his Crown
by clear and indisputable Inheritance, by the Sanctions of Law, by the
Consent, and with the Applause of a great Nation"; and for those who
might doubt the rightness of royal behavior he added that George "uses
his Power and Royalty, as becomes a King, that is, as a Trust for the
Public Good." In an address of 1745 he described George II as "a just
and Protestant King, who is of so strict an Adherence to the Laws of
our Country, that not an Influence [sic] can be pointed out, during his
whole Reign, wherein he hath made the least Attempt upon the Liberty, or Property, or Religion of a single Person." And as early as 1740
Herring was able to assert that there existed "an inseparable Connection between the Health, the Honour, the Prosperity of the King, and
that of the Community he presides over." If the only evidence on this
point were from sermons and addresses, one might wish to suggest that
too much was being made of pulpit commonplaces. But the private
Herring was as royalist as his public counterpart. In late 1755, with
France at the gates, he wrote to Hardwicke: "God bless the King. I see
no Safety for us but in making him our center."[15] As a simple description of Herring's political philosophy that expression would serve very
well.

Clearly Herring placed the greatest importance upon the Protestant
nature of the British monarchy. But why did that evaluation lead him
to support the Court Whigs? Why, that is, did Herring believe that an

15. Ibid., xxi, 95, 227, 229; British Museum, Add. MSS 35599, fol. 279.

evaluation of the monarchy that was rooted in religious conviction entailed a political commitment? Essentially, he became a Court Whig because the constitution, which was the chief support of the monarchy, rested upon what he called "Whig principles" and therefore could be sustained only by those men who called themselves Whigs. It was true that many in the opposition also assumed that title, but their readiness to cooperate with the Tories against a Whig government proved them to be, at the least, deficient in their grasp of the constitution. For however they chose to denominate themselves, their behavior showed them to be abettors of the cause of a Catholic pretender. In short, if the prerequisite of British safety was a Protestant monarch, then the party that most unambiguously endorsed the frame of government sustaining that monarch was the only political group deserving support. It was reasoning of this sort that led Herring to reject the superficially enticing notion that the king should be above parties, bestowing favor and power irrespective of partisan adherence. "This is a noble principle, it must be ownd, & I would to God it took effect truly," he explained to Hardwicke, "but what must be the consequence, when it is only made the vehicle of Jacobitism and tends to overturn a government, wch began & can only be supported upon Whig principles." To urge that the king should be oblivious to party in choosing his ministers was to advise him to bring traitors into his council. Thus those who resisted such suggestions—who told George to repose trust only in Whigs of proven fidelity—were the sounder constitutionalists. Thus too Herring could sincerely describe the struggle against those who worked to unseat George II as a fight for "the Cause of Truth and Liberty."[16]

A second basis for Herring's Court Whiggery was his belief that domestic peace and tranquillity constituted the chief prerequisites for happiness and the faithful practice of religion. A state beset by internal discord could not know contentment; indeed, the seventeenth century provided a host of examples of how political struggling brought misery. In a sermon on the anniversary of Charles I's death Herring warned that "our chief Concern is for the present and the future, and it is

16. British Museum, Add. MSS 35599, fol. 65; Herring, *Seven Sermons*, xxix.

extremely well for us, if we can grow wise upon the Experience of our Forefathers, and learn the Value of Peace, without the Expence of War and Bloodshed." What had provoked the mischiefs of those unhappy days? They "did not arise so much from any one Set of Men, as from a general Misbehaviour and Want of Temper in all." The value of "peaceful Government" lay in its being the foundation for all the good things a people might produce or do. "It is," he declared, "the Support of every thing safe and orderly, and beautiful in Society." And its opposites—"Anarchy and Confusion"—were absolutely destructive to those accomplishments. Internal disorder was, in fact, "a greater Evil to Mankind than Plague, or Famine, or open War,—a Distemper of greater Malignity, longer Continuance, and of more difficult Care."[17] These bold comparisons strikingly revealed how deeply Herring's fear and distaste of disorderliness had penetrated.

The importance of tranquillity often served Herring as a springboard to leap into one of his favorite themes: the need for altruism. And the line of argument was as recurrent as the theme. God had so designed the world that the courses of action enjoined by moral considerations were identical to those required by what he called "policy." This happy coinciding of the moral and the practical provided an invaluable guideline for choosing from among alternative governmental actions. In no sphere was the congruence more compelling than in that of social policy toward the indigent. Both the commands of religion and the wisdom of civil government recommended charity as an appropriate action by the rich. "The truth is," he explained to a London audience, "neither the Peace nor Welfare of the Public can in any Degree be preserved without a due Care of the Poor; and it wants but little Reflection to see, that the Rich, with all the Advantages that their Wealth could give them, would have a very uneasy Time of it, if the Children of the Poor were utterly untaught and ignorant, the Sick and Aged unprovided for, and the idle and vagrant Part of them let loose upon the Sober and Industrious." There was not a great deal the state could do directly to help the poor, though to encourage the sober and

17. Herring, *Seven Sermons*, 109, 111, 81–82.

industrious among them it should vigorously fulfill its chief function, "the Practice of distributive Justice, and proportioning Rewards, or Punishments, to the Merits, or Demerits, of Men."[18] But there was more it could do indirectly—and nothing deserved more emphasis than the steady fostering of charity and mercy within the political nation. A discontented class of indigents could bring tumult and then ruin upon a state.

But again a question must be posed. Why did such a high evaluation of order and domestic peace lead Herring to support the Court Whigs? The answer appears to be threefold. It had been the administrations of the late 1720s and 1730s, all led by Sir Robert Walpole, that had brought about the existing condition of "great Security and Happiness: And, when we consider, upon the Comparison [with the seventeenth century], the Blessings of a gentle Government, and a powerful State of things; if we have any Love for our native Country, a sincere and honest Zeal for our good Religion, or a Sense of the Value of our wise Establishment, it will put us, methinks, upon endeavouring, all we can, to enjoy that Happiness temperately ourselves, and to transmit it safe to our Posterity." Thus to Walpole's leadership went the credit for creating a stable and tranquil kingdom. And to his leadership and that of his successors, operating by similar principles, should go allegiance. The opposition had no similar record with which to commend itself, and it was, moreover, in the short run patently seeking to discommode rather than calm the state. The motives of the leaders of the opposition were not such as to portend a tranquil regime if they gained power, for at their worst they were men "perpetually intoxicated by Ambition, by Pride, by Covetousness, by Revenge, by Faction (which last is nothing else but a wicked Compound of Pride and Covetousness of Ambition and Revenge), united and knit together by Hypocrisy." Herring privately acknowledged that the motives of the Court Whigs were often as reprehensible, and, he once lamented, "ye great mischief is, ye true zeal for ye publick influences neither party." But even so, the argument that change itself would be disruptive and ought therefore to be foregone retained its force. "If that be really ye case," he continued, "& all

18. *Ibid.*, 74, 83.

mean to rob it the state, I think one may as well keep to ye gang in wch we were first listed."[19]

Thus, the achievements of the ministries of the 1730s and 1740s and the selfishness of the Patriots were two reasons for allowing a zest for peace to impel one toward support for Court Whiggery. But a third reason also existed. Nothing posed a greater threat to social tranquillity than an excited and deluded lower order. It was therefore imperative that the government conduct itself in a fashion that would keep these meaner people of society in their places. Happily, most of the people were by disposition quite prepared to accept their allotted roles and to look deferentially to their betters for leadership. But if "the spirit of the mob" flared up—if the people abandoned their accustomed readiness to seek direction from those above them—then all was brought into peril. It followed from such convictions that, among politicians, those who most clearly resisted the pretensions of the mob merited support. Again it was the Court Whigs who so qualified. The opposition regularly appealed to the mob for support, hoping with the weapon of an hysterical public opinion to beat down the government. It was a natural strategy for the Patriots to adopt, for they were seeking to compensate for their deficiency in royal favor with periodic surges of popular favor. The uproar over the excise bill in 1733 showed how potent the weapon could be. But in trying to bring the genii of mob opinion into national politics, the opposition recklessly courted danger. The Court Whigs resisted this appeal to demagoguery. They might be, it is true, every bit as self-serving in this stance as the Patriots: as the obverse of the opposition they stood to gain by resisting any strategy adopted by their foes. But even if their motives were no less sordid, their policy was correct.[20] The health of the state required that the *demos* be confined.

The third basis of Herring's Court Whiggery was his dislike of France. Rooted in his aversion to France's loyalty to the Roman Catho-

19. *Ibid.*, 81, 175; University of Nottingham Library, Pw V 120, letter 26.

20. No Court Whig action so embittered and disappointed Herring as their acquiescence in the repeal of the Jewish Naturalization Act in 1753. His attitude toward the mob makes this anger understandable. The party that should have resisted popular passion was instead submitting to it and thereby reinforcing it. British Museum, Add. MSS 35599, fol. 93; *Letters from Herring*, 138–39.

lic church, the dislike extended to almost everything associated with that nation. Britain, he warned, should avoid all but the most necessary contacts with the French. "The Vanity, the Looseness, the Perfidy, the Libertinism, the abject and fawning Manners of this People," he declared with the zeal born of the Church of England's unconscious appropriation of Puritan prejudice, "tend to spoil the Spirits of Men, and to break them gradually to an unmanly Government." Even trade and the grand tours should be curtailed as projects "hurtful to us, but a rich Mine to them." Nor was that all. Britain, he added, employed too many French women and men as servants, embraced too readily France's "fantastic Fashions," and betrayed itself with a "slavish Fondness for their Language, unbecoming the Freedom and Grandeur of the *British Nation*." Moreover, France was dangerous not merely as a bad example but even more severely as a fomenter of sedition and trouble. The French, he said during the height of the war, had "Designs" for Britain—namely, that "Popery and arbitrary Power come in upon us"— and His Most Christian Majesty was pushing those schemes in a "savage and bloodthirsty" manner. The bond between this attitude and a consequent high regard for Court Whiggery is not hard to find. The opposition, in its desperate pursuit of place, had sought various types of French support. Bolingbroke, for example, had accepted a French pension. Such behavior fatally compromised all Patriot hopes of appearing free of embarrassing foreign ties. Then, in the 1740s, the Patriots compounded their problem by arguing for alterations in military and naval strategy that would have eased France's lot. It did not matter to Herring that the Patriots felt they could use the French government without being used by it, or that they believed strategical shifts would help rather than hurt Britain. All that mattered was that the Court Whigs alone had the resolve to resist France in peacetime and defeat her in time of war.[21] This resolve merited the fullest support.

Herring made no effort to hide his political views. Publicly and pri-

21. Herring, *Seven Sermons*, xx, 220–21. There is no indication of Herring's opinion of Walpole's foreign policy for the 1720s through the War of the Polish Succession. Presumably he was, at the least, suspicious of it. But by the time Herring began to address himself (in extant works) to foreign affairs, the Court Whigs had shifted to hostility toward Versailles.

vately, through sermon and conversation, he sought to identify himself with the administrations in which Hardwicke served. He was known to be, in his own word, a "warm" Whig. But once enthroned at Canterbury and a spectator to the Pelhams' efforts to mute partisanship in the face of the growing inconsequentiality of the word "Tory," Herring subtly modified his role. He remained a loyal Whig, but now he took to calling himself an "Old Whig." Indeed, he tried to assume the informal post of spokesman for the Old Whigs. In appropriating this term, long a favorite among the principled Opposition Whigs such as John Trenchard and Lord Molesworth, Herring did not mean to identify himself with men whom he had always dismissed as republicans. Nor can he have meant to link himself with the writers of *The Old Whig and Consistent Protestant*, a journal of the late 1730s that was too egalitarian and hostile to the Church of England for Herring's taste. Instead he intended to imply that he and his kind were being faithful to the Whiggery of Sir Robert Walpole while the Pelhams, through inadvertence or ignorance, were sometimes abandoning it.[22] These Old Whigs objected above all to what they saw as the Pelhams' short-sighted policy of giving places to men of dubious loyalty to true Whiggery. As chief patronage agent in ecclesiastical affairs, the duke of Newcastle fell most blatantly and gallingly afoul of Herring's preferences. This doubtless accounted for Herring's decision to slight the secretary of state at his installation as chancellor of Cambridge University. Thus, though Old Whigs remained adherents of the administration in the early 1750s—there was nowhere else to go—their allegiance was now clouded by fears of an insidious Tory take-over carelessly promoted by incautious Whig ministers. And in this light it seems fair to conclude that Herring's self-proclaimed motto of 1747—"God bless the King & his present Administration!"—remained on his lips until his death but shifted in meaning from a thankful prayer for gifts received to a worried petition for an increase in ministerial wisdom.[23]

22. Robbins, *Eighteenth-Century Commonwealthman*, 241–42. For a brief exposition of the "Old Whig" view in these years, see *A Word in Season to the Old Whigs* (London, 1754).

23. British Museum, Add. MSS 35598, fol. 309, Add. MSS 35599, fols. 64–65, 200, Add. MSS 35598, May 20, 1747.

IV

A preacher is a teacher. And if this obvious remark remains true for the late twentieth century, it is far truer when applied to the clergy of the eighteenth, when no other professions could presume to rival the churchmen as recognized instructors of the people. The church was the classroom of the community, and the pulpit the lectern of the instructor. And although there were numerous variations in emphasis, in treatment of subjects, and in oratorical ability among the clergymen of England, their messages were generally similar. They spoke on the timeless concerns of pastoral care: of the need for charity, the dangers of pride, the uncovering of hidden good amidst pressing and personal trouble, the promise of salvation. But they also addressed themselves to political issues, and in this capacity they were splendidly situated to become—though many did not—spokesmen for the public ideology of the state, upholding its authority and defending it from the accusations of its enemies. It is likely that most figures in public affairs thought this instructional role of the clergy their most important function. Precisely because Herring was celebrated for his homiletic skills we may presume that he exercised more than ordinary influence as a preacher, even before the weight of title was added to his forensic talent. We may also presume that he paid the closest attention to what he chose to say to his assembled congregations.

What lessons did Herring wish to inculcate? How did his Court Whiggery help to shape his sermons? The answers to these questions cannot be advanced with total assuredness, for it is impossible to distinguish with certainty those lessons that sprang directly out of his Christian faith from those that, perhaps remotely emerging from the same source, had their immediate roots in Court Whiggery. But it is possible to identify certain dominant themes in his sermons that were highly congruent with his political views. And the effect of illuminating political doctrine with scriptural candles in an ecclesiastical setting was, naturally enough, to suggest a kind of divine sanction for that doctrine. Herring's overriding concern was to justify the subject's obligation to be civilly obedient.[24] It ran through all his sermons that have

24. For an examination of how this theme was seized by *Tory* divines in Anne's reign to combat *Whig* error, see J. P. Kenyon, "The Revolution of 1688: Resistance and Con-

survived and was best expressed in the text from I Peter 2:13–14 that he selected for explication in a sermon delivered before the House of Lords in 1740: "Submit yourselves to every Ordinance of Man for the Lord's sake, whether it be to the King, as Supreme; Or unto Governors, as unto them that are sent by him, for the Punishment of Evil Doers, and for the Praise of them that do well." The disciple's call for obedience to civil authority became Herring's call too, and most of the rest of what he said can be understood as glosses upon this core doctrine.

According to Herring, a subject of the king had an irrefragable obligation to submit to civil authority: the king must be "revered and honoured as Supreme, and the Subject must be dutiful and obedient." This obligation emerged from four considerations, each of which Herring regarded as independently compelling. Disobedience, he noted, had evil consequences for the state. It entailed divisiveness, and no state could long endure the existence of faction. So his reiterated prayer was for "union." Disobedience also had evil consequences for the disobedient. Herring asserted that he had often seen it end "in the Ruin of turbulent and unquiet Spirits" and counseled obedience "for the Peace and Comfort of your Life." Disobedience also threatened the violator with the wrath of the magistrate. The state had laws against rebellious activity and was not noted for its tolerance in judging accusations of sedition. A simple prudential judgment thus recommended obedience to the law, lest the power of the state lead to incarceration or worse. Finally, disobedience was wrong because it offended conscience. The sense of the natural law implanted in each man directed him to submit to authority. Every subject, Herring declared to the leaders of York in 1745, had sworn loyalty to the king. "You have entered into the most solemn religious Engagement and . . . your Obedience to the Government, under which you live, is become your indispensable Duty."[25] From this obligation the subject could not recede with impunity. God judged—and God punished.

tract," in *Historical Perspectives: Studies in English Thought and Society in Honour of J. H. Plumb*, ed. Neil McKendrick (London, 1974). By the 1730s it was no longer the property of one party alone.

25. Herring, *Seven Sermons*, 84. For a discussion of the manner in which postrevolution Anglicans retained their commitment to obedience, see Gerald M. Straka, *Anglican*

Herring acknowledged that a prince might become tyrannical, and he vaguely suggested that there were limits to the obligation to obey. But his extant writings give no indication of how he would have dealt with the difficult and central problem of determining at what point a monarch had become so wicked that his writ no longer carried authority. Indeed, every time Herring approached this thorny dilemma he shied away. For example, he asserted that St. Peter, in the cited epistle, did not give princes "a lawless and tyrannical Power," but then instead of saying what a nation should do with a prince who assumed such power he merely added that the disciple similarly did not confer "a loose and unsettled Obedience" upon the subjects. He obliquely returned to the issue when he distinguished between the attitudes of proper obedience and "servile terror," but again he avoided the central problem with a simple admonition to prince and subject to love each other. Yet the unspoken fascination of the dilemma drew him back once again. Submission, he avowed still later in the sermon, was not the same as "a blind and passive and implicit Obedience." But then, instead of demarcating the two, he shifted the grounds of the argument by declaring that human nature would not peacefully endure tyranny.[26] In fashions of this sort Herring avoided ever discussing how the subject should deal with the despot.

What then did Herring teach about liberty, that precious condition possessed almost exclusively by Britons? How did he reconcile his reiterated appeals for obedience with a manful respect for liberty? These too are crucial questions, for Whiggery had appeared on the seventeenth-century political scene essentially as a movement for liberty, and by accepting the designation of "Whig" Herring meant, among other implications, to suggest a tie across a generation between himself and the colleagues of Lord Shaftesbury. The Opposition Whigs drew heavily on precisely this legacy. Herring dared not, without repudiating the entire tradition, scorn or belittle liberty. But neither could he extol

---

Reaction to the Revolution of 1688 (Madison, Wisc., 1962). Herring's pulpit style was discursive. The identification of four lines of argument in this paragraph does not follow his own analysis but is rather my effort to give order to a series of related remarks that steadily amplify a rather vague argument. See also, *Seven Sermons*, 165–66.

26. Herring, *Seven Sermons*, 84, 88, 103–104.

it excessively. He chose, appropriately for the dilemma, a middle road in his definition of the term. Liberty was incompatible with "the Tyranny of Princes," but it was not to be confused with license. Having advanced this conventional Court Whig answer to the problem of simultaneously defending liberty and acclaiming royal government, Herring went on to assert that in his day the major enemy to liberty was the "Licentiousness of the People." This assertion had the virtue of justifying his manifest tendency to emphasize antipopular themes in his sermons. He acknowledged liberty to be "the most excellent Privilege of our Nature," but the essential thrust of his explorations of the subject was to cast doubt upon the fitness of Britons for this privilege. "That very Liberty," he declared, "(which, rightly treated, is in natural Friendship and Alliance with true Religion and the public Weal) we abuse, and prostitute most vilely to every Purpose of Faction and Immorality; as if we were studious to shew, that Liberty is a blessing too good for us, and that our Minds are too low and too sordid to enjoy so gracious and so divine a Privilege." Herring also believed an extensive liberty incompatible with the retention of truth.[27] This blessing and privilege, quite clearly, was to be enjoyed only in moderation.

In his effort to recall Britons to obedience Herring set forth a number of teachings that he saw as germane to his purpose. Cohering loosely together in a religious framework, they cumulatively taught that obedience was an expression of godliness and a prerequisite for fullness of life. "The more we know of God," he declared in a sermon not basically concerned with obedience, "and the better we understand ourselves and our Duty, the better and happier Men we shall be for it." What needed to be known of God? Above all, it was necessary to recall that God was a "God of Order, and made you for Society and Government." Since God created order, and since society subsisted as an ordered system, the obligation to submit to the king was nothing less than a "Duty to God." Such obedience served to uphold the world of order. And God of course punished disobedience. "God alone determines the Fate of Nations, who destroys or builds them up, according to his good Pleasure." Jesus, in Herring's depiction, became the mild-mannered

27. *Ibid.*, 94, 203; British Museum, Add. MSS 35598, fol. 436.

Whig of Galilee. He "both taught and practiced the important Doctrine of a quiet and peaceful Behaviour, as one of the most invaluable Blessings to Men; and for that Reason, doubtless, has made it one of the primary Precepts of his Religion."[28] With God sanctifying order in Herring's world and Jesus living it, the primate had created the appearance of a theological foundation for Court Whiggery.

Through what means did God send order to society? The answer to this question took Herring from the realm of theology to the realms of sociology and ethics. His view was in fact akin to the classical one that saw sociology and ethics yoked. Society continued to exist only insofar as the people who comprised it remained faithful to sound ethical doctrines. It could not endure, Herring proclaimed, "but upon the Principles of Morality and Virtue." Or, as he phrased it a few minutes later, "Government can subsist no otherwise than upon the Principles of Order, and Peace, and Justice, and a Sobriety and Temperance in the Morals of all its Members." The conduct that natural law enjoined was the foundation of social integrity. Given this line of argument, Herring was only being consistent when he disapproved of the "most wicked and licentious Principle," conventionally attributed to Machiavelli and recently advanced by Bernard de Mandeville, that probity could disable a prince and that morality should be prostituted to the interests of the state. Somewhat less predictably—and therefore indicative of how seriously he regarded good conduct—Herring declared that for Britain "a sober and regular, though weak and deluded *Romanist* is a character preferable to a loose and immoral *Protestant*." The chief component of this good conduct that he called for was the granting of respect to those in authority. And should this moral obligation be neglected, the consequence was inevitable. "Once a People have lost all Reverence for Magistracy," he grimly warned, "naturally speaking, there is no other Bond can hold Community together."[29]

In a properly ordered society, where respect for morality prevailed, there was a mutuality of interest between prince and people. This mutuality revealed itself through the demands for reciprocity in the duties that reason, policy, and religion imposed on ruler and ruled. The

28. Herring, *Seven Sermons*, 50, 82, 83, 218.
29. *Ibid.*, 92–93, 101, 202, 204–205, 215.

prince's obligation was to support true religion, to protect the nation he governed, to apply the laws impartially but with a tincture of mercy, to set a fitting example of goodness and faithfulness, to give mature thought before making decisions, and to execute his decisions steadily. The people, reciprocally, were duty bound to honor their prince, to pay deference to his character, to vindicate his name, to extol his virtues and honor, to obey his laws, and to act and speak at all times to his credit. Since such commendable behavior was unlikely to arise completely spontaneously, society created a system of laws to define the reciprocal duties and to add the motive of fear to that of devotion in the hearts of those upon whom the moral responsibility lay. Law was in fact the tool chosen by "policy" to secure compliance to morality. "There is Reason, and Spirit, and Liberty in Law," he declared, "and it is not only essential to every Man's Property, but, without it, there can be no such thing as Virtue or Religion in the World."[30]

If either prince or people blatantly broke the obligation of mutuality, society would experience the severest evils. But Herring issued a ringing warning at this point. Princes were men and subject to the frailties of the flesh. Thus it was unfair and ill judged to presume that every error they committed was a deliberate assault on the nation and an effort to avoid the commands of mutuality. The people, he urged, should not rant at "every little Miscarriage that they see," especially when "the main Points of Government are safe." Instead they should recall that erring was human and that charity in judgment was as appropriate in measuring kings as in assaying friends. The true poisoners of good relations between prince and people were not the princes themselves but either "bad Ministers" or "Faction." Here Herring fell back upon conventional categories of the day. Wicked ministers were those who "abused the Confidence" of their prince, advising him poorly while seeking to use his position to further their own selfish goals. As long as the Court Whigs remained in office, this danger was muted. Factions on the other hand rose from within the ranks of ostensibly faithful subjects. They implanted "base and false Notions of the best of Princes," hoping thereby to elicit "Contempt and Hatred" for

30. Ibid., 105–106, 222.

him from among their followers. Here was a very present danger. The response to either threat was a fuller commitment to allegiance to the monarch. If everyone—from the most influential duke to the meanest laborer—kept ever in mind the obligation to revere the king, the state would never be imperiled.[31]

The doctrines of the church and the predispositions of Court Whiggery combined to make Herring a forceful advocate of a forward policy toward both non-Anglicans and Americans. It is true that he represented himself as a friend of the Act of Toleration and declared his opposition to altering it in 1748. But prudential considerations constituted part of his grounds for conservatism—he feared perhaps the wrath of dissenters—and since the act was widely seen not as a peripheral piece of legislation lightly passed by the postrevolutionary Parliament but as a cornerstone of the revolutionary settlement, one can appreciate Herring's undisguised reluctance to tamper with it. Nevertheless, both religion and policy—again the yoking—argued for active efforts to bring the light of the Anglican faith to dizzy dissenters and benighted papists. The former would then learn that a respect for ordered liberty was a truer Christian attitude than a lusting after levelling; the latter would learn that a religious liberation conferred a new "Spirit of Labour and Industry," and that this gift in turn replaced indolence with diligence. America too should be brought to heel. Unless chastised and somewhat confined, the Americans threatened to pollute Britain with dangerous political and social ideas—to become, "not the Credit, but the Disgrace, not the Advantage and Security, but the Mischief and Ruin, of their Benefactors." Before an audience of members of the Society for the Propagation of the Gospel in Foreign Parts Herring was at his most explicit in explaining why the conversion efforts must be carried to Romanists and dissenters alike, in Britain, Ireland, and America: "every Convert to Christianity, or"—to speak more accurately—"Member secured to our Establishment upon Gospel and Protestant Principles, is a Friend to our Country and Government, as well as to our Religion."[32]

Herring was a manifestly inconsistent thinker, and there seems little

31. *Ibid.*, 88–94.
32. British Museum, Add. MSS 35598, fol. 342; Herring, *Seven Sermons*, 35, 149–53.

sense in making a closer analysis of his sermons simply to demonstrate what any reasonably attentive reader already knows: that he used words cavalierly, clothed murky logic in cloudy syntax, and wanted even originality to compensate for his inexact thought. All that can be said—and, in the present circumstances, all that need be said—is that he sounded certain themes again and again. Essentially he was a moralist. The reiterated themes tolled the conventional categories of Anglican morality: obligation and duty, respect and allegiance, truth and peace. Collectively the themes constituted a variation of Court Whig thought that was not uncommon in the age of Walpole and the Pelhams. Indeed, with Herring we come to a figure whose idea-world in the area of politics and constitutionalism might more accurately be called a farrago of attitudes than a philosophy. But even if the problem of internal consistency can thereby be put aside, there remains one final issue to deal with: has Herring been accurately understood by the one scholar who studied his political thinking?

William Dickinson wrote when many who knew Herring were still alive, and he thus was able to consult with some of the archbishop's friends before putting his views on paper. From such preparation Dickinson pronounced his verdict. He could affirm Herring to have been "certainly a very sincere Protestant," but he had "no hesitation in asserting, upon good authority, that his politics were monarchical, and his religion high church." Herring did not act upon "any very enlarged ideas of the British constitution." He simply believed a Protestant monarch essential to Britain and thus, though he may have found the Stuart claims more theoretically and abstractly satisfactory, he became a celebrated defender of the Hanoverian possession.[33] Clearly Dickinson had caught sight of the powerful authoritarian strand in Herring's pronouncements. But having seized upon an element that he, in the 1780s, had not expected in the thought of a self-proclaimed Whig, Dickinson proceeded to make too much of it. Above all, he seems to have misunderstood the grounds for Herring's monarchical professions. He recognized that the archbishop saw George II as the pillar of British

33. Dickinson, *Antiquities*, 250–51. This interpretation was adopted by R. Garnett, "Correspondence of Archbishop Herring and Lord Hardwicke during the Rebellion of 1745," *English Historical Review*, XIX (1904), 529–31.

Protestantism. But he missed another foundation stone of Herring's advocacy of the Hanoverian cause, namely, his fear of an over-mighty *demos*. And in his speculation that in the abstract Herring would have preferred the claims of a Stuart, he went beyond any evidence I know of. Herring was simply not concerned with theoretical claims to the throne. Whoever exercised authority did it by virtue of God's direction, and George's possession of the regalities was a sufficient argument for the rightness of his claim. If a further sign were needed, it could readily be discerned in the king's religious faith. He was a Protestant, of a family brought to the throne to protect the established Protestant church. And since that church held to the path of the apostolic faith while dissenters stumbled and papists fell, it would have been absurd to assume that any Roman Catholic pretender could have mustered acceptable grounds for displacing a Protestant incumbent. Samuel Squire, writing anonymously and eulogistically after Herring's death, had a sounder understanding than Dickinson: Herring viewed the Protestant monarchy as "the only Support of the Church of England; as the Bulwark of our Civil Liberty, and the surest Defence of the Independency of Europe."[34]

At the conclusion of his most extended treatment of his favorite theme of obedience Herring turned to the task of summing up his views in an easily apprehensible manner. There was, he announced, but "one plain and easy Rule" to follow—"To be quiet, and mind our own Business." It was the lesson of both Scripture and natural law. In his formulation he was paraphrasing St. Paul's advice to the Thessalonians, and the admonition recalls as well one of Plato's efforts to define justice.[35] But the purposes of the three men differed enormously. The apostle sought the advancement of Christianity and urged his coreligionists to avoid behavior that would discredit the faith in the eyes of the state. The philosopher hoped to fathom the moral foundations of community. Herring wanted to strengthen Great Britain, and his reasoning was straightforward. If people minded their own business, doing their jobs and fulfilling their duties, the kingdom would be united. And

34. Herring, *Seven Sermons*, lxii.
35. *Ibid.*, 113. Compare I Thess. 4:11; Allan Bloom (trans. and ed.), *The Republic of Plato* (New York, 1968), Bk. IV, 433a.

union was what Britain required. "For while *Great Britain* is in Union at Home, lives in Obedience to her Laws and Government, and in the conscientious Practice of the true Protestant Religion, the Providence of God, the Situation of her Islands, and the Genius and Spirit of her Country, as they have often preserved, so always will preserve her."[36] It was a voice we have heard before. It was, this time in the rhetoric of the pastor, yet another intoning by the authentic voice of Court Whiggery.

36. Herring, *Seven Sermons*, 117.

Chapter V

Samuel Squire (1714–1766): The Court Whig as Historian

I

Samuel Squire, D.D., combined the inclinations of a scholar with the ambitions of a place-man. It was an uneasy union. As a man of the university he studied and enjoyed languages, he believed history had lessons to teach, and he aspired to be counted a successor to the great Anglican scholars who flowered in the early years of the eighteenth century. But as a figure on the edge of politics he sought advancement with an assiduity remarkable even in an age of climbers, and for a while he was prepared to turn his considerable scholarship to the service of partisan propaganda. It was natural that such a man should seek a career in the church. Holy orders offered unusual opportunities for both the leisure that permits scholarly activity and the social occasions from which political liaisons emerge. He capitalized on the opportunities. While publishing two lengthy and Whiggish historical works, *An Enquiry into the Foundation of the English Constitution* and *Historical Essay upon the Balance of Civil Power in England*, and while assailing such Tory historians as Thomas Carte, Squire served the duke of Newcastle as chaplain, wrote a variety of political pamphlets, and finally in the first year of George III's reign became bishop of St. David's. Later historians have usually assumed that Squire was therefore a flunkey of the powerful. They have seen him simply as the paradigmatic careerist clergyman of the eighteenth century, sycophantically echoing the political views of important patrons. They have recalled William Warburton's famous comparison of Josiah Tucker and Squire: "One of them made Trade his Religion; the other, Religion his Trade."[1] That view is not so much wrong as incomplete. For if Squire pursued promotion with unbecoming fervor and was not backward in using the pulpit to give political instruction, it remains true—but less celebrated—that when his scholarly commitment to truth came into visible conflict with his partisan promptings, it was the latter that gave way. Squire was not a great scholar, but he was finally an honest one. That point should not be forgotten when assessing the man.

II

All historians make certain assumptions when they undertake their enterprise. Such assumptions—Squire called them "right notions"— define the reality the historian will deal with. Squire was no exception, and an examination of his political and constitutional thought rightly begins with a survey of the operative assumptions that controlled his historical investigations. The basic one postulated the fundamental changelessness of human nature over time. "Mankind have always been pretty much alike with regard to their inward frame. The same ruling-passions have ever influenced their actions, tho' they may have had different objects to work upon." Other assumptions added substance to the concept of an unchanging heritable nature. All mankind, Squire believed, simply by virtue of being human had a primitive sense of justice and could understand "natural equity." All were, moreover, prone to self-interestedness and the wickedness that follows from it— that is, all were finally to be regarded not as "saints" but as "sinners." And once racial divisions were acknowledged, there was still more to be said about heritable nature, or at least about the nature of all people of German origin. These people who had originally sprung from Teutonic forests shared an "invincible love of liberty" and a deep-seated

1. Nichols, *Illustrations*, II, 55. The chief sources for biographical information on Squire are the brief life in British Museum, Add. MSS 5831, fols. 162–64, and the longer, handwritten one added to the first volume of the British Museum's made-up edition of Samuel Squire, *Works* (4 vols.; London, 1741–63). The reader may also refer to the entry in the *DNB*; John Nichols, *Literary Anecdotes of the Eighteenth Century* (9 vols.; London, 1812–15), II, 348–52; and Reed Browning, "Samuel Squire: Pamphleteering Churchman," *Eighteenth-Century Life*, V (1978), 12–20.

aversion to change. They were, in fact, sufficiently distinct from other racial groups to allow Squire to speak of "the natural genius of our Northern ancestors."[2] In this manner Squire was in effect postulating the original national character of the English people whose past was the subject of his own historical studies.

If Squire's assumptions about human nature helped him explain individual and (sometimes) collective actions, his assumptions about the origins of civil society guided him in his understanding of political activity. In essence, he used John Locke as an anthropological source. It is true that he claimed his method to be Aristotelian, and insofar as he began his account of constitutional society with the family and continued on to larger groupings he employed a mode of analysis that Aristotle helped conventionalize. But it goes without saying that he missed Aristotle's subtlety, and he neglected as well the philosopher's appreciation of diversity. Instead, he invoked Locke's authority to assert that all civil societies arose from compacts or covenants concluded among independent and equal men. In his *Letter to a Tory Friend* he used such an argument to confute those who attributed the origins of civil society either to an act of coercion or to an amplification of the natural authority of the father.[3] In the *Enquiry* he followed Locke even more directly, explaining the emergence of civil authority among the Germans as a consequence of the need to create a power that could adjudicate disputes among free men. Squire thus employed Locke not simply as a social theorist but as an historian as well.

Once a society had been founded, Squire adverted to another "indisputable maxim" to account for the shifts in power that inevitably occurred in that society over time. "In whatever hands the overbalance of national property lies, there the great weight of national power will

2. [Samuel Squire], *Remarks on Mr. Carte's Specimen of His General History of England* (London, 1748), 11, 43; Samuel Squire, *An Enquiry into the Foundation of the English Constitution* (Rev. ed., 1753; London, 1745), v; [Samuel Squire], *Letter to a Tory Friend on the Present Critical Situation of Our Affairs* (London, 1746), 22; Squire, *Enquiry* (1745), 9, 118–19, 163. The terms "saints" and "sinners" are clearly drawn from a theological anthropology, and there is no denying that they bear certain doctrinal freight. But the context is unquestionably secular—i.e., a consideration of which people were most suitable as governors—and Squire is not covertly introducing metahistorical criteria.

3. [Squire], *Letter to a Tory Friend*, 34–39.

always be found." This was a principle made famous by James Harrington, who had been the first to use it to explain systematically the contours of modern English history. Thereafter, cheapened in the hands of the neo-Harringtonians, it became a commonplace. The principle underlay the *Enquiry* of 1745, but the notes in that work suggest that Squire had learned it from the writings of the Hebraist Moses Lowman.[4] The existence of numerous handwritten quotations from Harrington among the marginalia of Squire's personal copy of the *Enquiry* further indicates that he was not familiar with *Oceana* and the *Aphorisms* when composing the *Enquiry*. But by the time the *Historical Essay* was finished—and Squire had drafted it by the late summer of 1747[5]— he was imbibing his Harrington straight and quoting the master's words directly. For Squire this "indisputable maxim" meant that whatever group in society held the bulk of landed property would by virtue of that possession also exercise dominant power. It was upon the group, not the individuals within it, that Squire focused. Property invariably gave power to the group that held it, but not invariably to every individual within that group. Personal weakness, feckless activity, bad luck, or simple stupidity could all destroy the power of a man and his family. But if one wanted to understand why the franchise was wide or narrow, or why an aristocracy was in one era strong and in another weak, one needed only to identify those forces that were bringing about shifts in the pattern of landholding. It was a principle that reduced the inchoate data of history to a simple formula, and like Squire's other assumptions it could be used as readily to conclude as to begin a line of argument. For if the group that exercised dominant power was known, then the group that held the bulk of property was known. Or if the group that owned the preponderant quantity of land was known, then so too was the group that controlled society. The mastery of history thus required even less application than the mastery of simple addition.

Another principle that Squire accepted was the notion that the growth of wealth and "monstrous luxury" in a society entailed its moral

4. Samuel Squire, *Historical Essay upon the Balance of Civil Power in England* (Rev. ed., 1753; London, 1748), vi. Moses Lowman wrote *A Dissertation on the Civil Government of the Hebrews* (London, 1740).

5. British Museum, Add. MSS 4318, fol. 268.

corruption. Squire here drew on another Harringtonian conviction, central to the whole body of thought that has been called civic humanism. "Corruption" was a concept rich with implications. The key one for Squire was that a people grown accustomed to luxury, magnificence, titles, and great estates—and he held the English in recent centuries to have become such a people—had lost the inclination to submit the private to the public and therefore needed royal governance to maintain themselves. Without some unifying force an affluent people could not cohere. Their community would fragment under the pressures of heightened envies and ambitions. Conversely, a people inured to the simple life, self-reliant and cooperative, unriven by great discrepancies in wealth and the cupidity to which they gave rise, was a people able to rule themselves without feeling a need to submit to the power of a single individual. Squire believed the Anglo-Saxons to have been such a people, and he extolled them for their public-spiritedness and readiness to contribute from their own meagre resources toward the support of a prince. Their era, untouched by expanding riches, was one in which the private interest was defined in terms of the public interest. "It was dividing these two interests," Squire then concluded, "the public and the private, which both God and nature had so firmly united together, that first introduced the necessity of legal taxations, and all those other impositions, which are the great burthen as well as grievance of our modern governments."[6] This was an attitude widely held in eighteenth-century England, even by those—such as Squire—who supported administrations bent upon making England richer and who undisguisedly enjoyed the amenities that this corrupting wealth provided them.

These assumptions were the "right notions" Squire employed in the mid-1740s as he undertook to make sense of English history. Whether explicitly invoked or implicitly relied on, they allowed him to reconstruct what had occurred even when there was no documentary evidence. He knew what had happened because, privy to a wisdom that gave meaning to history, he could deduce what *must* have happened. Such a tool was particularly invaluable for fathoming the scarcely re-

6. [Squire], *Letter to a Tory Friend*, 24, 29; Squire, *Historical Essay* (1748), xxvi; Squire, *Enquiry* (1753), 60.

corded deeps of Anglo-Saxon days. He knew, for example, that ceorls had emerged in early England from foreign rather than English stock. It could not have been otherwise, for the English, imbued with an unconquerable love of freedom, would not themselves have accepted dependent status. He similarly knew that Anglo-Saxon thanes were identical to German companions, not because etymological evidence implied as much but because Tacitus had described German society in the first century and a people averse to change would not have altered their social organization. He asserted, *even against the tenor of evidence*, that the early English had chosen their governors through some method involving general approbation. This was, he argued, a legitimate inference from the "genius" of the German people. His understanding of Locke allowed him to know that the earliest Anglo-Saxon societies in England, though products of an era of dislocation and conflict, were nevertheless free and responsive to the will of all citizens. And his understanding of Harrington disclosed to him that the right to attend a general council (Mycelgemot) in Anglo-Saxon days was shared by all freemen, not just by some. It was, after all, impermissible to assume that those to whom ownership of property brought power would allow themselves to be deprived of the right to participate in decision-making. Squire was, it is clear, not fully cognizant of the epistemological insecurity of his "right notions," but he at least had some awareness that he was granting to certain principles of interpretation a preeminent status and thereby making them invulnerable to historical criticism. In a set of handwritten jottings apparently designed as a private commentary upon his *Enquiry* he identified the paucity of firm evidence about Anglo-Saxon days as the justification for relying on the "a priori" for guidance.[7] And that is exactly what he did: some of his historical truths emerged not from a posteriori reasoning but from a priori postulates.

The consequences for the historian of adopting such principles might well have been to drift further and further away from truths that could be empirically established. After all, taken together, the prin-

7. Squire, *Enquiry* (1745), 113, 118–19, 163, 9–10, 170–71; notes bound between the *Enquiry* and the *Historical Essay* in Volume III of the edition of Squire's *Works* in the British Museum.

ciples argued both for a diminution of the importance of mere facts and for the invariability of central historical processes. They held out the promise of revealing truths in history that were timelessly valid. Fortunately for Squire and his reputation he did not entirely yield to this momentum. There grew within his mental apparatus two countervailing tendencies. The first was an emergent willingness to submit to facts. The critical point in the conflict between the thrust of his principles and the accumulating weight of facts did not arrive until the years around 1750, and the nature and outcome of the conflict will not be spelled out until the next section. But by 1753 Squire was adopting a tone that would have been foreign to him eight years earlier and that showed a more cautious and empirical approach to historical understanding. For after leading the reader through a radical revision of his former views about the origins of the House of Commons, he declared in support of his new view that although certainty on obscure and distant matters was impossible, "a good degree of historical probability" rested with his interpretation. This was the language of the a posteriorist, not the rhetoric of the a priorist. "Right notions" had not been discarded, but they had been subordinated; the stubborn fact had slain the attractive theory. The second countervailing tendency was Squire's emergent historicist consciousness.[8] In the 1748 edition of the *Historical Essay* he mused skeptically about the possibilty of comparing different eras: "perhaps there is scarcely any foundation in nature, even for making the comparison, much less for giving the preference." So many things, he noted, had changed—manners, customs, laws, trade, wealth, science, and population. All, he concluded, "was in perpetual flux and variation." This Heraclitean mood recurs in his elliptical notes. "Y^e manners & customs of ye times almost toto caelo different from the present," he wrote. And he immediately drew the fitting conclusion: "we shd not fill our selves wth ideas of the present times lest we deceive & be deceived."[9] A man who could make statements of that

8. By "historicist consciousness" I mean to designate the awareness of diversity across time and the concomitant tendency to see historical eras as self-defining entities, in some ways radically different from and perhaps opaque to later generations.

9. Squire, *Historical Essay* (1748), 35; handwritten notes bound in Volume III of Squire's *Works*.

sort had armed himself against excessive reliance on universal historical truths. But since he had adopted both the increased respect for facts
and the heightened historicist intuition in the middle of his career as
historian, the new sensibility forced him to modify his view of English
history.

III

Squire's interpretation of English history—the rationale for his Court
Whig politics—is found primarily in two works. *An Enquiry into the
Foundation of the English Constitution*, first published in 1745, surveyed
German and Anglo-Saxon constitutionalism. It was less a history of
the pre-Norman era than a dissection of what he presumed to be the
essentially static pre-Norman institutions of government and the presuppositions upon which they rested. In its pages he focused analytic
attention on the Anglo-Saxon love of liberty. Three years later Squire
published his *Historical Essay upon the Balance of Civil Power in England*.
This study, though briefly overlapping the period covered in the earlier
work, moved quickly to the Tudor era and traced the dependence of
English liberty upon the existence of an equipoise among competing
institutions and groups. When such an equipoise had lapsed, an arbitrary government had appeared. The culmination of the struggle to
create an enduring balance had occurred in 1688, when Whig wisdom
had seized upon the recklessness of a would-be despot to secure and
perpetuate liberty. The *Enquiry* and the *Historical Essay* were reissued
in 1753, bound together to provide a continuous history of England
from the days of Hengist. The new editions were marked by numerous
changes, some simply stylistic, others designed to soften the transition
from the *Enquiry* to the *Historical Essay*; the most important, however,
revealed Squire's revised understanding of the middle period of English
history. In addition to these two major works several of Squire's tracts
provide information about his judgment of English history. And the
handwritten notes bound between the *Enquiry* and the *Historical Essay*
in Squire's personal edition of his works contain helpful generalizations
about major long-term developments in the kingdom's past, for in the
privacy of these jottings Squire indulged himself in more Olympian
utterances.

The English people, in Squire's view, first appeared on the world stage in the fifth century when Saxons, Jutes, and Angles from Germany, accepting the invitation of the hard-pressed Britons, began migrating to England. Squire thought these Britons not dissimilar in governmental institutions from the Germans who conquered them. But since little was really known of them, and since English constitutional continuity begins only with the advent of the Germans, Squire could ignore the still earlier British history. More was known about the Germans not because they left written records—they were a preliterate people—but because the perceptive Roman historian Tacitus recorded his observations of them. What Tacitus told of German government was, unless directly confuted by irresistible evidence, valid for the Anglo-Saxons as well. Above all, these unlettered people, living a rude but dignified life, valued liberty and glory. Wherever they went they created (or, strictly speaking, retained) a constitution grounded in "the free consent of the governed." It secured to all freemen living under it the "true ends" of government: peace and safety, the defense of private property, and the "natural liberty of individuals."[10]

The institutional framework that emerged in early England is properly viewed as tiered.[11] Each man of property presided over his own household and dependents, rendering justice to them through what was in later Anglo-Saxon times called the Hall-Mote. This function was the vital source of social order in England, for the poorer people—that is, the dependents—were prone to tumultuous behavior. But because there was also a need to adjudicate disputes among the propertied themselves, provincial institutions called Shire-Motes were devised. They were assembled at least semiannually and attended by all men of property in the province. The Shire-Mote had extensive power. It was a court of appeal and entertained pleas of the crown, it registered mortgages and conveyances, made new laws, administered oaths, and elected provincial officials. Above the Shire-Mote there was a still

10. [Squire], *Remarks*, 25–27; Squire, *Enquiry* (1745), 88, 80.

11. Squire's chief sources for the post-Germanic part of his *Enquiry* were a mixed lot: chiefly Sir William Temple, Moses Lowman, Sir William Petyt, James Tyrrell, Sir Henry Spelman, L. A. Muratori, Henri de Boulainvilliers, and William Prynne. Some were used only for comparative purposes. In the second edition he added some references to Montesquieu's *Esprit des lois*, which had been published in 1748.

more comprehensive body, "a general assembly of the whole nation"—
that is, of all the propertied men residing in the several counties that
comprised the kingdom. In 1745 Squire identified it as the Witenagemot, but by 1753 he had reconsidered his sources and equated it with
the institution called the Mycelgemot. Whatever its name, it func-
tioned as "the sovereign legislative power of the whole kingdom." In its
sessions both national issues and disputes among the counties were
"maturely examined, debated, and determined." It was competent in
both civil and ecclesiastical affairs. This great body was the capstone
of a "beautiful and lasting Gothic structure." It was both the "basis of
the Anglo-Saxon constitution" and "the foundation as well as the preservation of public liberty amongst them."[12]

The full rights of citizenship, Squire believed, were the exclusive
possession of men who held landed property. Squire was uncertain how
numerous this group might have been, though he had no doubts that
it avoided being parasitically small. He was clear, however, in his conviction that the distinction between those who held land and those
who did not was the fundamental fact of Anglo-Saxon constitutional
understanding.[13] Alternative lines through society might have been
drawn, but Squire explicitly finds the Anglo-Saxons rejecting them.
Thus, citizenship did not depend upon holding a title, for many who
had no title were yet fully citizens. Nor did it depend upon having the
status of a freeman, for there were men who were free (the ceorls) who
were yet not fully citizens. In short, the titled comprised too small and
the free too large a category. Only the possession of land conferred the
right to participate actively in the politics of the kingdom. These proprietors attended Shire-Motes and Mycelgemots by right, and they
made the laws. Below them were the ceorls and, still more distressed,

12. Squire, Enquiry (1745), 165, 186. In a handwritten note on page 291 of the Enquiry in the British Museum Squire declared, "I am of opinion that the word Wittena-
gemot always means ye regia curia, or lesser senate & ought always to be used in that
sense & y^t ye word our ancestors made use of to express ye assembly of ye nation was
micclegemot." He further noted that the earliest usage of Mycelgemot he could find dated
from 977, a not very helpful fact in view of his hope to apply the term to pre-Alfredian
institutions. In his puzzlement over this terminological point Squire simply shared the
confusion of the scholars who had preceded him.
13. This distinction was central for Harrington too.

the slaves, who together "were scarcely looked upon as members of the community." Yet even so, they were entitled—one must not expect total consistency from Squire—to give at least their "consent" to laws and ordinances.[14] Above the proprietors—or, more accurately, a select titled group chosen from among them—were the thanes. These men advised the king, were rewarded by him, and filled the great offices of the kingdom and the counties. Society was, briefly, hierarchical, and political capacity was correlated with property-holding.

The chief magistrate of the kingdom was the king. Initially he (or his forerunners) had been a "generalissimo," but early on in English history the title of king had been adopted. He retained the right to lead the troops in war and to divide the spoils of victory (after appropriate consultation) among his chief followers. But in calm times he was little more than a governor. For although he could summon extraordinary sessions of the Mycelgemot and was expected to execute the laws of the kingdom and supervise voting, he was constitutionally incapable of behaving tyrannically. The powers to make or alter laws, to impose taxes, to limit the liberties of freemen, or to deprive them of their property were not held by the monarch. And any king who attempted to exercise such illegitimate powers would promptly discover that the crown had not been irrevocably bestowed. Kings in Anglo-Saxon days served with the approbation of the people, and though convenience and reputation made recourse to successive generations of the same family the convention, in the final analysis it was not blood but ability and self-command that brought a man to the throne and kept him there.[15]

One other institution informed the Anglo-Saxon constitution. Since a Mycelgemot was a cumbersome body, too large to be easily

14. Squire, *Enquiry* (1745), 174. There is an element of simplifying selectivity in this account, for Squire was not entirely consistent. He suggests at times that all free-born Englishmen *must* be proprietors of land and hence that those who are free but not proprietors must be freedmen and of foreign origin. But elsewhere he makes clear his understanding that ceorls (foreign born) can be holders of land and that some Englishmen fail to keep their land.

15. Squire viewed England's Anglo-Saxon kings favorably. "Perhaps no nation," he wrote in his private notes, "can boast a better series of kings y^n England from Ecbert [sic] to ye Conqueror." He added, however, that Ethelred alone did more harm than the others together did good.

dealt with and composed of men whose local interests invested them with parochial outlooks, it posed potential problems. Unless wisely directed, such a body threatened to dissolve into tumult and disorder. The Anglo-Saxons therefore adopted the device of a senate or "preparatory council." In 1745 Squire called it the "King's Court." By 1753, in conformity with the shift he had accepted for the name of the national assembly, he designated it the Witenagemot. Composed of the wisest men in the kingdom—in practice, of the thanes—it served as the "eyes" of the legislature, superintending national affairs and proposing legislation to the Mycelgemot. Thus, although it could not make laws unilaterally, neither could the Mycelgemot enact legislation that had not been submitted to it by the Witenagemot. A marginal notation in Squire's hand shows that he found Harringtonian theory to bear out Anglo-Saxon wisdom. He appositely quoted the author of the aphorisms: "76. A popular assembly without a senate cannot be wise. 77. A senate without a popular assembly will not be honest."[16]

In only one major respect did the Anglo-Saxon settlers of England alter German practice. It had been the custom in Germany for the king, after consulting with his advisers, annually to redistribute the nation's land among the families who inhabited it. Thus the land always remained ultimately with the community as a collectivity, not in the hands of private persons. In England this practice was abandoned. The uneasiness of the times, the frequency of war, and the scarcity of good land required a more permanent settlement. The king therefore divided the land among his leading followers (each allotment becoming a county), and the followers in turn apportioned it to selected freemen serving under them. These allocations were not subject to annual review, confiscation, and redistribution. And, as was natural, such portions of land, now held permanently, were soon passed on from one generation to the next by inheritance. Furthermore, when a man had several sons, he divided his land among them. In this way "a natural agrarian" operated in society, preventing the accumulation of excessive quantities of land and hence of excessive power in only a few hands.[17] Squire knew that this break with German custom was important, and

16. Squire, *Enquiry* (1745), 180; Squire, *Works*, III, 69.
17. Squire, *Historical Essay* (1748), 38.

he acknowledged that the difference in the land laws led by degrees to other differences between Anglo-Saxon England and the Germany whence it came. But he nevertheless finally felt that the Anglo-Saxon decision to give permanence to land titles did not invalidate his broader proposition that the German people, including the Anglo-Saxons, were highly conservative and resistant to change.

From the fifth until the ninth century England was divided among seven different kingdoms. But the constitutions of all members of the heptarchy conformed to this same general pattern.[18] The introduction of Christianity at the end of the sixth century significantly modified various social customs (presumably most particularly those related to bloodletting), but it did not alter the constitution. Nor did the unification of the heptarchy under the house of Wessex. The Danish invasions dealt a superficially shattering blow. But the "great Alfred" linked "the most consummate valour" to "the most wise and prudent conduct" and "restored . . . the broad constitution to its primitive integrity."[19] He put all men back under some political authority—the trythings, hundreds, and tithings—to reestablish a means of securing order. He systematized and regularized older usages, resisting any impulse he may have had to create a novel regime and instead, faithful to the German love of liberty and reverence for custom, revivifying the older one.

For the sake of convenience I shall call the centuries from Hengist to Alfred the early period in English history. Of this period Squire's view never changed: the Anglo-Saxons brought popular government with them to England and planted it in English soil. But when he turned his attention to what may be called the middle period—the centuries from Alfred to Edward I—Squire found his views to be far less fixed, and positions he assumed in 1745 he steadily retreated from in his later publications. In the *Enquiry* of 1745 he argued that Alfred's reforms brought the Anglo-Saxon constitution to its culmination and suggested that thereafter, down to the very Hanoverian period from

18. Squire speculated on the existence of an assembly comprised of landholders from all seven kingdoms. He suggested calling it a Pan-anglicum but acknowledged that the evidence for it was meager. Squire, *Enquiry* (1745), 220.

19. Notes in Squire's *Works*, III, between *Enquiry* and *Historical Essay*; Squire, *Enquiry* (1745), 232.

which he spoke, that constitution, though not always honored, had always been the final and effective defense of English liberties.[20] The key Alfredian reforms had been the founding of boroughs and the decision to give them representation in the Mycelgemot, thus making that body virtually a ninth-century analogue of the Georgian Parliament. Squire knew the historical studies of Dr. Robert Brady and acknowledged that the matter was controversial. But Brady, infamously a Tory, he rejected, preferring instead the considered judgments of the Whiggish George St. Amand.[21] Alfred's wisdom, Squire argued, allowed him to grasp the importance of trade to national welfare. The dislocations of the times and the development of heritable lands conjoined to create a class of men who, though born of the landed, found themselves without land. Alfred worked therefore to overcome the traditional Anglo-Saxon contempt for the ways of the merchant. He encouraged the landless to settle in towns, he imported teachers to instruct in commercial activity, and he opened up avenues to honor through trading. Moreover, Squire continued (in his most extended exercise of deductive reasoning divorced from factual substantiation), since Alfred was organizing the rest of society into groups, he would not have neglected the new mercantile order he was sponsoring. He combined merchants into trading societies, and since these societies needed foundations upon which to begin their enterprises, he gave them land. But landholding entitled men in Anglo-Saxon days to a voice in the Mycelgemot. And since this land granted by the king was held in common by trading societies, it was but natural that the new merchant order participated in the great assembly not directly but through representatives or delegates. In this manner the last element of the eighteenth-century Parliament took its appointed place, and the

20. Squire did not deny that a Conquest had occurred, but he minimized its importance. Nor did he deny that something conventionally called feudalism had existed. But this too he minimized, even to the point of asserting that he could precisely date its inception—at the assembly of 1085. Squire, Enquiry (1745), 136n, and retained in 1753 edition.

21. Author of An Historical Essay on the Legislative Power of England (London, 1725). For a cautious evaluation of St. Amand as a historian, see D. W. L. Earl, "Procrustean Feudalism: An Interpretative Dilemma in English Historical Narration, 1700–1725," Historical Journal, XIX (1976), 33–51.

practice of representation, though perhaps experimented with earlier, first became regularized.

Squire later repudiated this interpretation in toto. He did so because, honest scholar that he was, he discovered that he could not deny the forcefulness of two destructive lines of counterargument. He had assumed that what Alfred had wrought had remained over the intervening eight centuries basically intact, "with little or no variation in essentials." But to make this bold claim was to deny that either the Norman Conquest or the long medieval interval of feudalism had altered Alfred's achievement, and this denial became increasingly difficult to sustain. Furthermore, he had asserted that something remarkably like the House of Commons had, in the persons of the mercantile representatives, taken part in the ninth-century Mycelgemot. To uphold this view when no relevant writs existed prior to the thirteenth century Squire had resorted to the ingenious contention that those thirteenth-century writs indicated not the origin of representation for the Commons but the end of the lengthy period in which such representation had been voluntary and uncoerced.[22] But once he had made concessions about the Conquest and feudalism and had explored the system of land distribution practiced under the Normans, Squire realized that he would have to yield on the issue of the Commons too. By 1753 his view of the middle period was recognizably close to the twentieth century's.

It is possible to trace in a broad manner both the timing and some of the specific causes of the shifts in Squire's views. As late as 1746 he continued to minimize the importance of the Conquest and any attendant changes in the rules governing landholding. By September of 1747, however, he was receding from such radical continuationism. William I, he asserted in the 1748 edition of the *Historical Essay*, made "a considerable alteration in . . . civil government," vastly extending the lands of the crown and imposing a "grievous yoke" upon the English people in order to deprive them of their "ancient rights." The Conqueror divided his new kingdom among his chief allies not as allods—the Anglo-Saxon practice—but as fees burdened with military

22. [Squire], *Letter to a Tory Friend*, 59; Squire, *Enquiry* (1745), 254n–259n.

obligations. Moreover, to assure that his vassals retained enough power to fulfill their military responsibilities, William ended the practice that permitted fathers to partition land among male heirs and insisted instead that the fees be kept intact from generation to generation. This requirement recoiled upon the monarchy, however, for with the abolition of the "natural agrarian" the estates that then emerged gave to their holders wide political power and an opportunity to cultivate the loyalty of dependents living on them. These developments in turn gave the barons a basis from which to struggle against Norman and Angevin authoritarianism. The subject English accepted the baronial direction because it promised to check "the exorbitant invasions of the crown." Ultimately the barons prevailed, confining the powers of the crown and instituting not the "popular-monarchy" of Anglo-Saxon days but a novel "aristocratical one." This new order received its enduring confirmation in the "last great and most solemn publication of the grand charter" in Henry III's reign.[23]

In some notable ways Squire had begun, in these opinions of 1748, to veer toward Brady's view. But Brady himself remained beyond the pale. His politics had been intolerable, and when Squire dismissed Carte in 1748 he did so with the prediction that Carte's books "will soon be as cheap, and as little regarded, as the voluminous labours of his friend Brady."[24] Some of Squire's terminology in the first edition of the Historical Essay, especially the reference to the "grievous yoke," suggests that his magnification of the Conquest drew more on Commonwealth literature than on the best medieval scholarship. In the next few years, however, he came not only to embrace the full feudal hypothesis but to acknowledge his debt to Brady. The work that effected the complete conversion was Thomas Madox's Firma Burgi. As Squire gently put it after reading Madox, he and St. Amand had been "somewhat too hasty in forming our notions."[25] And if Madox was right, so was Brady. In the 1753 edition of the Enquiry Squire described

23. Squire, Historical Essay (1748), 38–39, 41–43.
24. [Squire], Remarks, 47.
25. Squire, Enquiry (1753), 251. It must not be thought that hitherto Squire had rejected all of the best scholars. Much of the work of Sir Henry Spelman and George Hickes he found assimilable. But they, of course, were arguing for a view that Squire endorsed: that Anglo-Saxon England was not feudal.

a Norman England that had severed almost all constitutional continuity with its Anglo-Saxon past. "By this means," he wrote, referring to the Conqueror's land partition, "instead of the antient Anglo-Saxon laws, by which this country had been hitherto governed, the feudal customs and institutions were every where introduced, and by degrees grew into common practice." In a footnote Squire broadened the scope of the changes even more: "In truth, it is marvellous to see . . . so great an alteration in the course of law proceedings in this country, wrought in so short a time; and that so little, in effect, of the Anglo-Saxon law and usages were retained." He then described feudalism as an organization of society resting upon decentralized justice, decentralized and diversified laws and customs, decentralized administration, and localized money raising. The king in this society—excepting always that "tyrant and contemnor of all laws," William the Conqueror—was not a despot. Power rested instead with the small body of the king's great tenants-in-chief. But of Anglo-Saxon liberty and constitutionalism virtually nothing remained. And the praiseworthy authority of Brady was specifically and frequently invoked to validate this view.[26]

Nor was that all. In the *Historical Essay* of 1748 Squire had admitted that the power of the Commons under the Normans and Angevins could not have been very great. They had been reduced by the rise of the nobility—that is, of the great landholding barons—"into an inferior order . . . made up chiefly of tradesmen, yeomen, and the lesser land-holders," exercising very little power because they possessed very little property. But by 1753 even this major retreat from the Alfredian splendor of 1745 was insufficient. For if the Commons was demoted in 1748, it was expunged in 1753. Alfred was no longer the creator of even an incipient House of Commons. Towns had emerged as "parts and parcel of some private patrimony" and had not been regarded as "distinct members of the great community." Norman thinking on this point varied not a whit from Anglo-Saxon: men in towns were dependent and servile. As the post-Conquest era advanced, towns on the royal demesne slowly acquired some degree of autonomy, securing char-

26. Squire, *Enquiry* (1753), 271–73; notes in Vol. III of Squire's *Works*. Squire did not accept Brady's analysis of the coming of the Anglo-Saxons to England but retained his faith in Sir William Petyt's interpretation.

tered exemptions from various imposts or duties in recognition of their importance to the kingdom. But they remained subject to royal direction. They found their continuing obligation to pay tallage especially rankling, and they began protesting that unlike the barons they were not permitted to assent to the grants the crown exacted from them. At last, needing money and domestic tranquillity to wage war abroad, the king decided that it would be less disturbing to the peace to summon deputies from the towns to attend Parliament, where their approval of supply measures would guarantee easier collection of taxes. The Parliament of 1295, summoned by Edward I to raise money for the struggle with France, was the first Parliament to include delegates from towns. The men represented remained tenants and dependents and their power could only be viewed as circumscribed. But "another order in the state" had been acknowledged; the prototype for the House of Commons had been created.[27] And the institutional framework of the "ancient constitution," now seen as a product of the middle period, was finally complete.

Upon the third and final period of English history Squire made only one extended pronouncement. In his *Historical Essay* he explained how the late medieval Commons (it did not matter whether it were Alfredian or Edwardian in origin) attained to paramountcy in the modern constitution, why political parties emerged, and when English liberties were at last ineffaceably secured. The key to the growth of the Commons lay in the expansion of the number of property-holders in the kingdom. This explanation was Harringtonian not only in structure but even in its provenance: *Oceana* provided an analysis of English history that from the Tudor age forward seemed persuasive to Squire.[28]

27. Squire, *Historical Essay* (1748), 50; Squire, *Enquiry* (1753), 282, 302. Squire rejected the claims of 1265 for three reasons: 1) the civil war provided peculiar circumstances, 2) the manner of summoning was irregular, and 3) the events of that year were not immediately emulated. Squire, *Enquiry* (1753), 305.

28. Insofar as Harrington followed John Selden in failing to distinguish between Anglo-Saxon and Norman tenures, he was not serviceable to Squire—and was rejected. See J. G. A. Pocock, *The Ancient Constitution and the Feudal Law* (Cambridge, 1957). Other major sources for the *Historical Essay*—which lacks systematic citations—were Francis Bacon, Lord Bolingbroke, Machiavelli, René Albert de Vertot d'Abeuf, and perhaps David Hume.

The chief movers in the shifts in property-holding and hence power were Henry VII and Henry VIII. Propelled to authority by the Wars of the Roses, Henry VII diagnosed England's malady to be a case of too few nobles holding too much land. He further reasoned that the force of property might be weakened if land were more widely held. Exercising the extensive influence that his role as binder of national wounds temporarily gave him, he promoted two measures that collectively served to increase the number of men holding land. By permitting the nobility to break up and sell their estates, he created a supply of land. By curtailing the practice of retaining, he created a group of men—the discharged former retainers—who wanted land for purchase and who thereby provided a demand for it. In each case the indebtedness of the nobility, itself a consequence of a generation of fighting, made the nobles receptive to laws that might otherwise have seemed threatening to them. The men who now purchased land became "yeomen," and as their number waxed, so too did the significance of the House of Commons.

Henry VIII's contribution to the growth of the Commons was still less deliberate. By confiscating the monastic lands he provided himself with a basis "as must for ever have secured to [him] the absolute command of the whole national power." But he obeyed his passions, not his reason, and sold the lands. The purchasers again were commoners—"the middling, and lower, sort of people." A set of massive land transfers had thus ensued, with the Commons the chief beneficiaries in each instance. They had secured some land from the crown, more from the nobility, and still more from the church. And as their possessions grew, so too did their power in Parliament. They had the means to buy this land that was being put on the market because, in recoil from the convulsions of the late fifteenth century, the "provident and thoughtful" among the new yeomen eyed the Genoese, the Hansards, and the Venetians and recognized what advantages prosperity offered. From this period on, Squire asserted, "the people of *England* began to make proper use of their naval situation, and to exert"—he began to rhapsodize—"that universal genius, which fits them for the accomplishment of every thing, to which they will diligently apply themselves."

In brief, they took up trade. And trade in turn fostered liberty, for it encouraged the wider division of property, and "this preserved our liberties, as those upon the continent sunk."[29]

But as the kingdom prospered under Elizabeth, a fissure rent it. Some Englishmen accepted the faith of Geneva and became Calvinists. Others held to the moderation of the Elizabethan settlement. This division between "Puritans" and "Church-of-England men" provided the foundation for later disputes, and thus, in the reign of Good Queen Bess, "the two parties of *Whig* and *Tory* were virtually formed." The religious dispute acquired a political component in the seventeenth century when the first two Stuarts infringed upon the rights of subjects. The Whigs naturally attracted the aggrieved, since the Tories had close religious ties with the crown. Each party thereafter had both a religious and a political wing, but in the seventeenth century the political issues dominated. The Tories became proponents of the divine right of kings, the indefeasibility of the succession, and the obligation of the subject to absolute obedience. The Whigs retorted that government was the creation of man and could be circumscribed by man, that the succession was subject to limitation, and that in extraordinary circumstances even the supreme magistrate might be resisted. When Stuart aggrandizement persisted, a third group, the Republicans, emerged. They proposed the abolition of the monarchy and, though never very numerous or rich, they exercised wide influence among Whigs by virtue of their learning and high character. When the conflict between the crown and the Parliament broke into war, the Whigs and Republicans won because a majority of the people, especially the merchants, and the bulk of the property were on their side.

The Whigs, however, could not use their triumph to create a Whig world. They fell out with their Republican allies and found the more radical army unsympathetic to their pleas for moderation. The army turned on the Whigs, routed them, and put the king to death. The old constitution was thereby "utterly subverted." But Oliver Cromwell could not regather the nation because he dared not summon a fair

29. Squire, *Historical Essay* (1748), 53, 56–57; *Historical Essay* (1753), 346; notes bound in Vol. III of Squire's *Works*.

Parliament. If it were Republican it would ultimately oppose him; if royalist, it would immediately do so. He therefore ruled without one and, assisted by the army, was able for four years to hold out "against the balance of property and the general inclination of the people." But all men of property yearned for a return to the old constitution. Cromwell's death and the ensuing anarchy supplied the occasion; the Stuarts were restored. The great error at the Restoration was that no conditions were required of Charles II. So he and his successor James II reembarked on the reckless course that had undone their father and grandfather. Indeed, James II compounded his difficulties. Raised a strict Tory, he decided to use the full panoply of his prerogative powers to effect the restoration of the Roman Catholic church. Even for Tory stomachs this was too much. The king was asking them to draw conclusions from their principle of obedience that they found intolerable; the absurdity of their doctrine lay exposed. And so, to protect the church they loved, they joined the Whigs and forced James II to flee the throne. They then accepted the coronation of William and Mary.

It was this revolution, Squire concluded, that finally rendered the nation proof against royal aggrandizement. The English people had followed old Anglo-Saxon practice and behaved in accord with both natural and positive law in bringing in William and Mary. The blood royal had been recognized but the succession was not deemed indefeasible. Moreover, the monarchs had submitted to terms. The people drafted "a second *Magna Carta*, another *Bill of Rights*, and required the new king to accept it." The conditions ended for all time the Stuart notion that the monarch somehow stood apart from his people. Quoting Bolingbroke's *Dissertation upon Parties*, Squire stated simply that "he and they are parts of the same system." Moreover, the revolution finally lifted the Commons into regulated dominance within the constitution. It gave "the last and permanent establishment to the popular interest, and immoveably fixed the nodding balance of power to that side, whither it had so long been inclining." The Whig era had come at last, and Squire was not at all surprised that it bore a patent resemblance to the ancient constitution. It is true that in the modern era the greater dispersion of ownership meant that "the blessings of government are more general and diffused thro' all sorts of men"—that is, that more people qualified as citizens.[30] But in both regimes the constitution and the people stood together to defend liberty, protect property, and speed justice.

IV

This elaborate interpretation of English history was insupportable. Of course the twentieth-century historian can scarcely condemn the eighteenth-century Squire for not knowing what intervening scholars have uncovered and propounded. But no such reasons disable the reader of today from adjudging Squire accountable for his failure to consider the inconsistencies that marred his effort. Omission, ambiguity, and outright contradiction join together to enfeeble the very foundation of his historical edifice. And although such flaws doubtless tell us something about Squire's limited capacity to think perspicaciously on any subject, they also suggest how adherence to an ideology can blinker a man's vision.

His inconsistencies were of various sorts. Some, for example, were rooted in carelessness of exposition—in his tendency to enthuse over a subject, write hyperbolically of it, and then neglect the implications of such excess. Squire shared in his era's almost universal admiration for King Alfred, and the great monarch sparkles in the *Enquiry* as a man of consummate wisdom, extraordinary valor, and inexhaustible energy. But Squire had somehow to confine this dynamic monarch within what he believed to be a static constitutional system. The incursions of the Danes gave Alfred a credible opportunity for military exploits, but there was no arena in Squire's broad pattern of Anglo-Saxon history for constitutional novelties. Thus the author was trapped into commending Alfred's political wisdom, citing his vigorous programs of political systematization and encouragement of trade, and then concluding—in spite of all this argument—that Alfred was no more than a restorer. Another type of inconsistency arose when Squire introduced new entities onto his historical stage and then used them in manners that seemed at variance with the explanation for their ap-

30. Squire, *Historical Essay* (1748), 60, 75–76, 90; Squire, *Enquiry* (1753), 379; notes bound in Vol. III of Squire's *Works*.

pearances. His treatment of the political parties clearly demonstrated this failing. Leaving aside his decision to place their origins in Elizabeth's reign—a judgment we find puzzling today—one need only draw attention to the difficulties he incurred by simultaneously identifying the Tories as the Church-of-England party and imputing James II's catholicizing ambitions to his Tory upbringing, or by simultaneously seeing the Whigs as originally Puritans and himself as a Whig. All four assertions had significant measures of truth. But within the context of Squire's account, and despite his efforts to describe changes in the parties over time, they made little sense.

These however are minor flaws when compared with Squire's larger difficulties. It is initially tempting to think that the heart of his problem lay in the discrepancy of purposes between the *Enquiry* and the *Historical Essay*. The earlier work, after all, emphasized the popular nature of the early constitution and the ineradicable Anglo-Saxon love of liberty, whereas the later work showed how liberty had been lost and recovered and emphasized the importance of retaining a constitutional mechanism of balance as a means of securing a moderate liberty, even against the possibility of assault by the people themselves. The *Enquiry*, in short, glorified popular institutions and rooted them in a love of liberty; the *Historical Essay* feared them and their threat to liberty. But I believe that this inconsistency is more imaginary than real and that, though severe problems remain, the discrepancy in purposes is not one of them.

The Anglo-Saxon political community was, in Squire's view, unitary. The kingly office was a mark of honor, not an occasion for power. Thanes were not a class apart, since all men of property—the numerous political community—were equal. They were also, if not exactly poor, then certainly not rich. Politics therefore did not involve contention over wealth. Above all, liberty was respected, institutionally rooted in the pattern of widespread property holding and sustained in the Anglo-Saxon consciousness by the paramount role it played in civic deliberations. In such a state popular government and liberty were not incompatible. But then England changed. The Conquest destroyed the liberty of most and led to a consolidation of property-holding. A nobility thereby arose, splitting the hitherto unitary landed community into two rival groups. The monarch began to amass great wealth and to cultivate the hope that it might be used to acquire widened power. Increasing affluence privatized people, blighting their civic consciousness and choking their readiness to subordinate themselves to the community. In this inchoately pluralistic state the only way to restrain the various aspirants to power was to create a constitution that pitted them against one another and thereby sustained an equilibrium. And the people themselves could no longer be trusted as sole guardians of liberty because, conditioned to adversary politics and made grasping by wealth, they lacked the capacity to act in a communitarian spirit. Thus the real difference between the two works is not that their purposes diverge but that Squire approved of popular government when the citizens were civic-minded and feared it when they became self-serving.

All this would have been fine if he had not been so enthusiastic for the dictum about power following property. In the final analysis, it was his adoption of this central principle of neo-Harringtonian social science that fatally flawed his thesis. For all too often Squire was reduced to tortuous reasoning or embarrassing silence when dealing with those crucial occasions in which property did not confer power—when, indeed, it lost out to power. Squire acknowledged only one instance in English history when property was insufficient in the struggle with power; but Harrington had seen it too, and Squire simply followed Harrington in attributing Cromwell's ascendancy in that instance to the strength of an army during an anomalous institutional vacuum. Squire was wrong, however, in implying that the interregnum was unique. Examples of defeats for property abounded. Proprietors in Anglo-Saxon days began to accept service obligations in return for protection of the land they already held. This change would appear to suggest that they were losing power, but Squire could not accept that interpretation and stunningly argued that they were in fact, by virtue of expanding wealth, becoming stronger. They became so strong that they were able to overthrow the old German custom of allowing the king to redistribute the land annually. Instead, they kept the land for themselves and their heirs. But in return for such lands they agreed to accept military obligations under the king, and so attractive was the prospect of military life that even those who held unencumbered land voluntarily accepted such obligation. Behind this convoluted argument lay a simple assertion: the men were appearing weaker because they were becoming stronger. In the real world such behavior is not impossible, but in Squire's neo-Harringtonian world it is unacceptable. The issue arises again with William the Conqueror. It is never made clear why the Norman monarchs so quickly lost power. The Conqueror secured all of England for himself and alone exercised true power. He then chose to parcel the land out among his lieutenants to give them foundations upon which to build a military defense of Norman rule against the threat of English rebellion. But the fees were not distributed as allods. Each was burdened with obligations that the incumbent owed the crown, and ultimate rights of possession lay with the crown, enforceable whenever any one of a number of not uncommon situations arose. It might be legitimate to argue that his dispersion lessened the authority of a Norman king. It seems far harder—within a neo-Harringtonian universe—to sustain Squire's contention that a monarch defined in this manner exercised no more authority over his noble vassals than an Anglo-Saxon king did over the free proprietors.

Similar difficulties bedevil the Tudor and Stuart eras. Henry VII tamed a nobility that commanded far more acreage than he. It is true that the nobles were weighed down with financial obligations and hence prepared to accept sacrifices to lift themselves from indebtedness. But to make that acknowledgment—and it is precisely the explanation Squire advanced—is to introduce an independent variable into the simple mathematics of the neo-Harringtonian world. Henry VIII had an even easier time defeating another landed foe, the church. (One might cavil with the argument: the church after all was something quite different from a set of individual secular landed freemen. But again it would seem necessary at least to acknowledge that the dictum about power following property can be saved only by being further qualified and diluted.) Finally, the Republicans bear attention. Neither numerous nor rich, they nevertheless exercised wide influence in the mid-seventeenth century. Squire explained their authority as a consequence of their earnestness, their learning, and their rectitude. The explanation is unexceptionable—unless the explicator has already testified to his faith in neo-Harringtonian sociology. In truth, Squire tried to fit English history into an impossible mold. But since he would not deny his legacy from Harrington and could not deny facts, he wound up simultaneously asserting that power was a product of property and narrating a tale of propertied people regularly falling prey to tyrants. It seems legitimate, therefore, to speculate on why he fell so afoul of elementary logic.[31]

The question may be simply put: why, in the face of much contrary evidence, did Squire retain his faith in the proposition that (in the words of the Enquiry) "power is founded upon and always follows property" and (in the words of the Historical Essay) "in whatever hands the overbalance of national property lies, there the great weight of national power will always be found"? Part of the answer is surely that Squire lived in an age that made the principle almost canonical. Men of all views paid obeisance to it; far subtler minds than Squire's accepted it; and the conventional solution for apparent lapses in its application was the invention of another epicycle. Squire was a thoroughly unoriginal man, and in all ages the unoriginal have unquestioningly received the inconsistent conventional wisdom bequeathed them by the past. Squire probably never realized that neo-Harringtonianism and facts were incompatible companions. But another part of the answer is that the dictum was in a very positive sense serviceable to Squire. Upon its validity rested the validity of his rejection of both the Tory and republican oppositions to Court Whig administrations. If the dictum were invalid, a major line of Court Whig argumentation would collapse. And thus to complete an analysis of Squire's historical thought it is necessary to link his historical views to his political opinions.

V

Squire was a scholar by disposition and he turned to the study of history because it fascinated him. It cannot be demonstrated that his view of English history made him a Court Whig, but it is clear from his career that he believed the argument from history to be powerful ammunition

---

31. Harrington himself, it is essential to reiterate, was not so simple-minded. He applied his dictum cautiously and in the awareness that other considerations besides property might in the short run be crucial.

in the Court Whig armory.[32] Sometimes the support he found history offering was simply ad hoc: he would cite a particular incident or isolated development to clinch a discrete point. To those, for example, who feared that the king could use the Civil List funds to subvert the constitution Squire replied that public monies were appropriated for specific purposes and that even an ill-intentioned monarch—and George II, of course, had only good will for his subjects—could not draw enough money from a fixed Civil List in a kingdom of expanding private wealth to undermine liberties. For those who feared a standing army Squire noted how the state of technology and the temper of the nation had changed over the centuries. The citizens' militia was no longer satisfactory: it lacked the necessary skills for modern warfare, and its way of life was actually harmful to a people who had become "trading and free." National defense should therefore be the responsibility of professional soldiers who, being paid by Parliament, would be loyal to it. To those who feared that a bought Parliament would yield up all national liberties to a covetous king or minister Squire retorted—hypothetically, for he denied that Whig Parliaments were corrupt—that the Pension Parliament in the age of the exclusion crisis proved otherwise: if this most famous of corrupted legislatures set a limit to the number of royal abuses it would suffer, there was no reason to suspect that its Hanoverian successor would be less diligent. The gentlemen of England, he continued, "have too long tasted of the delicious sweets of a rational liberty" to exchange those sweets for pensions and places that would themselves thereby become vulnerable.[33] These replies met specific polemical needs. But Squire, like most historians of his age, was attracted by generalization. He was also an aspiring intellectual and by training and inclination was wont to ask questions. Although the questions lacked depth, when linked to his wish to synthesize they led him to try to justify the Court Whig position by systematic reference to some broader framework. In so doing

32. Both Dickinson, *Liberty and Property*, 61–65, and Kenyon, *Revolution Principles*, 35, underline the centrality of appeals to the ancient constitution in the polemics of the first postrevolutionary generation. Bolingbroke and Squire demonstrate that the mode of argument remained important through the mid-eighteenth century.

33. These arguments are drawn from the dedication of the 1748 edition of the *Historical Essay*, vii–xviii, transposed to the conclusion of the 1753 edition, 379–91.

he took precisely the opposite tack from Hervey: whereas the peer found the kingdom's long past irrelevant as a source of modern constitutionalism, the ecclesiastic found that past to be the vivifying soul of such constitutionalism.

The core of Squire's defense of Court Whiggery lay in his belief that the eighteenth-century constitution of Great Britain—"perhaps the most perfect plan of civil empire, which can be invented"—was the analogue of the "ancient constitution" of "Old England." Each constitution defined a regime of liberty; each caught the fitting mixture of freedom and restraint; each assured that government would hearken to the people but avoid popular follies. Squire did change his view about when that "ancient constitution" had appeared. In 1745 he fixed it firmly in the Anglo-Saxon era, but by 1753 he preferred to see it as a product of Edward I's reign. The shift—though it had important correlative implications to be discussed shortly—did not, however, injure his operating assumption that history provided the present with a model. In both the past and the present society was divided into two groups. One comprised the men of property—men who used land and, perhaps, trade to give themselves independence. These were the citizens of the state, whose property conferred on them the right to participate in decision making. The other group, those without property, were, simply, the dependent. Squire described them for the Anglo-Saxon period in terms that demonstrated his conviction that their condition and behavior were historical universals: they were the "poorer and meaner sort of people, whose want of proper education, and instruction in those sounder principles of religion and the public good, renders them ever obnoxious to the sudden starts of a licentious will, and makes them ready to seize every occasion of riot, tumult, and confusion."[34] The need in each society was for a means of maintaining freedom for the propertied and order among the poor. The "ancient constitution" had filled this need, and the modern, by conforming itself to the ancient, could achieve the same.

The process of conforming to the earlier model meant, first of all, employing similar institutions. And if one allowed for the transition from the medieval delight in warfare to the modern appreciation of the

34. Squire, *Historical Essay* (1748), 34; Squire, *Enquiry* (1745), 151.

arts of peace, Squire believed that the two constitutions bore manifest similarities. The Hanoverian monarch was the reincarnation of the monarch in the ancient constitution. Each held authority for the execution of laws and presided in some manner over the nation. Each could choose his own ministers and, in time of war, lead the armed forces. But each was also limited: neither unilateral lawmaking nor unilateral powers of judicial decision rested with the king. He served at the wish of the people, ever subject to dismissal if he proved thoroughly unsatisfactory. He was, finally, the great symbol of communality, but he was not arbitrary, still less despotic. George, in sum, equaled Alfred (or Edward I), and those who mocked the equation only bore witness to their ignorance of English history. The Hanoverian legislature stood in a similar relationship to the past. To it repaired the men of property. It deliberated upon the great matters of the day, and without its assent no proposal could become binding. Its power extended to both the civil and the ecclesiastical spheres. It was, moreover, in both its modern and ancient guises, essentially a two-headed body. Squire could only be vague in trying to justify this particular point. In his earlier view he acknowledged that the precise relationship between the Houses of Commons and Lords of his own era and the Mycelgemot and Witenagemot of Anglo-Saxon days was not clear. Commons and Lords were separate bodies, whereas the Witenagemot seemed best understood as part of the broader Mycelgemot. In his later view he was even more reticent. Clearly Edward I's legislature had not been bicameral, and Squire was reduced to distinguishing between the confined role of the burgesses and the broad role of the peers in what met as a unitary body. But whether an Alfredian Mycelgemot or an Edwardian Parliament, the assembly of the ancient constitution corresponded in principle to the duality of the Hanoverian Parliament. Finally, both constitutions required a body of royal counselors. Thanes had advised the Anglo-Saxon king—"the checks as well as the executioners of his power"—and "great men" had given the same service to Edward. In the era of the Georges the ministry performed an identical function for a similarly circumstanced monarch. And Squire left no doubt that the description he attached to the companions of ancient German kings remained generally appropriate to their various English successors—"a choice and select band of the wisest, most robust, and hardy native-freemen of the country."[35] Only such men were fit to serve a nationally acclaimed king and guide an assembly of proprietors.

From the perspective of Squire's simple assertion that the modern constitution conformed to the ancient, it did not matter whether the ancient were placed in the ninth or the thirteenth century. But the lines of argument that were thereafter required to turn historical parallel into historical injunction could not be the same. Squire realized this, though he may not have realized some useful additional implications of the change. In 1745 the argument, because it was so simple, could remain implicit. Squire claimed to be describing "the first origin of those excellent laws and maxims of government, which, under the present establishment, have grown up to maturity, and are maintained in their utmost vigor and perfection." The structure of the present was simply the structure of the past. The nation's history needed the most attentive scrutiny because "each party confidently appeals to the antient constitution of the kingdom for the truth of the opinions it maintains and pretends to make that the measure of its political principles."[36] If the English constitution had been so felicitous in Anglo-Saxon days, and if it had remained intact down to Squire's day, then it seemed thoroughly plausible to suggest that one might measure the worthiness of political parties in the eighteenth century by assessing their fidelity to the principles of the ninth. Faithfulness to the ancient constitution was thus the standard of merit. Those who sought change could not be heirs of the true tradition; but those who sought to perpetuate the beneficent legacy of Anglo-Saxon wisdom were worthy of trust, respect, and authority. There were many other polemicists who advanced the same sort of argument in early Hanoverian days. What made Squire's essay interesting was that he invoked the Anglo-Saxon past to glorify rather than denigrate the Court Whigs. He showed that a weapon conventionally used by the opposition to flail the Court Whigs could also be used to support them.

By 1753, however, Squire no longer believed that the Anglo-Saxons

35. Notes bound in Vol. III of Squire's Works; Squire, Enquiry (1753), 334–38; Squire, Enquiry (1745), 184–85, 30.
36. Squire, Enquiry (1745), v.

had completed the constitution or that English constitutional history had flowed unchanged to the present. He knew instead that the My-celgemot of Alfred's day had lacked anything resembling a Commons and that the Conquest had then shattered the Anglo-Saxon state. He knew that "the whole system of feudal constitutions" separated Anglo-Saxon from modern days. This was awkward knowledge: it deprived him of the use of the type of historical reasoning his contemporaries found most compelling. Squire had therefore to soften and readjust his argument from history. He set up the age of Edward I as the era in which the modern constitution had appeared, and though he did not deny that it had changed in important and valuable ways since then, he was unembarrassed by those changes, because he now rooted the Court Whigs' claim to authority not in their putative fidelity to the constitutional structure of the past but in their commitment to the leading constitutional principle of that past. This principle was simply a statement of the necessity of maintaining balance within the constitution. It had become the dominant principle in Edward's day, and the protection of liberty depended upon respect for it. The Whigs, Squire insisted, had never receded from this principle. They stood, at the middle of the eighteenth century, as always, "for maintaining a due balance of power between the several orders of the legislature, well knowing, that in a constitution poised as ours is, the safety of the whole must consist in the reciprocal dependence of all the parts upon one another."[37] In this manner Squire found a new argument to bind past and present. No longer sharing a structure with the past, the present still retained the capacity to be informed by the principles of the past. Beyond that achievement, his new view had two advantages over the initial one. It showed that the Court Whig interpretation could be upheld in historical terms without rejecting Brady, Madox, and the best of historical scholarship.[38] It also introduced into English history

37. *Ibid.* (1753), 280; *Historical Essay* (1753), 396.
38. Kramnick, *Bolingbroke and His Circle*, 111–36, shows that Walpole's defenders had already found justifications for Court Whiggery that did not require rejecting Brady. But their views, unlike Squire's, were fundamentally ahistorical. That is, for the Walpole school identified by Kramnick, and represented in this study by Lord Hervey, relevant history began in 1688, not 1295. The useful past contained two generations, not four-and-a-half centuries.

a phase of radical decentralization—the feudal period—and thus gave historical reality to an evil against which Court Whigs regularly inveighed. Squire did not advert to these advantages and perhaps was not aware of them. It cannot be denied, however, that they helped to make his second version of Court Whig history ultimately more effective than his first.

But since all political commentators of his age agreed with Squire in understanding the constitution in terms of balance, it was not sufficient for him simply to assert that the Court Whigs were the best guardians of that balance. A bare assertion invited a bare retort. Proof was required. It was at this point, then, that Harrington's dictum became crucial to Squire. The Tory opposition—those who stood for the presumptive right of the gentry to govern Britain—bewailed what they believed to be the decline of the power and influence of the landed class. Harrington permitted Squire to reply that such decline was impossible: the land was the gentlemen's, and as long as they held it, the power was theirs as well. From the other direction the republican opposition, intent upon weakening the inhibiting and unjust authority of kings and nobles, decried the enforced weakness of the House of Commons. To them Squire could reply that the Commons could not be weak because it represented the untitled landed, and the untitled landed controlled four fifths of Britain. Indeed, on the basis of this argument it became possible for Squire to assert that the only true threat to balance and liberty came not from the crown but from the House of Commons. The king was confined by law. If he passed beyond the legal he would provoke an outcry he would find invincible, for he lacked the landed power to make good any challenged claims to undue authority. But the Commons was not so confined. Not only did the line between liberty and license remain undefined, hence vulnerable to unnoticed transgression, but beyond that difficulty lay the transcendent problem of the modern constitution: the Commons spoke for the overwhelming bulk of the land. The Court Whigs were therefore indisputably correct in fearing the powers of the Commons and in acting to create laws and precedents that could restrain that body or make it more susceptible to guidance. Concretely, they were right in resisting place bills. A radical separation of crown and Commons would remove from the popular chamber precisely those elements that gave it an understanding of national policy and most disposed it to moderation.[39]

There was one further way in which the popularity of the notion of balance gave Squire ammunition in his struggle against the enemies of the Court Whigs. An Aristotelian conception of political virtue underlay eighteenth-century discussion of balance. The rhetoric of balance inevitably suggested that those on the extremes were bad and that the mean defined the good. In the mid-eighteenth-century political world that Squire portrayed, the Whigs had preempted the middle ground. To one side of them stood the Tories, caught up in contradictions between their professions and their actions. Their language retained some of the resonance of Stuart principles, and though they were not really like the Tories of old, they were still, *pace* Bolingbroke, not true conservators of the principles of the revolution. To the other side stood the republicans (and some Tories, who, in a manner inexplicable to Squire, had shifted across the middle). They posed the threat of utopianism. They believed that perfect government was achievable and were therefore prepared to sacrifice the existing fine edifice for a dream.[40] Court Whigs were wiser than those on the extremes. They knew that either a king or a Commons could become "overbearing, domineering." They believed that a society should work to retain and build on what it held and valued, not to pursue imagined perfection at the expense of existent good. "In short," Squire concluded, "a true and confident *Whig* is a balancer, and a mediator; always against violence, and against encroachment from whatever quarter it is derived . . . but still a friend to law, truth, justice, and the establishment."[41] In short, Squire wanted us to add, the Court Whigs merited the continued confidence of the electorate.

Squire presented his readers with a more complex view of politics and the constitution than did Hervey, Hoadly, or Herring. But it was in the last analysis an inconsistent view. The discussion in this chapter has focused on Squire's resolute pursuit of Harringtonian explanations

39. Squire, *Historical Essay* (1753), 385–91.
40. Squire rejects political utopianism in both the *Enquiry* (1745), 81, and the *Historical Essay* (1753), 393.
41. Squire, *Historical Essay* (1753), 396.

and on the tension that arose between that pursuit and the brute facts that Squire needed for his historical narratives. But as was noted in the chapter opening, Harringtonianism was not the only transhistorical principle by which he sometimes ordered his material. Like Herring, Squire had a compelling sense of the difference between the natural and the unnatural. It was the former that helped to define the right. Thus, when Squire spoke of a "natural agrarian" or of an innate sense of "natural equity" or of "natural genius," he was invoking nature to set standards for humankind. Men could, he believed, order their lives by applying their "natural reason" to discern what he at various times called the "law of nature" or the "plainest principle of nature."[42] He seems not to have realized that his deterministic Harringtonianism, already ill at ease with the stubborn testimony of awkward historical facts, would find consorting with ethical principles a no less difficult task. Had Squire confined himself to a single mode of analysis he might at least have produced an internally consistent narrative. As it was, he chased facts with Hervey, accepted determinism with Harrington, and embraced natural moral law with Herring. We ought not to wonder that with the joint publication of the *Enquiry* and the *Historical Essay* in 1753 Squire abandoned the writing of history. Not wise enough to disentangle the various principles at war within his work, he may nevertheless have been perspicacious enough to realize that the enterprise was beyond his capacity. History is rarely the friend of ideologies.

42. Examples of uses of these quotations may be found in Squire, *Historical Essay* (1748), 34, 38; Squire, *Enquiry* (1745), 53; [Squire], *Remarks*, 27; and handwritten notes inserted in British Museum edition of *Enquiry* and *Historical Essay*.

Chapter VI

Lord Hardwicke (1690–1764): The Court Whig as Legist

I

The most important figure in British politics between Walpole's decline and Pitt's rise was an accidental politician. Trained in the law and ambitious chiefly for his legal reputation and his brood of talented sons, Philip Yorke, earl of Hardwicke, preferred the bench to the closet and his chambers to the cockpit. But the same qualities that made him a good jurist—an analytic and orderly mind, a sober awareness of operative constraints, a capacity to frame arguments compactly and powerfully—made him a highly useful counselor. Thus, after Walpole's resignation deprived the political scene of its one giant, Hardwicke stepped forward as the most reliable and capable of the Court Whigs emerging from Sir Robert's shadow. With the Pelham brothers he formed a triumvirate to direct affairs. Henry Pelham headed the treasury, the duke of Newcastle took the seals of a secretaryship, and Hardwicke presided over the House of Lords and affairs judicial as lord chancellor. His close friendship with Newcastle and his respect for the abilities of Henry Pelham made him an ideal mediator whenever the quarrelsome brothers embarked upon one of their notorious family disputes. He was, moreover, a purveyor of moderate, forcefully argued political advice. On two occasions he took the lead in legislative matters, seeking first in the aftermath of the Forty-Five to end those legal customs that reinforced Scottish particularism and then pushing in 1753 for the passage of the marriage act that conventionally bears his

151

name. Meanwhile, for two decades—the longest tenure of the century—he was lord chancellor, using his high office to preach to the kingdom and especially to those professionally involved with the law his beliefs about the fundamental interests of the nation. And while in all these ways he was helping to confer stability on the political life of Britain, Hardwicke was simultaneously giving unprecedented order and coherence to that branch of jurisprudence called equity. It is the judgment of many legal historians that Hardwicke above all others deserves the credit for fixing the chief substantive principles of equity. His legacy thus becomes doubly impressive. As a politician he was the great conciliator; as a jurist, the great consolidator.[1]

II

One of the timeless questions of political life is whether government should be of men or of laws. In harmony with the large majority of political thinkers who preceded him and, more particularly, with the Whig tradition that conceived of man as weak by nature and therefore vulnerable to temptation, Hardwicke spoke out for law. Aristotle had committed much of Greece to the side of law: "He who commands that law should rule may thus be regarded as commanding that God and reason alone should rule; he who commands that a man should rule adds the character of the beast." Henry de Bracton had declared that the "King himself ought not to be subject to any man, but he ought to be subject to God and the law, since the law makes the King. . . . There is no King where will rules and not the law." Machiavelli had proclaimed law to be the indispensable element of an enduring state, "For a Prince who knows no other control but his own will is like a madman." John Locke had sweepingly concluded that "No Man in

1. Unquestionably the best study of Hardwicke's life is the massive biography written by Philip Yorke (a descendent of the subject), *Life of Hardwicke*. This is a work of surpassing distinction, the finest biography of an eighteenth-century figure produced in our century. It alternates sections of analysis or narrative with sections composed of lengthy and numerous extracts from the Hardwicke papers in the British Museum. The best analysis of Hardwicke's work in chancery is in Sir William Holdsworth, *A History of the English Law* (16 vols.; London, 1903–66), XII, 237–97. See also Yorke, *Life of Hardwicke*, II, 420–45. For a sharply critical assessment of Hardwicke's judicial mentality, see E. P. Thompson, *Whigs and Hunters: The Origin of the Black Act* (New York, 1975), especially 208 and 265.

Civil Society can be exempted from the Laws of it." And James Harrington explicitly endorsed what he took to be the view of Aristotle, calling for "an empire of laws and not of men."[2] No one of importance in Georgian Britain would have dissented from these professions. Governments were framed to be perpetual, Hardwicke asserted. Even should a good ruler appear, he could not live forever and his successor might be made of baser stuff. It was therefore folly to assume that it would be the good man who always held power. But if regimes could not rely for their maintenance on the recurring accident of good rulers, they must rely instead on good laws.[3] Thus it was the inevitability of mortality that mandated a recourse to legality.

"The laws," Hardwicke wrote early in his career, "are the Birthright and Inheritance of all the subjects of England." The English, that is, lived in the society of laws that Hardwicke, like any Whig, deemed preferable to a society subject to arbitrary rule. But what—another timeless question—was the end or purpose of these laws? What, most fundamentally, were the laws supposed to provide for the people of England and, by extension, of Great Britain? To this question Hardwicke had an answer simple and yet dual. In the most direct sense the laws were to provide quiet, to assure tranquillity, to abate incipient unrest—in a word, to secure *peace* for the kingdom. But laws achieved this goal in two different manners, or rather, they fulfilled two different functions in British society—functions which, when simultaneously pursued, secured peace. One function was the upholding of morality. Laws, Hardwicke believed, were the appropriate instruments by which to define and realize the moral order. The second function, however, shows Hardwicke moderating the authoritarianism implicit in the first:

2. Ernest Barker (trans. and ed.), *The Politics of Aristotle* (Oxford, 1973), 1287a; Henry de Bracton, *Tractatus de legibus*, in *Bracton De Legibus et Consuetudinibus Angliae*, ed. George E. Woodbine (New York, 1915–42), fol. 5[b]; Niccolo Machiavelli, *Discourses on the First Ten Books of Titus Livius*, in *The Prince and the Discourses*, ed. Max Lerner (New York, 1950), Bk. I, Chap. LVIII; John Locke, *The Second Treatise of Government*, section 94; Harrington, *Commonwealth of Oceana*, 26. Thomas Hobbes, it should be noted, dissented from this line of thought. See *Leviathan*, ed. Michael Oakeshott (London, 1970), Chaps. 26 and 46. And Plato, in discussing the philosopher king, also stood with the minority. See *Republic*, Book V, 473 c–d.

3. *Cobbett's Parliamentary History of England* (41 vols.; London, 1804–20), XIV, 19–20.

laws provided protection for the subject against governmental incursions and thereby served as the chief defense of "the lives, liberties and estates of Englishmen."[4] Despite his use of these Lockean categories, Hardwicke did not share Locke's belief that a regime founded solely to protect individual rights could endure. He did not, that is, accept a simple equation of pursuit of private interest with pursuit of public interest. For if the laws that protected subjects helped to secure tranquillity by reducing the restrictions placed on the subjects, the laws that enforced morality made clear that there were identifiable limits to the types of unusual behavior the regime would tolerate from its citizens and that the might of the government would be used to deal with those who transgressed the limits.

Since one function of the law was to inculcate and encourage right behavior, it is understandable that the relationship of law to the moral order was an issue to which Hardwicke often adverted. At times he spoke as if he were a legal positivist: he seemed, that is, to assume that man-made law was essentially arbitrary and that such arbitrary laws defined justice. To make such a Hobbist reading of Hardwicke, however, is to misunderstand him. Even when suggesting that practical considerations could sometimes warrant the retention of legal rules that might seem to the impartial observer unjust, he noted that the standard by which statutes were properly to be assessed was that of "natural reason." Here we have a significant term. The idea of natural reason is central to the doctrine of natural law, a theory of jurisprudence that, in opposition to the theory of the positivists, sees legislation as an activity not of creation but of discovery—an activity characterized not by the arbitrary making of idiosyncratic rules but by the thoughtful search for universally valid precepts. Hardwicke stood with the natural lawyers. He argued, in agreement with Chief Justice Holt, that Christianity was part of the law of the kingdom. And he wished to extend that argument to cover not merely the body of doctrinal teachings which Scripture and reason enjoined, but also the larger body of moral directives which reasonable men knew to be binding. Certain activities—unhappy consequences of man's sinful nature— were always wrong, and the task of law was ever to resist them. Thus

4. Yorke, *Life of Hardwicke*, I, 94–95; British Museum, Add. MSS 36115, fol. 103.

Hardwicke warned the House of Lords that "if you take away the law, every man will become a law to himself—*lust* will become a law, & *envy* will become a law—*covetousness* and *ambition* will become laws." A lapse of law would unleash "all the worst passions that can warm the head—misguide the judgment—or corrupt the heart of man." Sometimes Hardwicke assumed the stance of a modern-day Jeremiah, lamenting "the degeneracy of the present times, fruitful in the inventions of wickedness." On other occasions, with a mellower Machiavellian tone, he decried the "corruption of manners" that threatened to enervate the citizenry and thereby destroy trade. But whether the evil was vice or indolence, the remedy was the same. It was to the salvific power of legislation that the regime must turn. Thus in his public career Hardwicke endorsed laws designed to regulate marriages; to suppress the evils of gambling, swearing, inebriation, and sabbath-breaking; and to measure the loyalty of teachers. Above all, he believed that the law should be employed to preserve "not only the name and outward form of the Protestant religion amongst us, but the real uniform belief and practice of it." The scriptural maxim remained, he averred, a sound principle: "Fear God and Honour the King."[5] The fundamental duties of mankind were thus antecedent to human law codes, and in the best of human regimes the laws were but translations of timeless moral truths.

The maintenance of liberty was the other function of law, for "Law without liberty," Hardwicke asserted, "is tyranny."[6] What he meant by "liberty" must be determined by inference, since he did not, to my knowledge, define the term. Clearly he meant something less extensive than the broad freedom associated with the arguments of John Stuart Mill. Two essential components of Hardwicke's notion of liberty are distinguishable. First, drawing on the English tradition, he believed that liberty comprehended security—security of one's own property against arbitrary demands or exactions, and security of one's person against arrest. Second, turning to the older classical tradition, he held

5. British Museum, Add. MSS 36115, fol. 101; Yorke, *Life of Hardwicke*, I, 81, 146, 574; British Museum, Add. MSS 35876, fol. 370, Add. MSS 36115, fols. 78, 102, 259, 278.

6. British Museum, Add. MSS 35878, fol. 40.

that liberty was the right to do right—the condition of being able to do what one ought to do. Neither component entailed a strong advocacy of a wide range of personal rights, and Hardwicke, as already noted, found no incompatibility in simultaneously endorsing liberty and recommending legal inhibitions to a variety of actions. Just as he did not define the term, so he does not seem to have examined at any length the grounds for assuming liberty a good.[7] But he knew and concurred with his countrymen's love for it. Indeed, the English were notorious as the people who, of all Europeans, placed the highest valuation on liberty. Hardwicke believed that if they sensed their liberty to be under assault, they would strike back forcefully against the offender. Thus, if peace was to be fostered, liberty would require protection. And the chief source of protection could only be law. "The law," he told the House of Lords, "is at the same time the standard and guardian of our liberty. It both circumscribes and defends it." He shared with Montesquieu, whose authority he invoked, the view that "we are then free because we live under laws." "Liberty without law," he noted, in a declaration that completes the argument with which this paragraph opened, "is anarchy and confusion."[8]

A major question naturally presents itself at this point: how were these laws that upheld the moral order and protected liberty to be created? Hardwicke had a conventionally imprecise British answer. In one sense Parliament was the legislature, the sovereign body entrusted with the power to make law for the kingdom. This Parliament was three-headed, comprised of Lords, Commons, and crown, and the consent of all three was necessary to produce statutes. It was, he noted briefly, the "duty of the legislator to make good laws," and as the regular author of the speech from the throne he contrived to have Parliament frequently reminded that its purpose was to promote "union & good harmony" in

7. On occasion he argued that liberty promoted trade. But he nowhere (to my knowledge) suggested that that connection should be the prime justification for liberty. More generally, though trade figured regularly (but briefly) in the speeches from the throne that Hardwicke composed, the theme and treatment seem simply conventional in that context. In his private writings Hardwicke's allusions to the world of commerce are infrequent.

8. British Museum, Add. MSS 35878, fols. 40, 47.

the kingdom. But in another sense, even more important than statute law for Hardwicke was the common law, which he characterized as the "result of the wisdom of the ages." In expressing this view he adopted the widely held notion that the common law was the product of the collective sagacity of anonymous men toiling across the centuries. To these men, at once attuned to the needs of their fellow citizens and versed in legal tradition, there had come the insights that allowed English law to incorporate justice. Infused with reason, the precedents they established came collectively to constitute a structure of timeless wisdom. Despite superficial appearances, therefore, common law was not a disordered aggregation of arbitrary decisions. It was a complex and intricate reticulation of moral injunctions that commended themselves to perspicacious observers by virtue of their reasonableness.

Hardwicke put great store by precedent and followed Sir Edward Coke in allowing it the capacity to invalidate statute. "A series of precedents," he asserted on one occasion, "against the plain words of an Act of Parliament have made a law."[9] With statements of this sort Hardwicke, the prudential natural lawyer, further defined his distance from the positivists. The crown in Parliament was not the ultimate lawmaker, for convention and tradition, as embodied in the common law, could legitimately claim to set limits on the legislature. Hardwicke was here adopting the doctrine of prescription—the notion, later made famous in an expanded form by Burke, that long usage in and of itself was sufficient to confer authority on a practice or custom. The legislature, in Hardwicke's view, had no legitimate power to alter the oldest and most basic of British legal and constitutional practices. In the last analysis the common law, operating prescriptively, had woven the legal fabric that cloaked all Britons. The fabric, to pursue the metaphor, was designed to specifications provided by the interplay across the centuries of "natural reason" and historical circumstance. To Parliament remained only the important but subordinate function of mending rents in the fabric which the wisdom of the past had neglected or not known of.

9. Yorke, *Life of Hardwicke*, II, 427–28; British Museum, Add. MSS 35869, fols. 326, 332, Add. MSS 35878, fol. 39, Add. MSS 36115, fol. 101.

The application of law is a matter analytically separable from the act of legislating.[10] Hardwicke saw the responsibility for application resting with two groups: the trained judges and the common-sensical juries. Like many mid-century legists, he was particularly concerned to see the functional distinction between the two retained in full clarity. If it should be abandoned, he warned, the English legal tradition would be severed from its natural and historical roots. "If ever they come to be confounded," he stated on one occasion, "it will prove the confusion and destruction of the law of England." Juries he held, were convened to determine *facts* and facts alone. In origin they had been bodies of witnesses. This original function remained the justification, touchstone, and explication for such broader powers as they had later secured. Specifically, they were not to intrude upon the duties of judges—that is, they were not to presume to determine points of law. Judges, for their part, although obliged to apply their learning and wisdom to their determinations, were bound to honor the "declared intent of the legislatures, provided the words of the law will bear it." Hardwicke "utterly disclaimed the power of legislation" for judges.[11] Thus the discretionary power of the judges was confined to interpreting law and did not extend as far as making law. In none of these views was Hardwicke in any way out of step with informed opinion of his time.

Hardwicke insisted that there was a radical distinction between the attitudes appropriate to the creating and the applying of law. Lawmaking, he felt, was a prudential activity, to be carried through cautiously and in full awareness of the limits of human wisdom and power. Because human natures were at once individually complex and collectively diverse, simple calculations were grossly inadequate in efforts to predict the full effect of proposed laws. Since no human institution could be entirely free from imperfections, "it requires great judgment and foresight," he was quoted as saying, "to choose that which shall be exposed to the fewest and least dangerous consequences." On one occasion Hardwicke proposed three questions that he believed should be answered affirmatively of every piece of proposed legislation before a

10. Upon this distinction seventeenth-century constitutional thought about separation of powers had been built. See Vile, *Constitutionalism*, 30.

11. Yorke, *Life of Hardwicke*, I, 125, II, 542, III, 465.

vote.[12] Was the grievance in fact amenable to cure by law? Would the removal of the cited grievance not create a greater one? Was the law drafted clearly enough to effect the desired end? But if legislators should be cautious, those who applied the law should be rigorous. "It is this," he told a grand jury, referring to strict enforcement, "which gives life to laws and without it they will be but a dead letter." "Dangerous consequences" were the product of allowing people "to get the better of the Laws" and in effect "overrule the Acts of the Legislature." Violators must be made to know that illegalities would not be tolerated. It was a theme to which Hardwicke often and deliberately returned. "The chief office of government," he remarked on one occasion, "is to secure to us the regular course of law and justice." People who successfully flouted the law, he warned, "go on from invading the property to taking away the lives of their fellow-subjects; and from an obstinate contemptuous opposition to the regular decisions of the ordinary courts of justice they advance almost to open rebellion." His view was summed up in his aphoristic and oft-quoted dictum: "Certainty is the Mother of Repose and therefore the Law aims at Certainty."[13]

Here then was a philosophy of law—or rather, a philosophy of society in which law was the crucial element assuring stability. A government would find its support among the citizens chiefly to depend upon the effective handling of its judicial obligations. "I look upon the administration of justice as the principal and essential part of all government. The people know and judge of it by little else." Law was to be enacted with "wisdom and prudence," precisely defined, and strictly applied. It was both a teacher of morality and a defender of liberty, and for no decision was the prudence of the legislature more necessary than when it was compelled to adjudicate between the individual's demands for protection and the societal claims of morality.[14] It is only by keeping

12. *Cobbett's Parliamentary History*, XV, 740–41. Hardwicke is quoted as proposing *four* questions, but the elided one—is the law necessary for the intended program?—is vague in import and embraced by questions number one and three in the text.

13. Yorke, *Life of Hardwicke*, II, 423; *Cobbett's Parliamentary History*, XIII, 67, XIV, 20; British Museum, Add. MSS 32690, fol. 84, Add. MSS 36115, fols. 81, 91, 101.

14. *Cobbett's Parliamentary History*, XIV, 20; British Museum, Add. MSS 36115, fol. 101. Hardwicke often denounced *jus vagum et incertum*. For a markedly different judgment

all these considerations in mind that we can begin to understand Hardwicke's constitutional theory. For if his legal views were unexceptional in themselves, they had most interesting consequences when used to underpin some conventional Court Whig language about the constitution.

III

The eighteenth century was the golden age of the "balanced constitution." Like all his thoughtful contemporaries Hardwicke pointed to the concept of balance when identifying the key to Britain's constitutional order. "Balance" was in fact a cant word of the era. It suggested—though generally in an unparticularized manner—that the success of the constitution in fostering stability while safeguarding liberty lay in the existence of a condition of counterpoise among conflicting constitutional elements, whereby various nodes of power were kept in check by being kept in equilibrium in the act of legislation. There was, however, no consensus on the identity of these key equilibrated elements. Some theorists envisioned Britain as composed of *orders* or *ranks*, not unlike the estates that were believed to define France. From this point of view it followed that the constitution balanced the programs or interests of these socially differentiable ranks—specifically, of the crown, the aristocracy, and the people.[15] Other theorists saw the legislature composed of three *institutions*—a crown, a House of Lords, and a House of Commons—and argued that the balance was effected among these three to prevent any one from dominating the other two. A third group of theorists stressed the *functional differences* among these three elements—the crown administering, the Lords evaluating (or judging), the Commons providing money—and conceptualized a balance among the three functionally differentiable agencies. Clearly the three theories were similar. Not surprisingly, many explanations of the constitu-

---

of the role of law in the eighteenth century, see Douglas Hay, "Property, Authority, and the Criminal Law," in *Albion's Fatal Tree: Crime and Society in Eighteenth-Century England*, ed. Douglas Hay *et al.* (New York, 1975).

15. See Corinne Comstock Weston, *English Constitutional Theory and the House of Lords, 1556–1832* (New York, 1965), for the peculiar notion that the crown was an order. More generally, see Vile, *Constitutionalism*, 33–34, and Gwyn, *Separation of Powers, passim*.

tion confused or conflated several of these views. What was remarkable about Hardwicke was that he conceived of balance in a far different fashion. He did not so much disavow any of the three—for sometimes his language suggests endorsement of one or another view—as intimate that "balance" might be a richer image than it was usually taken to be and that beneath (and supportive of) any tripartite division within the constitution was a more fundamental bipolar conflict between two principles. The success of the constitution, he proposed, lay in its capacity to keep these two conflicting principles in balance.

What were the two principles? They may be called the prerogative principle and the democratical principle.[16] The prerogative principle emanated from the crown and sought to secure order, prosperity, regularity, and protection of property for the kingdom.[17] The democratical principle on the other hand emanated from the people. It sought to protect them from an overweening crown and to assure that decisions affecting the public would be made in consultation with that public. It will be readily seen that these two principles coincide with—but are more inclusive than—the two peace-securing functions that Hardwicke ascribed to law. That is, the preservation of a moral order was a task of the prerogative principle whereas the protection of liberties was a task of the democratical. What may be less immediately obvious are the implications that this view of balanced but conflicting principles has for the institutions of Britain.

Hardwicke's interpretation rose above the usual constitutional analysis of his day when he specified how the two principles found expression in the conduct of national life. Unlike most commentators, he did not assign particular principles to particular institutions, which institutions were then to represent and advance the claims of those principles in all public affairs. Nor did he confine his notion of balance to the act of legislation alone. Instead, making again the fundamental distinction

16. The designations are drawn from Hardwicke's vocabulary, though he did not use them (or their alternatives) with complete consistency in his discussions of the underlying balance. "Democratical" is undoubtedly a difficult term, for it suggests much to a twentieth-century reader that Hardwicke would not have understood by it in the eighteenth. Still, the adjective is his, and the suggestion is that the principle so named is the principle of the people.
17. British Museum, Add. MSS 36115, fol. 98.

between creating law and applying law, he argued that the constitution was so framed as to allow each principle to find sufficient expression in both activities and under several different constitutional guises.. When laws were made, he argued, the concurrence of crown, Lords, and Commons was necessary. The crown spoke for the prerogative, whereas the two houses stood for democratical interests. Respective subfunctions on the democratical side could, moreover, be distinguished. The House of Lords was the wiser body, the House of Commons the more accurate judge of public opinion. Thus their lordships were summoned by writ "ad consulendum" whereas the knights and burgesses were summoned "ad consentiendum."[18] Then when laws were applied both principles were again represented. The prerogative principle was embodied in judges, chosen by the crown for their wisdom and skill and therefore serving the purposes of the prerogative principle. The democratical principle lay in the juries, without whose assent no subject could be found in violation of the law. In a charge to a grand jury, after advancing the conventional argument that the element of consent by the people in the process of legislation assured the protection of British liberties, Hardwicke added that "as no law can be made to concern any of those valuable liberties without their consent, so no law can be adm[ini]stered to affect any of these but either originally or finally by the verdict or presentment of a jury, that is by judgment of their fellow-subjects upon their oaths." This type of analysis allowed Hardwicke to conclude that "the uniformity of the constitution, & due ballance of it, is preserv'd thro'out": the crown had a hand in both the creation and the administration of the laws, but no law could be made without the consent of the representatives of the people in Parliament and no law could be wielded to touch upon them without the consent of their representatives on juries.[19]

Hardwicke often waxed enthusiastic on the constitution. He regularly described it as "excellent" in the speeches from the throne that he

18. *Cobbett's Parliamentary History*, XV, 735.
19. British Museum, Add. MSS 36115, fol. 103. This is a central document for understanding Hardwicke. It is possible that the bipolar nature of the balance he sees has been missed by commentators because his treatment of the institutional manifestations of the democratical principle is not as full as one might wish. See also *ibid.*, Add. MSS 36115, fol. 75.

composed. Britain, he reminded the convicted Scots peers in 1746, was celebrated for its "mild and gracious government" and for the "best constitution, formed and established upon the justest balance." The kingdom's government, he asserted on another occasion, was the "best constituted of any in the world—administered over us and secured to us by the best body of Laws that human wisdom can frame." Drawing on a conventional image of the era, he argued admiringly that the mechanism of the constitution was a complex one in which the various components fitted together with the intricacy of a complicated machine. Embracing another traditional image he spoke of Britain's "happily mixed government."[20] In all these expressions he revealed at once his respect for the constitution and his belief that it merited such respect by virtue of its balance.

Precisely because balance was the heart of the constitution, Hardwicke was forever on the alert against changes that might threaten that balance. The metaphor of the machine suggested to him the attractive argument that exquisitely refined mechanisms should not be tampered with, for fear of destroying them even while seeking only to remedy a minor flaw. What seemed to him the danger most to be guarded against was the disproportionate growth of one of the two principles. And throughout most of his public career he was inclined to believe that the graver threat loomed from the popular rather than the royal flank. In accounting for his opposition to the militia bill of 1756, which included provisions designed to confine the crown's control of the militia, Hardwicke asserted that "the scale of power in this government has long been growing heavier on the democratical side." He warned that the militia bill, if enacted, would "throw a great deal of weight" onto that democratical side. "What I contend for is this," he bluntly concluded, "to preserve the limited monarchy entire, and nothing can do that but to preserve the counterpoise." But even if disposed to look toward the democratical camp when searching for enemies, he was prepared, late in his career and after Lord Bute and Henry Fox had driven Pelhamites from numerous offices, to acknowledge that the balance might also be prey to prerogative nibbling. The central constitutional

20. *Cobbett's Parliamentary History,* XI, 921; Yorke, *Life of Hardwicke,* I, 566; British Museum, Add. MSS 35878, fol. 47, Add. MSS 36115, fol. 103.

issue, he told Newcastle in the aftermath of the purge, was nothing less than "the freedom & independency of Parliament."[21] It would be an exaggeration to state that Hardwicke thought the balance fragile. But clearly he did not think the constitution entirely self-equilibrating, and he therefore felt obliged to serve as a watchdog, ever poised to warn his fellow countrymen whenever—through thoughtlessness, conspiracy, or ambition—the balance appeared in danger.[22]

IV

Hardwicke's theory of the constitution had some important implications for his political behavior. Indeed, many of his actions in the political arena—and many of the suggestions he offered Newcastle or the king—were grounded in his constitutionalism. He was, for example, an advocate of strong ministerial government. Against those who complained of new forms confounding old distinctions between crown and Parliament Hardwicke argued for the necessity of a capable ministry, entrusted with the task of finding common grounds between the plans of the monarch and the hopes of his Houses of Lords and Commons. By some theories of balance the three bodies should ideally have been kept separated. But for Hardwicke this view was both a misconception and an error. He sought a balance, not between two (or three) institutions, but between two principles. In the making of laws—that function of government which above all others defined the regime—he envisioned the ministry, drawn as it was from the membership of the houses but acting for the monarchy, as the agency of mediation between the two principles. Balance was effected not by the clash of contrary institutions or the counterpoise of forces but by the intelligent merging of royal schemes with plans congenial to the houses. It required men of uncommon understanding and prudence to discern the grounds upon which such mergers were possible. It required men who

21. *Cobbett's Parliamentary History*, XI, 921; British Museum, Add. MSS 32953, fol. 52, Add. MSS 35877, fols. 296–97.
22. For obvious reasons—their alertness to the importance of law being the primary one—Hardwicke thought those who followed the profession of law to be the most important bulwarks of constitutional balance. History, he asserted, showed that lawyers had defended the people when the crown became arbitrary and the crown when the people became clamorous. British Museum, Add. MSS 36115, fols. 94, 97–98.

had the trust of the monarch and credit with the houses. Only men so qualified should be chosen as ministers. And by virtue of being ministers they should then exercise wide authority, but always in conformity with the practical limits imposed by their peculiar state of owing simultaneous obedience to two separate masters.

Hardwicke was a realist. He knew the resources that ministries required if they were to succeed. They needed, first of all, to be composed of men of independent stature—in Hardwicke's phrase, "weight and influence." They needed, that is, to draw upon the recognized leaders of the national community. Only such men, trained to leadership, could command wide enough respect to be able to guide national affairs amid numerous quarrelsome groups characterized by a general inability to disengage their personal concerns from public affairs. But ministries needed as well royal support—"authority, confidence & credit from His Majesty." A monarch should appear neither to resent his ministers nor to rely on nonministerial friends for important advice, for when he did, the ministers in turn were unable to perform their mediating task effectively. George II is a monarch notorious for resisting these particular Court Whig views on the ministry. The king felt that Hardwicke and the Pelhams simply wanted to confine him within an ever-narrowing prerogative. "Ministers," he growled one day to his lord chancellor, "are Kings in this Country." Hardwicke, however, thought otherwise: they are, he had already told the chafing monarch, "only your instruments of government." In a sense, each man was right, though only Hardwicke knew it. The government was still conventionally spoken of as the king's, and the king's right to nominate his ministers was unchallenged. But precisely because ministers could only be effective if mediators, and only be mediators if respected within the political community, the king's options in choosing ministers were narrow, and their authority, once appointed, far-reaching.[23]

The task of the ministry, abstractly conceived, was to secure balance

23. *Ibid.*, Add. MSS 35411, fol. 11, Add. MSS 35870, fols. 90, 117. In a difficult but important article devoted to this aspect of Hardwicke's constitutional thought, Herbert Butterfield demonstrates how rich in implication the lord chancellor's view is. "Some Reflections on the Early Years of George III's Reign," *Journal of British Studies*, IV (1965), 78–101.

or complementarity or reciprocity between the prerogative principle and the democratical principle. In practice this meant that the ministers were obliged to direct national affairs in the manner most propitious for the maintenance of tranquillity. Hardwicke knew that the democratical principle had been growing in prominence. What he called "the prudence and temper of modern times" had quietly been sapping the strength of the crown. Consequently the sensibilities of the House of Commons could be neither ignored nor affronted. Hardwicke was, as noted earlier, prepared to stand resolutely against further institutional concessions to the democratical principle, but he believed it quite consonant with the mediating role of ministers that they be ready to advise the monarch to yield to that principle on an *ad hoc* basis. Britain was, he noted, "liable . . . to popular turns, which sometimes made it necessary for Kings to ply for their own sakes."[24] But whether counseling firmness or tactical retreat, the ministry held a central if undeveloped position in Hardwicke's constitutional thinking. Most constitutional theories of the day had trouble accounting for it, but not Hardwicke's. The ministry emerges implicitly from his statements as the body that, at the level of sovereign national government, sought to identify and then secure national compliance with policies that served both the goals of the prerogative and the hopes of the *demos*. It made practicable the conception of the king in Parliament.

Because a ministry existed in Britain, capable of yoking the crown and the houses, Hardwicke was an advocate of a strong standing army and an opponent of the militia. His view represented a reversal of earlier Whig thinking. In the days of James II Whigs had regarded the standing army, a force under royal control, as a manifest threat to liberty. As an alternative fighting force they had thus glorified the county militias, bodies seen too often through the distorting lenses of the writings of the civic humanists but unquestionably far more under the control of men of local importance than of the king. Hardwicke could not share the alarm of earlier Whigs. He thought the militia inept. The standing army, he therefore argued, was the only effective defense of the constitution against foreign enemies bent upon subverting it. He

24. Yorke, *Life of Hardwicke*, III, 38–39; British Museum, Add. MSS 35422, fol. 243, Add. MSS 36182, fol. 421.

knew that it would be necessary to retain civilian control of the army, but he did not believe such control difficult to enforce, and he saw no threat to the regime in a military body controlled by the king in Parliament. Indeed, he wanted it to be still more professional. Too many officers, he declared, were men of "great quality[,] rank, and distinction." What were needed were "soldiers of fortune" and "foreigners of service and distinction." Hardwicke had a second reason to dislike militias: he thought them pernicious in their effects on Britons. "The people of this country have been gradually wean'd from arms—habituated and formed to commerce, manufactures, & arts." To encourage them to become proficient with arms would be to inculcate "a love of idleness, of sports, & at last of plunder." Hardwicke had a Puritan's dread of inactivity. In a speech from the throne drafted by the lord chancellor this line of reasoning was amplified: "audacious crimes of robbery and violence, which are now become so frequent . . . have proceeded, in a great measure, from that profligate spirit of idleness, extravagance, and vice, which has of late extended itself in an uncommon degree, to the dishonor of the nation & to the great offense and prejudice [of the ?] industrious part of the people."[25] If arms begot idleness, and idleness crime, Hardwicke could only oppose a militia. Britain would be best provided for if it chose to leave its defense to those electing to make a career of the military. But Britain had the luxury of this choice only because it had a constitution so framed as to render nugatory earlier arguments about the dangers that standing armies posed to liberties and therefore to permit the issue to be decided solely on the grounds of military efficiency and national morality.

If a standing army was a body that his constitutional views permitted him to applaud, political parties were organizations that, again on constitutional grounds, he could only deplore. The problem of factions within the regime is one of the oldest of political issues, and Hardwicke knew the classical texts. Moreover, he grew to adulthood during the years of savage struggle between Whigs and Tories, rose to eminence in the period of Whig triumph and hegemony, and lived to see the Whigs dissolve into a set of successor factions. He styled himself a Whig, but

25. Yorke, *Life of Hardwicke*, II, 54, III, 190; British Museum, Add. MSS 35869, fol. 198, Add. MSS 35877, fols. 298–99.

by that appellation he simply meant to denominate his cast of thought. He believed in Whig principles and assumptions—the principles and assumptions this study attempts to specify—but he did not favor organized political factions. Like most of the political philosophers, he thought faction dangerous. He modified his view somewhat in the years just before his death, but the modification was a natural adjustment to an altered political landscape and suggests simply that the exercise of prudential judgment was a central component of Hardwicke's thought.

Two years before the accession of the Hanoverians Hardwicke had had occasion to explain his reasons for deploring "the unconscionable power of faction." It duped good men who ordinarily understood and pursued the kingdom's interests into adopting partisan stances and resisting sound ideas simply because of their provenance: it induced men to reject beneficial ideas out of partisan hatred for those who advanced them. From this judgment Hardwicke never receded. Participating in an organized opposition, he later asserted, would be to undergo "slavery" and to share in "guilt." And a few years before George II's death he assailed "wicked combination," announcing his intention to stay free of party and maintain his liberty to support right measures and oppose wrong ones. "I am sensible that this is not the political way to keep a party together, but that is not an objection against doing what I think in my own conscience to be right." Even in 1763, when George III's elevation of Bute and campaign against Pitt and Newcastle portended a royal war against the residue of the Court Whigs, Hardwicke did not so much recant his views as expand them. In an anticipation of Burke he asserted that there were "in this country . . . such things as honourable connexions" which were, in effect, "necessary engagements in order to carry on and effectuate right and necessary measures." What distinguished an honorable connection from a faction was the purpose for which men combined. Hardwicke continued to believe his Whig ideas were sound. In the years in which the ideas had easily held sway, this conviction had had no implications for party organization. Now that they had been put on the defensive, those who rallied to them should, Hardwicke believed, stand together. It was the same sort of practical logic that had led Bolingbroke in the 1730s to denounce faction in general but to suggest the need for a national party to save the kingdom. During Walpole's day Hardwicke called for a transcending of "little private divisions and resentments" so that all who "act upon the same honest principles, who mean the same thing," might unite. "'Tis a duty we all owe our Country, to give up private piques and animosities, to the public—to the interest of our Country." His declared view of the later Pitt-Newcastle coalition government—"His late Majesty's affairs never went on more prosperously" than in those days—expressed the approval that an old Court Whig, active in the post-Court Whig era, could feel for a national government that comprehended within its ample folds almost all who engaged in politics.[26] Only when Court Whig principles manifestly no longer informed the government and only when men of wicked principles secured power did party—"honourable connexion"—finally become justifiable.[27]

This case against party is a logical consequence of Hardwicke's view of the constitution. For if the role of the legislature is to determine by wisdom those laws that will contribute most to the kingdom's interest, and if partisan attachment leads men to embrace folly and eschew wisdom, then to the extent that the legislature is divided by party it will be disabled from fulfilling its constitutional task. Hardwicke once characterized the two houses of Parliament as "the great Council of the nation."[28] The deliberative capacity of that council could only be impaired by factional division. Hardwicke had faith that reasonable men—consulting together, invoking sound principles, and looking to the past for guidance—were competent to lead the nation. It was faction that made consultations acrimonious and recourse to principle or precedent prejudiced. Faction thus threatened the very capacity of a regime to endure. Hardwicke had no choice but to assail it.

Hardwicke's view of the constitution also led him to support the centralization of power. And in no respect does Court Whiggery stand at greater variance from Country Whiggery than in this one. The Country Whigs had an abiding distrust of power. They saw it as ever

26. Yorke, *Life of Hardwicke*, III, 362; British Museum, Add. MSS 32870, Fol. 399, Add. MSS 35352, fol. 396, Add. MSS 35422, fol. 243, Add. MSS 35584, Fols. 141–42, Add. MSS 36115, fol. 108.
27. See Brewer, *Party Ideology*, 70–76.
28. Yorke, *Life of Hardwicke*, I, 567.

preying on liberty. They viewed men as morally unequipped to exercise power, they believed that to confer power was to confer an opportunity for confining liberties, and thus—since they could not dispense with government entirely—they favored the decentralization of power, the multiplication of nodes of power, and the fostering of competing powers. Hardwicke unequivocally dismissed all these notions. In his conception of the political order the tendency of man to use political power for personal ends and to the destruction of liberty was best restrained not by the proliferation of small and competing powers but by the law and its agencies of enforcement. Therefore, to maximize the protective efficacy of the law all impediments to its applicability needed to be eliminated. The law was to be allowed to run with its full force wherever the Georges were sovereign. The impediments that existed in the eighteenth century were of diverse sorts. There was the Church of England, claiming for itself jurisdiction in a sphere of national life to which the common law did not apply. There were the territorial dependencies, asserting rights of self-government beyond the limits that tradition or expediency had sanctioned. There were the powers of personal jurisdiction that some in Scotland still retained. Hardwicke was a foe to all these rivals of the power that the king in Parliament alone should exercise. "I assure you," he wrote to Duncan Forbes, "with the strictest truth, that there is not a man in the United Kingdom who considers it as *one*, more than I do."[29]

Hardwicke was a devout man, but his view of the Church of England was at root constitutional. He tended to think of the faith of the reformation as "the great basis of civil government and liberty" and "the surest barrier of our civil constitution." He was, however, less sanguine about the ecclesiastical structures produced by the reformation. Like the Church of Rome from which they sprang, they could be dangerous—and he did not exclude the Church of England from that indictment. "Ecclesiastical usurpation," he said, in words that applied to all established churches, "seldom fails to end in civil tyranny." Thus although he favored legislation to enforce Protestantism in the kingdom

29. British Museum, Add. MSS 35446, fol. 4. The manuscript gives the clearest evidence that Hardwicke was thinking juridically, not culturally or racially: after "*one*" he initially inserted "people," but he then crossed it out.

as thoroughly consonant with his view of law as a promoter of morality, he also supported measures designed to weaken the capacity of the church to establish independent power. As chief justice in the celebrated decision *Middleton v. Crofts* he held that though spiritual courts could exercise jurisdiction over laymen, they did so only by virtue of parliamentary authorization. His famous marriage act suppressed the jurisdiction of the church over matrimony by rendering null a merely religious ceremony unaccompanied by the specified legal forms. And his support of the mortmain act, a measure that placed obstacles to the making of bequests to the church and other charitable institutions, was predicated on his acceptance of the Harringtonian dictum that power followed property and his consequent determination to prevent the church, an immortal body, from securing an immoderate amount of property.[30]

He was no less rigorous, though a bit more prudential, in dealing with imperial dependencies. His son, Charles Yorke, is most noted for his advocacy of the Declaratory Act of 1766, and the son was, in this respect, the spiritual as well as the biological offspring of the father. Hardwicke's first recorded speech in the Commons was an attack on the asserted rights of the Irish peers to certain ambiguously defined appellate jurisdictions and a defense of the supremacy of the House of Lords at Westminster in such matters. As legal officer for the crown he doubly restricted the financial powers of colonial legislatures, first by specifying that they could tax only when properly assembled by crown authority and then by prohibiting them from disposing of such monies on their own, requiring instead a governor's warrant for their issue. As lord chancellor, though presented with fewer opportunities to deliver opinions, he was no less determined to see the authority of the king in Parliament upheld in the colonies. When public uproar threatened the smooth operation of trials in New Jersey in 1751, Hardwicke vigorously insisted upon colonial enforcement of the applicable British statutes. "The King's Government," he admonished Governor Jonathon Belcher, "& the authority of his Laws must, & will be supported."[31] Colonies were dependencies and Britons residing in them were entitled to the

30. Yorke, *Life of Hardwicke*, I, 81, 121–23, 148, 574, II, 74–75.
31. *Ibid.*, I, 67–68, 89; British Museum, Add. MSS 35909, fol. 148.

rights of Britons at home, but the chief defense of these rights—whether the Briton be in Middlesex or Massachusetts or Munster—was the sovereign authority of the king in Parliament. Any obstruction to that authority could only be an obstacle to the defense of liberty.

Similar reasoning was equally forceful when applied to the existence of the heritable jurisdictions in Scotland. Hardwicke's views on this issue, though consistent with his expressed views about the pretensions of the church and the colonies, are nevertheless of considerable interest because they run contrary to a powerful strand of constitutional wisdom that received endorsement from no less a commentator than Montesquieu. In the years after the Forty-Five Hardwicke moved to suppress these traditional private jurisdictions by transferring the heritable powers to the baron's court. He argued that the destruction of the heritable jurisdictions would allow the powers to be "restored" to the crown and thereby enable the crown to secure the allegiance of the people subject to them. "The people," he was quoted as asserting, "will follow those, who have the power to protect or hurt them." Therefore, it was incumbent upon the ministers of a constitutional monarch to take all possible steps to remove that power from the hands of private persons. A formidable body of opinion dissented from Hardwicke on this question. In the House of Lords the duke of Argyll advanced the older Whig view that the decentralization and proliferation of jurisdictions was in itself a major safeguard of liberty. It followed from his argument that the heritable jurisdictions should be retained. Montesquieu himself was concerned about Hardwicke's reasoning. In 1749 he entertained Charles Yorke and, after inquiring for and receiving an explanation of Hardwicke's views, declared his own preference for the notion that multiple jurisdictions were a barrier against the crown and therefore a defense of liberty. Against both Argyll and Montesquieu Hardwicke was prepared to advance a counterargument. Their views were, for Britain, old fashioned and out of date. Hardwicke acknowledged that a multiplicity of jurisdictions might be a defense against the powers of an aspiring despot operating from a base of ill-defined constitutional power. But in Britain the crown had already been checked and the prerogative hedged. A constitution had been developed that could mediate between the will of the monarch and the will of the people. Liberty was therefore already secured. The only consequence of letting private jurisdictions "encroach" on the legal authority of such a crown would be the exposure of liberty to the danger of "petty tyrants."[32] For these reasons George II, surveying the legislation that suppressed the jurisdictions in Scotland, commended the acts as measures—the words are Hardwicke's—for "better securing the liberties of the people there."[33] Liberty, in sum, was best protected by a fully sovereign king in Parliament, not by the existence of competing nodes of authority.

From the perspective of the late twentieth century we can see that Hardwicke's theory was ultimately a dangerous one. A Parliament operating without inhibitions, fully supported by the monarch, could itself become a source of despotism. It could even do so, as the American Revolution dramatically showed, while professing a commitment to liberty and covering itself with arguments directly from Hardwicke's armory. Hardwicke himself, however, did not view the king in Parliament as operating without restraints. It is true that he could sometimes advance scarcely veiled threats of sweeping governmental actions against those the regime identified as wicked: the king, Hardwicke warned during the profligate 1730s, will use "*extraordinary*" as well as "*ordinary*" powers to suppress crime. It is also true that in 1744, fearing a Jacobite descent, he supported measures designed to confiscate estates from heirs of the disaffected, thus encroaching even on the sacrosanct ground of private property. But in fact Hardwicke set two types of limits to what Parliament could do. The first type was theoretical. As an exponent of natural law Hardwicke held that the legislature could pass only those laws that conformed to "natural reason"; statutes violating it were illegitimate. The second type of limit was practical. As a prudential man Hardwicke held that public opinion could not be systematically and deeply offended. "However much the people may be misled," he declared when supporting the repeal of the Jewish Naturalization Act in 1753, "yet in a free country, I do not think an unpopular mea-

32. *Cobbett's Parliamentary History*, XIV, 20; British Museum, Add. MSS 35353, fols. 92–93. The terminology is Charles Yorke's in his description of his talk with Montesquieu. Yorke, *Life of Hardwicke*, II, 173.
33. British Museum, Add. MSS 35869, fol. 144.

sure ought to be obstinately persisted in." He went on to compare the politician to the physician: each prescribes what he judges the best treatment for the diagnosed malady, but each should be ready to abandon a treatment that manifestly upsets the patient. Hardwicke was not afraid to use force to impose a law, but he knew that there were occasions in which force itself would be ineffective. "This is a law," he said of the militia measure of 1757, "which it is impossible to cram down the people's throats by force. You can never raise a militia by the compulsion of a standing army. . . . You may raise a rebellion."[34]

The final words set the outer limits to the effective power Hardwicke would give to the British Parliament. The king in Parliament existed to foster and sustain tranquillity. All the efforts of this sovereign body—whether legislative or executive—were to be directed to that end. The maintenance of a moral order and the protection of liberty, both achieved through and under law, were its chief responsibilities. The success and wisdom of its decisions could be measured only by the yardstick of domestic peace. And for this reason Hardwicke did not believe that the sovereign legislature, even if it chose to ignore the commands of natural law, would finally become despotic. The people would not remain quiet under a harsh, unfair government. They would rise up, expressing their discontent and sense of grievance. At this point the legislature would be obliged to retreat. And it would be yielding to the final and most powerful (if generally sheathed) weapon with which the democratical principle could make itself known. If peace was the goal of policy, then peace was the criterion by which to assess policy. For Hardwicke, in the last analysis, the matter was that simple.

34. Yorke, *Life of Hardwicke*, I, 327–29; *Cobbett's Parliamentary History*, XV, 102; British Museum, Add. MSS 35353, fol. 223, Add. MSS 35585, fol. 303, Add. MSS 36115, fol. 91.

Chapter VII

The Structure of Court Whig Thought

I

The central five chapters of this work present the individualized Court Whig views of five persons who found in Court Whiggery a reasonable account of or prescription for political life in Britain. But if such studies allow us to see the potential for idiosyncratic diversity within the Court Whig camp, they do not, in and of themselves, present a clear picture of the generalized Court Whig position as it emerged from the pamphlets and journal articles which for a full generation in the days of Walpole and the Pelhams flowed from the pens of proministerial writers.[1] The polemical skills of these writers were not insignificant. The conventional judgment that they could not equal opposition essayists in either verve or style is true, but the gap between the two camps was not nearly as wide as is sometimes supposed. William Arnall, the single most effective Court Whig essayist, is a case in point. He was an accomplished political writer, commanding a clear style and evincing a capacity for irony, satire, and vituperation whenever such tactics suited his polemical needs. Lord Hervey, Sir Robert Walpole, James Pitt, and

---

1. Pamphlets in the eighteenth century filled the role played by journals of opinion today. In tranquil times they appeared regularly. In times of controversy or crisis they surged to a flood. One ministerial tract, appearing in 1733, drew attention to the "Reams of Paper that have been prostituted" by the Patriots and to the "Vast Inundation of Words" they had poured out. *The Proper Reply of a Member of Parliament* (London, 1733), 9. Lord Hardwicke knew how difficult it was to keep abreast of the full range of these pamphlets: "One may wast [*sic*] all one's time reading such stuff." British Museum, Add. MSS 32949, fol. 91.

many of the thoroughly anonymous Court Whig writers were only slightly less proficient. They all stood in the shadows of their chief opponents, Lord Bolingbroke and William Pulteney, but neither they nor their message was therefore lost from the view of their contemporaries. Our scholarly need is to recover that message.[2]

Three general but fundamental assertions, reiterated almost beyond measure, constituted the axiomatic framework within which the Court Whig view took on plausibility. They provided a context that, once accepted, predisposed the accepter to assent to the validity of more precise Court Whig pronouncements. The first general assertion posited the essentially nonutopian nature of politics. It has already been noted how Hervey, Hoadly, Herring, Squire, and Hardwicke to a man denounced utopianism. All Court Whigs concurred. The perfect regime, they declared, was unattainable. The Patriots were depicted as utopians, and insofar as the description was deemed accurate, it damaged the credibility of opposition assaults.[3] A tract of 1722 asserted that "there's no Government without its Inconveniences, and it wou'd

2. This chapter covers much of the ground that Dickinson covers in Chapter IV ("The Defence of the Whig Establishment") of *Liberty and Property*. The reader will notice that, though we agree on many discrete points, we have organized our discussions in significantly different ways and come to rather different conclusions. It seems to me that Dickinson's analysis involves four major distorting elements. First, it assumes the primacy of the Court-Country axis in an age in which, by my view, the Whig-Tory axis remained at least of equal significance. Second, Dickinson's treatment assumes that the protection of property was the central concern of the Court Whigs. By my reading it was not. Court Whigs certainly valued property, but only a reader who is a priori committed to the notion that Court Whiggery was a cover for the protection of property could ignore the considerable evidence that makes property merely one of a cluster of goods. Third, Dickinson's treatment virtually ignores the ministry. Yet much of Court Whig apologetic was designed to defend and explain the ministry's decisive role in directing policy and harmonizing relations between crown and Parliament. Finally, Dickinson relied heavily on sources that, though certainly interesting, are not really Court Whig— Adam Smith, Adam Ferguson, Robert Wallace, William Blackstone, and David Hume. Hume, absolutely central to Dickinson's analysis, actually declared that he would vote against Sir Robert Walpole's retention of office. M. M. Goldsmith, "Faction Detected: Ideological Consequences of Robert Walpole's Decline and Fall," *History*, LXIV (1979), 17.

3. In truth, many in the opposition were not at all utopian. They believed that there was ample room between the utopian vision and the morass of Court Whig ineptitude and turpitude for an improved though nonutopian regime. See Kramnick, *Bolingbroke and His Circle*, 75.

be unjust to impute That as a Crime to the Administration, which
flows from the very Nature of the Constitution itself." The message
remained identical in 1731. "Since no Government in the World, no
System of Polity that ever was invented, can be otherwise than imperfect, no Administration infallible, there will for ever be Defects to be
complained of, Mistakes to be rectify'd." The early 1740s brought no
change. "Whoever aims at more Perfection in either [the form or
method of government] than consists with human Establishments and
human Frailties, must be looked upon as a mere Visionary, or something worse." Moreover, this Court Whig assertion embraced the so-
bering notion that many problems lay beyond the capacity of human
government to rectify or ameliorate. "There are many civil Maladies,"
wrote one Court Whig, "which by no Man's Sagacity could be foreseen;
or, if foreseen, could by no Man's Prudence be prevented, and when
establish'd, can by no Man's Virtue or Talents be remov'd, but must be
left to Time and Accidents." These were consistent themes in Court
Whig writing, and their purpose is obvious. If the exercise of power
invariably entailed errors and difficulties, and if many of the trials of
civil life were irremovable, then the responsibility of the ministers presiding over affairs for the problems arising during their ministry was
thereby diminished. "Shall I throw away my Coat," asked a ministerial
pamphleteer, "or rend it from Top to Bottom, because I cannot take
out a Spot, or mend a Fray in it?"[4]

The second fundamental assertion proclaimed that liberty in excess
became licentiousness (or license). Again the theme was hoary: the
Greeks and Romans had long before wrestled with the perplexities of
fostering liberty without destroying social cohesion. But the Court
Whigs were not concerned with the intricacies of the classical dilemma. Their one central though dual message was that true liberty
was not licentiousness and that licentiousness was destructive of all
good. Lord Egmont, in his famous prominsterial tract of 1743, Faction

4. [Matthew Tindal(?)], A Defense of Our Present Happy Establishment; and the Administration Vindicated (London, 1722), 5; The Popularity of Modern Patriotism Examined (London, 1731), 9; A Vindication of the Honour and Privileges of the Commons of Great-Britain
(London, 1740), 4; [William Arnall], Clodius and Cicero (London, 1727), 26; [John Perceval, Lord Egmont], The Thoughts of an Impartial Man upon the Present Temper of the
Nation (London, 1733), 12.

Detected by the Evidence of Facts, explained the relationship of the two. "Even Liberty itself, the more perfect it is, produces these Effects more strongly; for Wantonness and Licentiousness, which are its evil Genii, tempt all depraved Tempers to abuse it, and expose many to the Lash of the Laws, and to the just Indignation of Power." A less lofty tract, written in the electoral heat of 1734, expressed the conviction that "the Pulse of this Nation will ever beat high for Liberty" but quickly added the qualifying hope that that pulse not become so fevered as "to border upon Lunacy." In 1747 George Lavington, bishop of Exeter, put the relationship considerably more concisely: licentiousness, he stated, is "liberty run mad."[5] The purpose of these and many similar admonitions is no more obscure than the purpose of the Court Whig affirmation of antiutopianism. Against a Patriot front that incessantly assailed the ministry for its presumed infringements on liberty, it was necessary—though not finally sufficient—to argue that liberty could not be boundless and that too much freedom was as pernicious to the individual and society as too little.

The third fundamental assertion was that the Court Whigs held the middle ground in politics between those who would return to the royal authoritarianism of prerevolutionary days and those who would yield all power to the House of Commons. The terminology they employed was blatantly self-serving, violently distorting the real views of their opponents. In Court Whig rhetoric the opposition consisted of a wicked combination of Jacobites and republicans. Few among the opposition in fact espoused anything like a return to seventeenth-century Stuart government, and even fewer sought the unchecked rule of the Commons. But precisely because such views were unpopular and those who held them were regarded as foolish, it was useful for the Court Whigs to try to implicate as many of the moderates among the opposition as they could in immoderate schemes. Thus again and again the Court Whig pamphleteers denounced their opponents as craven Jacobites and cunning republicans.[6] The Jacobites, sometimes designated as

5. [Lord Egmont], *Faction Detected by the Evidence of Facts* (London, 1743), 6–7; *A Review of the Controversy* (London, 1734), 6; George Lavington, *A Sermon preached . . . May 29, 1747* (London, 1747), 25.

6. See, *e.g.*, *The Ordinary of Newgate's Account of the Parentage, Birth, Education, Strange Life and Behaviour, of Caleb D'Anvers, esq.* (London, 1734), 3; *Vindication of the*

papists,[7] were described as bitter enemies to the Hanoverian establishment: "as one Revolution sour'd their Tempers, so it is in vain to hope
they will ever be sweeten'd again,—but by another." The republicans—
"Wat Tylers" or self-styled "Old Whigs"—were opponents of social hierarchy and could be identified by their advocacy of schemes that
would unsettle the constitution by enhancing the power of the House
of Commons while binding that chamber more closely to the electorate. The unseemly union of these two discontented bands produced a
"coagulated Crew." But because this crew consisted only of the political
extremists in the kingdom, the middle ground was left to the Court
Whigs. They alone eschewed the extremes; they alone remained
sound. Because the center was increasingly the only respectable position in Georgian politics, the Court Whigs sought to monopolize it.
"True and lasting Enjoyment of Liberty," one ministerialist proclaimed,
is found only "in the Mean."[8] They never succeeded in persuading all
in the political nation that their own vision of politics was the only
valid one, but they forced the Patriots to deny the charges of extrem-
ism[9] or to try to throw the charges back on the Court Whigs[10]; in so
doing the ministerial writers helped to confine the range of the permissible in British politics within increasingly narrow and moderate limits.

Having posited this framework of centrist, antiutopian politics that

---

Honour, 34; Thomas Wingfield, *The Mischiefs of Unreasonable Opposition to Government.
A Sermon preach'd . . . January the 30th, 1748–9* (London, 1749), 10; *An Address to the
Freeholders of the County of Oxford, on the Subject of the Present Election* (London, 1753).

7. *The Landed Interest Consider'd: being serious advice to gentlemen, yeomen, farmers,
and others, concerned in the ensuing election* (London, 1733), 5–7; *The Present Measures
prov'd to be the Only Means of Securing the Balance of Power in Europe, as Well as the Liberty
and Independency of Great-Britain* (London, 1743), 26.

8. *A Complete View of the Present Politicks of Great-Britain* (London, 1743), 29; [Sir
William Yonge], *Sedition and Defamation display'd: in a Letter to the Author of the Craftsman*
(London, 1731), 43; [Horace Walpole], *The Interest of Great Britain Steadily Pursued* (Lon-
don, 1743), 59; [Horace Walpole], *The Rise and Fall of the Late Projected Excise, impartially
consider'd* (London, 1733), 32–35; *Plain Matter of Fact; or, Whiggism the Bulwark of the
Kingdoms* (London, 1742), 15; *A Coalition of Patriots Delineated, Or, A Just Display of the
Union of Jacobites, Malecontents, Republicans* (London, 1735), 6; *The Freeholder's Alarm to
His Brethren; or, the Fate of Britain Determin'd by the Ensuing Election* (London, 1734), 6.

9. For example, a Patriot writer of 1733, stung by Court Whig accusations, signed his
antiexcise tract "Neither a Jacobite, nor Republican." *A Letter from a Merchant of London
to a Member of Parliament* (London, 1733), 32.

10. This was the burden of Lord Lyttelton's anonymous *A Letter to the Tories* (London,
1747), especially 3.

identified the extension of liberty as particularly dangerous, the Court Whigs were armed to do battle with the Patriots on the issues that the latter raised.[11] They had no quarrel over the doctrine of constitutional equilibrium, and they joined the opposition in showering praise upon that doctrine. Innumerable examples of encomiastic references to the balanced constitution stud Court Whig writings. James Pitt, using the nom de plume "Francis Osborne," declared that "the Excellency and Perfection of our Constitution consist in the Balance of the Powers divided among the three Parts of our legislature; which Balance, while it is preserved, will keep us from falling under the Tyranny of One single Power." George Lavington proclaimed that "by the gracious appointment of the Almighty, our Government is hereby settled on its proper basis of a just and happy *medium*, and become the *best-balanced Constitution under heaven.*" A pamphleteer soliciting votes for ministerial candidates in an approaching election announced that "Our Constitution or Form of Government Established among us, composed of King, Lords, and Commons, is the most Excellent of any in the Universe." Another writer praised the constitution as "a happy Medium" which placed Britons "at the Tip-top of a *mixed, limited, well poised Government.*" Court Whig scholars lent their support to this evaluation. Thomas Gordon, whose *Works of Tacitus* was dedicated to Walpole, used one of his introductory discourses to describe Britain's "happy ballance" as the type of constitution Tacitus most applauded. And Thomas Blackwell, who dedicated the first volume of his *Memoirs of the Court of Augustus* to Henry Pelham and the second volume to the duke of Newcastle, waxed still more enthusiastic for equilibrium.[12] However much Court Whigs might have dissented from Patriots on most issues, they were at one on the constitution. "Balance" was its glory and the source of its perfection.

---

11. The order of items in the following discussion corresponds to the order in which they were treated in Chapter I.

12. London *Journal*, February 23, 1734; Lavington, *Sermon*, 24; *An Address to the Freeholders of Great Britain, in Favour of our Constitution* (London, 1734), 8–9; *The Difference Computed, in a Brief History of Arbitrary Power* (London, 1735), 40; Philip Williams, *The Love of Our Constitution in Church and State . . . A Sermon preached . . . 11th of June 1738* (Cambridge, 1738), 6; Thomas Gordon, *The Works of Tacitus* (2 vols.; London, 1728–31), I, 92; Thomas Blackwell, *Memoirs of the Court of Augustus* (3 vols.; Edinburgh, 1753–63).

But "balance"—and this point needs emphasis—was so vague a con-cept as to be almost empty. This indeed is why Patriot and Court Whig alike could embrace the notion. It has already been noted that the term was impossibly imprecise as employed by Lord Hervey; other Court Whig writers were scarcely more exacting in their usage. Corbyn Morris, exploring the same dualism that Hardwicke had placed at the heart of the constitution, found the forces in balance to be the crown and the people. The appropriate policy on any particular issue would be determined by judging which actions would best promote a contin-uation of the balance. Another writer saw not three but four agencies in balance—the crown, the lay Lords, the bishops, and the Commons. In the view of a commentator of the mid-1740s, the conventional tri-partite division was adequate but incomplete, missing much of the complexity that subordinate agencies and bodies in the constitution provided. "The principle Wheels of our constitutional Clock are the three Estates of the Realm, under them in their respective Stations many lesser." Several articles by Francis Osborne in the London *Journal* examined Bolingbroke's contention that the agencies in constitutional balance were not totally independent of each other, since such a situa-tion could produce only a stalemate. Osborne agreed, distinguishing between an "absolute" independence that would be intolerable and a "constitutional" independence that allowed the constitution to func-tion. But this agreement on principles did not entail any agreement on prescription. Whereas Bolingbroke feared that the Walpole administra-tion was trying to bring the House of Commons into subordination to the crown, Osborne worried about Patriot schemes that would turn the crown into a pawn of the elected chamber. Drawing on Harringtonian ideas, he noted that the Commons held about 85 percent of the land in the kingdom. The appropriate conclusion, he added, was not that the power of the House of Commons should be further enhanced, but that it should be stoutly restrained.[13] Otherwise balance would be de-stroyed. In sum, the Court Whigs made no effort to rebut Patriot con-

13. [Corbyn Morris], *A Letter from a Bystander to a Member of Parliament* (London, 1742), 30–31; [Egmont], *Thoughts*, 16; *A Continuation of the Plain Reasoner* (London, 1745), 50; London *Journal*, September 28, 1734. See the seventh letter in Lord Boling-broke's *Remarks on History*, published in Isaac Kramnick, ed., *Lord Bolingbroke: Historical Writings* (Chicago, 1972).

tentions about a balanced constitution precisely because the same constitutional model that allowed the opposition to attack enabled the
ministers to defend themselves. Neither side evidenced much penetration in its analysis. Everyone could agree about the value of balance
because no one could be sure what it meant.

Toward the other basic ideas of their "Patriot-Jaundice" opponents
the Court Whigs were not so accommodating. The Patriots, it will be
recalled, tended to see human nature as unredeemed and unworthy of
trust. The Court Whigs were in general more sanguine. To be sure, the
polemical requirements of political pamphleteering did not afford frequent occasion for analyses of human nature. But now and then, in
asides or brief summaries, Court Whig writers made clear their basic
adherence to a less pessimistic reading of human nature than that accepted by many in the opposition. If Thomas Hobbes and John Calvin
gave the Patriots their anthropology, it was Hooker, Shaftesbury, and
Francis Hutcheson who performed the same service for the Court
Whigs. William Parker, chaplain-in-ordinary to George II, founded his
political views on his Anglican understanding of human nature.
"Man," he preached, "is of a mixt, and middle nature, made up of
excellencies and imperfections." Rather than naturally hostile to fellow
members of his species, man was fundamentally sociable. He was also
capable of clear and effective thought, by means of which he could
comprehend both his world and himself and act in accordance with
such understanding. "Man is a Reasonable Thinking Creature," wrote
an early Court Whig (perhaps Defoe), "and his Actions must always be
accounted for by some one Principle or other." In the view of another
ministerial writer humankind was good by nature and acquired evil
traits only by virtue of poor education. All these considerations taken
together allowed a late Court Whig to depict man as rational and men
who employ this rationality as Whigs. "Whig-Principles are Principles
of Reason, of Liberty, of universal Benevolence, unclouded by Ignorance, unwarp'd by Error, unnarrow'd and unrestrain'd by local Preju-
dices. They are the Principles of rational Beings acting as such."[14] By

14. An Apology for the Conduct of the Present Administration (London, 1744), 4; William Parker, A Sermon preached . . . January 31, 1757 (London, 1757), 15; Loyalty to Our
King (London, 1745), 3; Popularity of Modern Patriotism, 7; [Daniel Defoe?], The Wicked-

this writer's enthusiastic reckoning not only was man rational; he was, insofar as he exercised his rationality, a Whig. This contrast in views about human nature between the Court Whigs and the Patriots is of fundamental importance. Some men who gravitated toward the opposition did so because they saw man as wicked; hence they held the possessors of power to be peculiarly dangerous. Others, who adhered to the Court Whigs, did so because their notion of human nature made them proof against excessive fears of what men entrusted with power might do.

It was for this reason that the Court Whigs were also unable to share the Patriots' deep concern about the effect power might have on liberty. They did not deny that power had an appetite and that, left unrestrained, it might seek to consume the liberties of the subject. But they believed that such restraints in fact existed. One forceful restraint was the character and public standing of the men of high rank upon whom public office was conferred. Such men gloried in their reputation as conscientious leaders. "All power," declared one Court Whig, "is a delegated Trust. . . . Wherever it is lodged, there will always remain some Danger . . . of its being abused; and a good moral Assurance to the contrary, is what, in many Cases, we must be content with." But since a mere moral assurance might seem insufficient for all situations, there existed constitutional restraints as well. The Court Whigs pointed to the checking nature of the balanced constitution. William Arnall, for example, reproached the opposition for failing to distinguish between a "power" to destroy and an "inclination" to do so. Such "power" existed, he acknowledged, but the "inclination"—and here he meant the capacity of a single agent in the state to destroy it—did not. The constitution had distributed power among several bodies. Only by acting together could they bring forth the weight of that power. And thus each body served as a barrier against the illegitimate or harmful exercise of power. Arnall's position coincided with Lord Hardwicke's. "Power *divided*," the lord chancellor wrote, "takes a regular course;

---

ness of a Disregard to Oaths; and the Pernicious Consequences of it to Religion and Government (London, 1723), 31; London Journal, July 5, 12, 1729; Some Thoughts upon a Bill for General Naturalization: addressed to those of all denominations who act upon Whig-principles (London, 1751), 3.

when it is exorbitantly exercised it operates & produces its own checks, & remedies. But power *undivided* naturally begets perpetual contention." The Court Whigs' confidence about the capacity of British liberties to withstand the nibbling of power was thus rooted in the twin beliefs that men of honor, wealth, and reputation were unlikely to abuse a trust and that the balanced constitution offered adequate protection against that unusual individual who might disregard such considerations of reputation. "Opposition to Power," Arnall stated summarily, "is far from being a sure Proof of the Abuse of Power."[15]

To the Patriots' jeremiads about a general corruption and decay in society the Court Whigs offered no united resistance. Some, such as Samuel Squire, thoroughly agreed. Wealth had corrupted the British, and it was this corruption of manners and morals that made them unfit for republican self-government. Others as firmly dissented. Francis Osborne, for example, held that freedom checked corruption and that a free state was far abler than an authoritarian one to elicit just thinking and just actions from its citizens. Most Court Whigs, however, adopted medial views. They saw corruption to be an ever-present danger, but they believed that a firm and fair system of laws could forestall corruption and decline by promoting public-spirited conduct. The threat of decay was implicit in what Court Whigs discerned to be a peculiar proclivity of Britons to embrace mindless change. A ministerial poetaster used pentameters to diagnose the national malady.

> See, Love of Change the *British* Race betray,
> And Heav'n's best Gifts delight but for a Day;
> With their own Choice ne'er can they long agree,
> Too wise for slaves, nor yet content when free.

And old Horace Walpole, alluding to the most celebrated instance of a nation in decline, drew the likeliest Court Whig conclusion. "Menaces and tumults"—the deliberate products of wicked faction—loomed as enemies of public order, he noted. "Faction (as ancient *Rome* found to its cost) may prove as subversive of a free Constitution, as Tyranny can be." But Britain had a resilient defense. " 'Tis the Happiness of our

15. *Vindication of the Honour*, 27; [William Arnall], *Opposition No Proof of Patriotism* (London, 1735), 24; British Museum, Add. MSS 35877, fol. 298; [Arnall], *Clodius*, 3.

own constitution in particular . . . to be governed by *Law*, and that only." Rather more grimly, Alured Clarke, chaplain-in-ordinary to George II, exhorted Britons to honor their laws; without such fixed landmarks of power and obedience, he insisted, society underwent inevitable and destructive decay.[16] It is clear from these and numerous other examples of Court Whig reflection upon the relationship of decay to law that the majority of ministerial writers tended to see social decay as virtually synonymous with social dissolution. Moreover, the most distinguishable symptom of decay or dissolution was a neglect of proper individual conduct—a disregard of manners and morality. But Court Whigs were likelier than their opponents to see law as a remedy for such decay.

II

It was not sufficient for the Court Whigs to try to turn back most of the basic ideas of the Patriots. They needed as well to deal with the range of more concrete criticisms raised by the opposition. At the center of this range was the contention that the Parliament was too much the prisoner of the executive, a contention that embraced both the insistence that Parliament should not be a tool of the crown and the demand that it be more responsive to the will of the political nation. Court Whig writers disputed both prongs of the contention. The independence of Parliament, Osborne reminded his readers, was not imperiled, for it was assured by the riches and estates of the eight hundred men who comprised it; their wealth made them proof against blandishments from any source to forfeit their liberties. Consequently the opposition's efforts to push a place bill through Parliament were treated as misconceived. The holding of place was not in and of itself corrupting, and to prohibit individuals from sitting in Parliament simply because they held places under the crown would be not only to deny electors the right to choose the candidate they might wish but also to separate two "trusts"—the representing of the people in Parliament and the executing of public office—which were best fulfilled when united

16. Squire, *Enquiry* (1753), 60; London *Journal*, April 1, 1733; *An Essay on Faction* (London, 1733), 4; [Horace Walpole], *Rise and Fall*, 33–35; Alured Clarke, *A Sermon preached . . . January XXXI, 1731* (London, 1731).

in one person. One writer pointedly reminded his readers that a place bill was the Hanoverian analogue to the notorious Self-Denying Ordinance. The readiness of Parliament to concur with the proposals of the king's servants, far from being a sign of Parliament's subjection to the ministry, was actually "an happy Evidence of the Integrity and Abilities of the Administration." Occasionally Court Whig writers dealt more candidly with the issue and in the process anticipated the judgment of David Hume. A famous tract from the early 1740s acknowledged that the administration employed electoral influence and the bestowal of places to procure friends in Parliament. But the writer justified these activities on the ground of necessity. Hints of such an argument were often dropped. With his prerogative curtailed by the Glorious Revolution, the king needed alternative ways to cultivate the affection of his subjects and to keep in some type of harness a House of Commons that already represented most of the kingdom's land. Moreover, a minister would be neglectful of duty who did not work to secure a House of Commons responsive to the king's wishes. For all these reasons the ministry could legitimately resort to political and electoral methods that the Patriots denounced. Only by such methods could excessive parliamentary independence be restrained and constitutional balance between crown and Parliament maintained.[17]

The Court Whigs were no less scornful of opposition demands for a surer measure of Parliament's responsiveness to the people. They gave short shrift to two major Patriot proposals—a return to triennial Parliaments and the instituting of constituency instruction of members. The case against triennial Parliaments was simple. Court Whigs advanced the argument from "Peace and Unity." Elections, they conceded, fulfilled the vital constitutional function of protecting liberty. But because they inevitably fostered "Riot, Excess, or Party Rage," it was best that they be employed as infrequently as possible. A septennial act met the needs of British society more adequately than a triennial act: it pre-

17. London *Journal*, February 19, 1732; *An Enquiry into the Danger of Multiplying Incapacities on the Gentlemen of England to sit in Parliament* (London, 1739); *Vindication of the Honour; An Apology for Government According to Law* (London, 1735), 19; *A Second Letter to a Member of Parliament Concerning the Present State of Affairs* (London, 1741), 60–63; compare London *Journal*, September 28, 1734, and *Freeholder's Alarm*, 37–38.

served liberty but gave no undue occasion for tumults and confusion. The case against the instruction of members was somewhat more complicated. The excise crisis had triggered an effusion of instructions to members of Parliament. In the view of Court Whigs the real danger of a program of instruction lay in its democratic implications. To instruct was to bind—at least implicitly. But members ought not to be bound. They were representatives, not deputies or attorneys or agents. Their task was to deliberate and then to decide on the basis of these deliberations, not to be mindless conduits for the views of their constituencies. The constitution reposed the power of legislation in the king in Parliament. Any scheme that infringed upon the right of Parliament to act for and by itself was destructive of the constitution and a harbinger of democracy.[18] To readers who shared the conventional eighteenth-century evaluation of the balanced constitution, these were weighty and often compelling arguments.

The Patriots often denounced the ministries' management of finance, seeing in it the clearest evidence of governmental corruption. They viewed the national debt as an insidious mechanism for shifting wealth from the landed to the commercial class, and they depicted the staff required to service the debt and to collect the revenue as an army of court-directed leeches. To these charges the ministerial writers responded with increasing boldness as the Court Whig era advanced. Even the conversion of the sinking fund into a reservoir to support new debt did not inhibit them. They noted, first of all, that with the landed interest comprising so large a part of the electorate, no ministry dared to ignore its needs and wishes. Then they dealt with the handling of the national debt itself. In the late 1720s a conventional defense sought to identify compensating considerations that would outweigh Patriot criticisms of the debt. Supporters of the government were at this time still wary of viewing the debt precisely as a blessing, but they could remind their readers that the stock market was again under control, the interest rate was falling, smuggling was being suppressed, and Scotland was being made to pay its fair share. In the middle of the next decade Sir Robert Walpole was among those who took up the pen in

18. *Address to the Freeholders of Great Britain*, 47–48; *Letter to a Member of Parliament*, 2–3; *Second Letter to a Member of Parliament*, 21–35.

behalf of the ministry, defending his management of the sinking fund, the Civil List, and votes of credit against what he construed as a barrage of opposition lies and innuendoes. Meanwhile, the argument that debt itself could be advantageous was slowly taking shape: a national debt made creditors unwilling to contemplate revolution and thus served as "an adventitious Security and Protection to our *Liberties* and Establishment." By the late 1740s, in the age of the Pelhams, the view had become still more sanguine. Debt allowed credit to flourish, and credit constituted the foundation of most of the nation's happiness and strength. Moreover, since so many in the landed class had themselves purchased government bonds, thereby blurring almost to invisibility the old distinction between the interests of the City and the interests of the landed, it was plausible to dismiss the bulk of the national debt as nothing more than money that the British owed to themselves. As for the rest of the debt—the portion owed to foreign bondholders—it helped to promote foreign trade. A decade of war, it is true, had increased the debt, but since the war was necessary to the defense of all that Britain held dear, the British should be pleased that their past record of debt management had made it possible for them to contract new debt so readily.[19] Within a generation the national debt had been transformed in Court Whig polemics from an unfortunate but necessary institution into a useful and productive one. And if it was indispensable, then the staff that managed it was also indispensable.

The Patriot assertion that the ministry fomented party division and hence disunity was dealt with in the most direct of manners: it was emphatically denied and then hurled back upon the accusers. The opposition, however, had patent grounds for so indicting the Court Whigs. Time and again, and especially as general elections drew near, the Court Whigs issued appeals for Britons to support Whigs and disavow Tories. Party distinctions, the Court Whigs declared, were natural in a free state. But not all parties that emerged merited approbation.

19. [William Arnall], *A Letter to a Freeholder, on the late reduction of the land tax to one shilling in the pound* (London, 1732); *A Letter from a Gentleman in the Country to Sir R— W—* (London, 1729), 10–13; [Robert Walpole], *Some Considerations concerning the Public Funds, the Public Revenues, and Annual Supplies* (London, 1735); [Robert Walpole], *Some General Considerations concerning the Alteration and Improvement of Publick Revenues* (London, 1733); *An Essay upon Publick Credit, in a Letter to a Friend* (London, 1748).

"Faction is a mischief, that as infallibly grows up with *Liberty*, as Weeds abound most in the richest Soil." Thus, the London *Journal* proclaimed that all who loved their country "will keep up the Distinction of *Whig* and *Tory*, while Men are distinguish'd by their publick Principles and Sentiments, that so the Sons of Liberty may be upon their Guard against the Enemies of Liberty." An electoral tract of 1734 concluded with an exhortation to Whig unity: "as *Tories* will be *Tories* in all Events, and perhaps *Jacobites* likewise; it is the Duty of *Whigs* to be WHIGS IN EARNEST, and to renew their first Principles of Zeal and Affection, if they would renew the Strength, and confirm the Establishment of the Protestant Succession." With declarations of such manifest partisanship issuing forth from ministerial sympathizers, one might think it rather brazen of the Court Whigs to deny that they encouraged party divisions. But their denial acquired a certain plausibility when conjoined to the notion that the regime established by the Glorious Revolution was at root Whiggish. If true, the notion implied that the Whig calls for Whig Parliaments were legitimate appeals for adherence to constitutional principles, whereas the Tory calls for Tory Parliaments were traitorous assaults upon a popular and free regime. Tory principles, the Court Whigs asserted, had the effect of transforming the Glorious Revolution into a "down-right Rebellion." And Tory pretensions to represent broad national interests were similarly discredited: "Is it possible . . . to conceive, that a *Rebel to our Constitution* can be *Reconciler* of our Parties?" In a Whig regime only the Whigs were constitutionally legitimate.[20]

To the famous Patriot accusations that the Court Whigs deliberately encouraged authoritarianism by supporting a standing army and inhibited foreign trade by persisting in unsound economic and diplomatic policies, the ministerial writers replied with heat and effect. The mili-

20. *The Danger of Faction to a Free People* (London, 1732), 5; London *Journal*, December 5, 1730; *The Sense of an Englishman on the Pretended Coalition of Parties, and on the Merits of the Whig Interest* (London, 1734), 51; *A Full and True Account of the Strange and Miraculous Conversion of All the Tories in Great Britain; by the Preaching of Caleb D'Anvers, prophet and apostle to these nations* (London, 1734), 13; *Sense of an Englishman*, 44. Bolingbroke advanced the converse argument in behalf of the opposition. Kramnick, *Bolingbroke and His Circle*, 157–60. But the argument was still more formidable in the writings of Court Whigs, for they had the manifest support of the monarch.

tia, they asserted, was insufficient for national defense needs. Yet, in an age that found a Catholic pretender roaming Europe in search of support, a foreign war would endanger not only the colonial holdings and maritime supremacy of Britain, but its very constitutional regime. Thus a strong standing army was essential. If Parliament did not permit recruiting it from among Britons, the government would be compelled to use subsidized foreign troops. "Strange," mused a Court Whig pamphleteer, "that Patriots should vote against putting their Country into a posture of defence, and think their Liberties safer in the hands of mercenary Foreigners than in their native Forces." Patriot fears of the army becoming a tool of despotism, the argument continued, were baseless. What was misleadingly called a standing army was in fact a *national* army, raised by law rather than princely edict and paid from the public rather than the royal purse. It owed its obedience to its parliamentary paymaster and could be construed as a threat to liberty only if Parliament itself could be so regarded. Against the accusations about trade the Court Whigs had the task of simply citing facts. Trade was expanding; traders were prospering.[21] In time of peace the Court Whigs warned of the deleterious consequences that war would have for trade as grounds for resisting belligerence. In time of war they justified much of what they did as an effort to open foreign markets. It remained ever possible for the opposition to say that trade would be still more vigorous under a Patriot government; it was impossible to say credibly that trade was flagging.

The collective thrust of this wide array of defenses against the whole range of opposition assaults was to blunt the force of the fundamental Patriot contention that the Court Whigs were creating in the cabinet a body that was unknown to the constitution, directed through a system of personal government (bitingly called Robinarchy in Walpole's day) that threatened to rival the authoritarianism of Stuart days. Such charges, in Court Whig eyes, were absurd. The cabinet was simply the

21. *Letter from a Gentleman in the Country*, 13; London *Journal*, February 12, 1732; *The Anti-Craftsman: being an Answer to the Craftsman Extraordinary* (London, 1729), 20–21; *A Letter to William Pulteney, esq., concerning the administration of affairs in Great Britain* (London, 1733). On the changeless nature of the debate over a militia, see Lois G. Schwoerer, *"No Standing Armies!" The Antiarmy Ideology in Seventeenth-Century England* (Baltimore, 1974).

traditional body of advisers that every monarch selected. The fears of
authoritarianism were unfounded, since no British government could
act without parliamentary approval. "The Ministers," William Arnall
complained, "have been abused for every good Action which they did
or attempted, and even for bad Actions which they neither attempted
nor intended." Court Whigs took exquisite delight in chiding the Patriots for protesting against infringements on the press by means of that
very press.[22]

For their leaders—Walpole and then the Pelhams—they had ful-
some praise. One pamphleteer commended Sir Robert as a "steady Patron of Liberty" and a "faithful Servant of a gracious Majesty" and attributed the abuse he received to the irritation of his opponents that
"he has been in the Right too long." Another writer eulogized Walpole
in his dedication: "It is, Sir, Your peculiar Glory to have baffled the
Rage of Power when out of Place, and by just Measures to have supported Your Self against all the Arts and Clamors of Faction since You
have been in." Then, as if that encomium were insufficient, the writer
continued, "Your Eloquence and Your Innocence have rendered You
victorious over all Your Enemies, and You have none now, but such as
are at the same Time upon [sic] Enemies to their Country." Poets too
vied in bestowing praise. One enthused over Walpole's steadfast pursuit
of the public good:

> So shines the Chief, who is his Country's Friend;
> Whom Terrors cannot warp, nor Favour bend;
> Nor sordid Avarise, nor Envious Hate,
> Debase his Soul, and make him meanly Great;
> But true to Honour, and in Action Fair
> The general Good exhausts his every Care.

Another celebrated the multiplicity of his virtues:

> This the Sovereign Man, compleat;
> Hero; Patriot; glorious; free;
> Rich, and wise; and fair, and great;
> Generous WALPOLE, Thou art He.

22. [Arnall], *Opposition No Proof*, 3; *The Case of the Opposition Stated, between the Craftsman and the People* (London, 1731), 39 and following; [William Arnall], *Observations on a Pamphlet* (London, 1731), 22.

In light of such effusions it is not surprising that several writers likened Sir Robert to Lord Burleigh. If the Pelhams received less adulation it was because they were less vitriolically abused. But Henry Pelham became "the greatest British Patriot" and Newcastle became a "Political Atlas." And one defense of the brothers, admittedly light hearted, suggested that they were "the greatest politicians, *Britain* ever produced."[23]

Ministerial writers meanwhile leveled assaults on the motives of their opponents, hoping thereby to deprive the Patriots of any aura of moral superiority that intensity of statement or professions of disinterestedness might otherwise confer. The most popular ploy was of ancient vintage. The Patriots, according to the Court Whigs, resorted to such vituperation simply because they were out of office and wanted to force their way in. They were disgruntled at deprivation, not enflamed over injustice. Theirs was not "a Struggle for Liberty, but a Contention for Power." Walpole himself labeled them "*Mock Patriots*, a Combination of the Chiefs of the *Disappointed* and *Discontented*; a numerous Train in all Ages!" Arnall turned one of their favorite assertions back on them: "If the Possession of Place influences Men, does not want of Place influence them as much?" But that argument was only the starting point of Court Whig vilification. The Patriots were "like those Wretches who live upon dangerous Coasts, whose Profit arises from Wrecks, who subsist by the Calamities and Misfortunes of their Fellow Creatures." They were "infamous Retailers of Lies, Scandal, Sedition, and Treason," whose chief mode of address consisted of "scurrilous Language," "groundless Aspersions," and "*Billingsgate* Appellations." They were "Incendiaries, who set Houses on Fire, that they may rob and plunder unobserved, in the Tumult and Confusion that such Accidents

---

23. *The Country Correspondent. Being, a Letter from a Country Gentleman to a Friend in Town* (London, 1739), 3; *The Crafts of the Craftsmen* (London, 1736), vii; *Essay on Faction*, 7; London *Journal*, May 4, 1728; [Thomas Gordon], *An Appeal to the Unprejudiced, concerning the present discontents occasioned by the late convention with Spain* (London, 1739), 21; Blackwell, *Memoirs*, I, 4; *The Political Magnet: Or, An Essay in defense of the late revolution* (London, 1745), iv; *The Conduct of the Two B—rs Vindicated* (London, 1749), 11, 29. In the hope of securing the support of some who had opposed Walpole, the defenders of the Pelhams sometimes wrote as if they distinguished between the excellencies of the brothers and the corruption of Sir Robert. But the policies defended were Walpolean. *A Serious Address to the Electors of Great-Britain on the present Election* (London, 1747).

naturally occasion." They were like "Whitefield the Pilgrim," who "wou'd destroy, if he cou'd, the whole System of the New Testament."[24] Court Whigs also resorted to allegories. In one instance they provided the *Craftsman's* pseudonymous Caleb D'Anvers with a choice biography. Product of an incestuous relationship between a tawdry mother and her own son, D'Anvers was raised in Billingsgate and briefly committed to a madhouse. Afterward he lurched from career to career, mastering such crafts as masquerading and pretending, brewing potions from the bones of dead traitors, and excelling at demagoguery. Another light pamphlet took up an image that Bolingbroke had employed in his public and self-exculpating letter to William Wyndham: Parliament became a kennel and the Patriots became a pack of dogs led by such hounds as Ranter, Snarler, and Babbler. A still later excursion into Court Whig humor proposed a "College of political Physicians" to treat the various disorders of the Patriots: logomania, "an intemperate Desire of Speaking"; krysophilia, the love of treasure and gold; cleodipsis, the thirst for honors and titles; and such unhellenized afflictions as "melancholy Madness" and the "Sullens." The ministerial writers found satire, savagery, sententiousness, and sarcasm all useful for lacerating a hated foe. "*The Truth is*," remarked one Court Whig, "that THEY who complain of *Grievances*, are themselves the *greatest Grievance* the Nation knows."[25]

In their efforts to discredit Patriot motives Court Whigs found it

24. *Case of the Opposition*, 15; [Robert Walpole], *Some Considerations concerning the Public Funds*, 6; [Arnall], *Opposition No Proof*, 5; [Sir Robert Walpole], *Observations upon the Treaty between the Crowns of Great-Britain, France, and Spain* (London, 1729), 4; [Yonge], *Sedition*, 2, 21–25; *Present Measures*, 4; *A Serious Remonstrance to the Publick. In regard to the many bold uncommon insults and reflections lately publish'd against the government* (London, 1740), 34. Bertrand Goldgar, *Walpole and the Wits: The Relation of Politics to Literature, 1722–1742* (Lincoln, Neb., 1976), 220 and *passim*, argues that many of Walpole's most celebrated literary foes—Alexander Pope, Henry Fielding, John Gay, and others—sided with the opposition because, among other motives, they did not receive the recognition they thought their due.

25. *Ordinary of Newgate's Account*, 5 and following; *A Hue and Cry after Part of a Pack of Hounds, which broke out of their Kennel in Westminster* (London, 1739), 3–8; *A History of the Rise, Progress, and Tendency of Patriotism . . . With a Curious Dissertation on the Diseases and Cures of Patriots* (London, 1747), 54–64; *The Conduct of the Ministry Compared with Its Consequences: or an Impartial View of the Present State of Affairs* (London, 1733), 6.

immensely useful to remind readers of the pasts of the opposition leaders. William Pulteney had been born to advantages and favored by
those he now assailed. But ambition had driven him to envenomed
opposition. This career proved him, in Court Whig eyes, to be "a Man
absolutely void of Principles, Gratitude, Truth and Honour."[26] Dryden's
famous couplet served on several occasions to preface works about him:
"In friendship false, Implacable in Hate / Resolv'd to ruin, or to rule
the State."[27] And if Pulteney was a useful target, Lord Bolingbroke was
ideal beyond the possibility of Court Whig invention. His career repudiated all he asserted, his record obliterated his pronouncements.
And thus scurrility knew no bounds when Court Whigs turned their
attention to "this Man, this Monster rather." Bolingbroke, by one
Court Whig estimate, "betrayed his Country, bribed and bullied the
Parliament, broke the publick Faith, brought Dishonour upon the Nation; and at last sold her to her worst Enemy." He was, wrote another,
a "Cameleon [sic] of a Statesman." "They must have stronger Stomachs
than mine," Arnall gasped, "who can bear to wallow in all that Filth,
which a thorough Scrutiny of that Man's Actions would necessarily
lead them into." Of all the opposition leaders only Bolingbroke was
regularly converted into a minion of the prince of darkness. He was "a
fall'n Angel." "Like Lucifer," he "fell through Pride, and has since rose
through Malice." On at least one occasion it was Lucifer's chief who
provided the most apposite parallel. Bolingbroke was a "haughty, ambitious, and revengeful Spirit, like Satan driven from his Power." "Has
he not," the writer asked, "even dared to cloath himself in the borrow'd
Rays of an Angel of Light?"[28] By implication the contest between the
Court Whigs and the Patriots took on the appearance of an apocalyptic
struggle. Court Whigs thus relished the opportunity to link Boling-

26. See the very similar biographies appearing in pamphlets published over a decade
apart: [Yonge], Sedition (1731), iii–iv; The Patriot and the Minister Review'd (London,
1743), 40.

27. See, e.g., Remarks on the R-p-n of the H— of C—ns to the K-g; and His M-y's A-f-
r (London, 1728); [Arnall], Observations.

28. Conduct of the Ministry Compared, 22; A Final Answer to the Treasonable Invectives
of the Craftsman (London, 1734), 32; The Conduct of the Late Administration with regard to
Foreign Affairs, from 1722 to 1742 (Dublin, 1742), 20; [Arnall], Observations, 9; A Dialogue between Sir Anthony Freeport and Timothy Squat, esquire, on the Subject of Excises
(London, 1733), 46; Crafts of the Craftsman, 4; Plain Matter of Fact, 7.

broke with their foes: whatever the polemical strengths he contributed to the enemy, his presence in the arena made clear which of the contending sides was truly in league with the forces of darkness.

III

Most of the Court Whig writings were defensive in nature and intention because they appeared as responses to opposition challenges.[29] This condition conferred an advantage on the Patriots that Court Whigs could only hope to reduce by publicizing. They accounted for the superior vigor of Patriot writings by declaring that "All ministerial Writings must be defensive." They reminded readers that ministers were often obliged to keep certain activities secret, even though a full rehearsal of the matter might disprove "facts" that the opposition adduced. They noted that opposition leaders had far more leisure than the ministers to devote to political writing. In addition, the full range of essay styles was not available to Court Whigs. Public opinion would countenance the "most *pathetic Figures of Rhetoric*" from Patriot pens, but the Court Whigs, fearing ridicule, dared "not venture at a single Trope."[30] Although exaggerated, these points were in general accurate. But even though largely defensive and ad hoc, and despite inhibitions on rhetorical versatility, the writings of Court Whig apologists provide materials for constructing a roughly coherent Court Whig interpretation of British society and government. The model about to be outlined may not have been the view accepted by every Court Whig. But it is consonant with a wide selection of Court Whig statements, and it covers most of the important controverted constitutional issues of the day.[31] Court Whiggery, through this process of distillation, emerges as a crude but consistent theory of the constitution.

29. A significant proportion are defenses of foreign policy. These have not figured prominently in my analysis since they usually raise strategic or tactical considerations, not political or constitutional arguments.

30. *A Modest and Impartial Reply to a Pamphlet Lately Published* (London, 1749?), 44; *The Occasional Patriot* (London, 1756), 5.

31. Several statements of Court Whiggery are justly celebrated. See, *e.g.*, [Arnall], *Opposition No Proof*, [Gordon], *Appeal*; [Morris], *Letter*; *Second Letter to a Member of Parliament*; [Egmont], *Faction Detected*. The reader will also find good summary statements in such less-known works as Edward Bentham, *A Letter to a Young Gentleman of Oxford*

The starting point of Court Whig thought was the acceptance of the notion of sovereignty. By embracing the view that there existed within every state a final and absolute authority Court Whigs secured for themselves the mantle of modernists and began to erect their defense against the Patriot charge that they were despots. Their adoption of the theory of sovereignty was trumpeted in unequivocal language. In the words of an early Court Whig apologist, the legislature of the kingdom—that is, the king, the Lords, and the Commons together—possessed an "absolute unlimited authority." William Hay was still bolder in his choice of words: "Supreme Authority," he declared, is "Unaccountable and Uncontroulable." But it was William Arnall who found the comparison that made the point most dramatically: "the Legislature entire is unlimited, and its Powers as ample and extensive as that of the Great Turk, over the Lives, Persons, and Properties of Men." The avowal of these arguments, however, did not mean that the Court Whigs sought some form of tyranny. It was true that all governments were absolute—it inhered in the definition of government that they be so—but it did not follow that all were arbitrary. Thus Patriot accusations that the government exercised sweeping powers were beside the point, for all governments did. What needed determining was whether the government exercised these powers in an arbitrary manner. In the view of the Court Whigs it did not, since it rested "upon constitutional Principles."[32] This fact—that Britain operated by constitutional principles—was for them decisive. For however much scholars might gloss classical texts, the Court Whigs averred, there were in reality but two types of government: arbitrary and lawful. Since in Britain laws emanated constitutionally from the crown in Parliament, the kingdom was a lawful one. And if lawful, it could not be arbitrary.

Still, in principle there was a wide range of possible lawful regimes, and it was thus necessary for Court Whig thinkers to define the precise

---

(London, 1749); Williams, *Love of Our Constitution*; *Address to the Freeholders of Great Britain*; *Complete View*; *Occasional Patriot*; *Sense of an Englishman*; *An Humble Address to the People of England. Being, a demonstration that the land-tax is more prejudicial to trade and liberty, than an inland duty on wine and tobacco* (London, 1733).

32. *Letter from a Gentleman in the Country*, 18; William Hay, *An Essay on Civil Government* (London, 1728), 30; [Arnall], *Opposition No Proof*, 24; *Occasional Patriot*, 15.

nature of the lawful government in Britain. This task they accomplished by noting that the British constitution—the instrument that specified what lawfulness meant in a British context—was a product of the two central events of recent history: the Glorious Revolution and the Restoration. That the events of 1688–1689 should be celebrated is scarcely surprising. The Whigs had appropriated them as peculiarly their own. They constituted "that glorious *Revolution*, which is now become the Basis of all our Rights, Liberty, and Happiness." "Our Government was made," proclaimed the *Daily Gazetteer*, "by the Revolution, as perfect as human Wisdom could contrive, or human Power execute." The Patriots, another Court Whig declared, made "one capital Mistake, which, like a wrong Principle in Mathematics, widens the Absurdity of the Proposition in its Progress. . . . This Mistake consists in supposing, that the Constitution was left imperfect at the Revolution."[33] But thoughtful Court Whigs yoked the revolution to the earlier Restoration. For if 1688 marked Britain's escape from despotism, 1660 marked the escape from republicanism. The balanced constitution of the eighteenth century, constituting a repudiation of both interregnal anarchy and Stuart tyranny, represented the fruit of both experiences. Samuel Croxall, one of George II's chaplains, saw potent significance in the decision by Parliament to appoint for celebration the anniversaries of both Charles I's death and William III's arrival. The two events "seem to be founded on two contradictory and incompatible Principles"—but they were not. In the proper encompassing view each symbolized an aspect of the existing constitutional order. The Court Whig regime rested upon both monarchy and liberty. The redoubtable Benjamin Hoadly agreed, indeed giving primacy of significance to the events of 1660. The Restoration had taught the value of the "Middle Way of Wisdom and Happiness." It had reestablished the legal government which the Glorious Revolution had then secured. And in his correspondence Lord Hardwicke concurred. What he sought, he ex-

---

33. *Conduct of the Late Administration*, 14; *Daily Gazetteer* (London), August 9, 1735; *An Historical View of the Principles, Characters, Persons &c. of the Political Writers in Great Britain* (London, 1740), 41. See also, B— G—, *The Advantages of the Revolution* (London, 1753).

plained, was "y^t this limited monarchy as establish'd [by?] y^e *Restoration* and *Revolution* taken together, may be preserved."[34]

Because the Restoration figured no less prominently in Court Whig thought than the Glorious Revolution, the Court Whigs were not embarrassed to magnify the monarch. The king symbolized the regime; he even, in a metaphorical sense, incorporated it. It was easy for Court Whigs to indulge the ruler in this manner for both of the first two Georges were themselves Court Whigs. George II, monarch during the heyday of Court Whiggery, was celebrated as "A PRINCE who is the Nation's great Security against all open Attacks, and secret Efforts, and an abundant Assurance, that no Artifice shall prevail to its Detriment." Patriots were rebuked for disseminating ideas that alienated subjects' affections from their monarch. Britons were chided for being ungrateful to a ruler whose sagacity, in the face of ignorant complaining, directed his kingdom along the course of wisdom in international affairs. The clergy happily took up the Whiggish *thèse royale*, linking the glorification of the monarch to the superintendence of God. Edward Young, the renowned literary figure in the Court Whig camp and another of George II's chaplains-in-ordinary, besought his audience to revere their king as "God's anointed" and as "a God (says God himself) of his People." One powerful basis for such enthusiasm was the monarch's devotion to Protestantism, "the natural Guardian, because it is the genuine fruit, of Liberty." The spectre of a Catholic king coming to the throne and undoing liberties was enough to unnerve any Court Whig. George embodied a right religion and a respect for sound constitutional government, and these incorporations made him invaluable. "The Cause of the King," explained one writer, "is the Cause of God and of our Country; and their Interests are inseparable." Inseparability might extend further. The ministry hoped to have itself linked in the popular mind to this cluster of indivisible entities. "The CAUSE of the *present Administration*," declared an essayist in the year of the excise crisis, "is the CAUSE of GOD and the KING." This conjunction of God and king

34. *Address to the Freeholders of Great Britain*, 10; *Complete View*, 7–8; Samuel Croxall, *A Sermon preach'd . . . January XXX, 1729* (London, 1729), 3; Benjamin Hoadly, "Sermon XII," in *Sixteen Sermons, formerly presented, now collected into one volume* (London, 1754); British Museum, Add. MSS 35877, fol. 294.

was congenial to the supporters of Walpole and the Pelhams. Court Whigs were, in a clear sense, Protestant royalists. No state could exist without a proper religious foundation, and George, with his devotion to Protestantism, provided such a foundation. For Court Whigs therefore the scriptural injunction retained its force. "To fear God, and honour the King, are our indispensable Duty."[35]

In addition to hailing the monarch, the Court Whigs dwelt heavily upon the subject's duties. And the foremost duty, they repeatedly affirmed, was obedience. There was need for Court Whigs to speak cautiously at this point, for in admonishing their readers to proper obedience they did not want to appear to be advocating the doctrine of passive obedience. The distinction they sought to draw, however, between a fitting and an unfitting obedience was rather murky. Indeed, Court Whigs often seemed to proclaim a distinction without a difference. Their rejection of passive obedience was, to be sure, unambiguous. The teaching that all subjects owe absolute obedience even to a despotic monarch they held to be "foolish" and "dangerous." It was foolish because it rested upon what one writer stigmatized as "a set of unintelligible Notions, in which Religion and Politicks were strangely blended."[36] It was dangerous because it undermined the basic justification of the Glorious Revolution, converting that act into a lawless rebellion. But having rejected passive obedience as an untenable doctrine, Court Whigs quickly proclaimed the need for an obedience from subjects that—in practice—seemed as uncompromising as the passive obedience they had just disallowed.

Their difficulty can be readily understood. Although in repudiating passive obedience the Court Whigs might have appeared to be endorsing the belief that subjects could on occasion disobey their rulers, this was scarcely the conclusion the ministerialists wanted propounded.

35. *Conduct of the Ministry Compared*, 32; [Robert Walpole], *Some Considerations concerning the Public Funds*, 6–7; *The Advantages of the Hanoverian Succession* (London, 1744); Edward Young, *An Apology for Princes . . . January the 30th, 1728/9* (London, 1729); Thomas Hayter, *A Sermon Preached . . . June 11, 1746* (London, 1746), 29; *Coalition of Patriots*, 25; *Conduct of the Ministry Compared*, 52. Compare Thomas Sherlock, *A Sermon preach'd before the Queen* (London, 1735). The command paraphrases Proverbs 24:21 or I Peter 2:17, both popular texts of obedience.

36. *Full and True Account*, 6–13; *Complete View*, 8.

And so, appealing to their argument that whereas James II had assailed liberties George II was defending them, they concluded that "*Obedience is the Duty of Whigs now*, as *Resistance* was their *Duty* then." The obedience they urged was, in their view, not passive but rational—appropriate because the government was lawful. But it was nonetheless extensive. Bishops and other Court Whig clergy found this theme especially congenial. Edmund Gibson, bishop of London, adjured the citizens of the City to support all magistrates. John Potter, when bishop of Oxford, reminded his auditors that Scripture called kings "Vice-regents of God" and that Christianity taught that obedience to authority was required by God and conscience. Thomas Hayter, bishop of Norwich, and Thomas Sherlock, bishop of Salisbury, advanced still other variations on this exceedingly popular theme.[37] Two scriptural texts placed the force of revealed authority behind this view. In Romans 13:1 St. Paul called upon every soul to "be subject unto the higher powers. For there is no power but of God: the powers that be are ordained of God." In I Peter 2:13–14 the chief of the apostles commanded: "Submit yourself to every ordinance of man for the Lord's sake: whether it be to the king, as supreme: Or unto governors, as unto them that are sent by him." Not everyone considered these two texts strictly compatible, and Hoadly's celebrated sermon had managed to confine even the Pauline injunction, but most clergy usually averted their eyes from the more recondite problems of interpretation and proclaimed the biblical message to be clear: the magistrate was to be obeyed.[38] Natural religion, speaking to those Court Whigs who believed that the Glorious Revolution had successfully and properly de-

37. London *Journal*, July 14, 1733; Edmund Gibson, *The Lord Bishop of London's Third Caveat Against Sedition* (London, 1731); John Potter, *A Sermon Preach'd at the Coronation of King George II* (London, 1727); Thomas Hayter, *A Sermon Preach'd . . . January 30, 1749–50* (London, 1750); Sherlock, *Sermon*. So absolutist could these Court Whig advocates of obedience sound that Thomas Sherlock's sermon, *A Caution Against Speaking Evil of Our Governors and of One Another* (London, 1733), provoked a prompt satirical response, *An Excellent Sermon in Defense of Passive-Obedience and Non-Resistance* (London, 1733).

38. See, e.g., Thomas Sherlock, "Discourse XIII," in *Several Discourses preached at the Temple Church* (4 vols.; London, 1755–58), IV, 371–72; John Mason, *Subjection to the Higher Powers . . . a sermon preach'd . . . November 5, 1740* (London, 1741); Wingfield, *Mischiefs*.

sanctified and demystified monarchy, taught a parallel lesson. It might be true, they acknowledged, that God had not decreed kingly government to be the only legitimate type, but He had warranted the existence of government itself. Thus, though the forms of authority might vary according to choice or chance, the institution of civil authority rested on divine sanction. It was, therefore, "a safe and prudent, and pious Conclusion, to acknowledge Him *who beareth the Sword, to be the Minister of God.*"[39] Again the message was clear: it was the subject's duty to obey.

Still, despite this insistence on obedience, the Court Whigs did not forget the British boast that Britain was a land of liberty. They thus portrayed themselves as the guardians of that liberty. But the liberty they protected was regulated, for they were wont to regard their fellow Britons as inclined to forays into licentiousness. "Were it not for the dread of Punishment," one ministerialist declared, "there would be no living in *England*. It would be a constant Confusion, Anarchy, Sedition, and Rebellion. There would be no such thing as Property, any more than there would be Religion and Freedom." The wise citizen—the man who aspired to lead others—was advised to moderate any undue zeal for liberty. "An unguarded warmth for Liberty, may be commendable in the fire of Youth," cautioned another Court Whig, "but it is no becoming character in one, who is chosen to represent his country in Parliament." In general, the Court Whigs believed that the law was the remedy to which the kingdom should turn in hours of simmering national licentiousness. The ordinary Briton was too apt to stray beyond the frontiers of a regulated liberty, "and so written laws are circumscribed around him, only to keep him right within his sphere; yet free within that sphere."[40] Locke had argued that liberty exists only where it is defined by laws—that laws, far from being the foe of liberty, were its foundation. The Court Whigs agreed. Liberty was the glory of

39. See, *e.g.*, Zachary Pearce, "Sermon XVIII," in *Sermons on Several Subjects* (4 vols.; London, 1778), IV, 383–99; Bentham, *Letter*, 25; *A Church of England-man's Reasons for taking the Oaths to His Present Majesty King George* (London, 1723); *Loyalty to Our King*.

40. *Advantages of the Hanoverian Succession*, 49; *A Letter from a Gentleman in Worcestershire to a Member of Parliament in London* (London, 1727); Parker, *Sermon*, 15. The phrase about "an unguarded warmth" is repeated verbatim in *Letter from a Gentleman in the Country*, 26.

Britain, but the liberty they celebrated was—like much else in Court Whig thinking—a medial entity. Both despotism and license were its enemies. It abhorred the regime that left too much to the discretion of the subject as heartily as it abhorred the regime that left too little.

It is easy to understand how one might regard the Court Whig insistence on the need to impose restraints on liberty as simply the product of an uneasiness about the reliability of the lower orders. This distrust and even fear of the poor marked almost all mid-eighteenth-century political and constitutional thought, whether ministerial or antiministerial. It was founded on the belief that the poor were incorrigibly irrational and passionate, and that they thus embodied in abundance the very characteristics which most endangered social order and civilization. Sometimes the message was muted. In such cases the writer might merely accuse the opposition of seeking to stir up "the *lower* Class of People against all Administrations" or remind the reader that the "Multitude" was too readily duped and led astray. But often the message became strident and vicious. Then the lower class was transformed into "the infuriate Scum and Dregs of the People." And Court Whigs believed that they knew what such unlettered, irrational creatures might do. "Let any Man be assur'd," warned one writer, "that if he can get the Mob on his Side, he stands a fair chance to have his Fooleries or Knaveries overlook'd for many prudential Reasons." With this quotation the deepest Court Whig fear about the character of demagogues and their followers rose to visibility. "Every knave, as well as every fool," the argument continued, "is a leveller."[41] The multitude, led on by such men, found their dangerous, egalitarian inclinations thereby encouraged. The mob threatened Whig notions of social hierarchy. It is true that the Court Whigs who accepted the leadership of Sir Robert Walpole and then Henry Pelham were not captives of the aristocratic presumption that would later characterize Whig apologias in the age of Burke. The ministerialists of the 1730s and 1740s were led by commoners and men of recent ennoblement, and they therefore had no reason to extol the peculiar wisdom of an older, Whiggish

41. *Popularity of Modern Patriotism*, 7; [Gordon], *Appeal*, 28; *Freeholder's Alarm*, 6–7; *History of Patriotism*, 28; *The Conduct of the Ministry impartially examined* (London, 1756), 6.

peerage.[42] But they still accepted the view that society was graded and that men of eminence—landed, wealthy, and perhaps enterprising—should direct affairs. At root, therefore, the Court Whig fear of the lower orders was the fear of radical disorder and overwhelming confusion.

But despite all the evidence that the Court Whigs shared with the entire landed class this fear of the lower classes, it is important to realize that their insistence on the need for restraints to liberty was not simply a response to their dread of lower-class leveling. It was a position that followed naturally from their recognition that good governance aimed at several different ends. If liberty were the only good, the purpose of government could be easily understood as the maximization of freedom. The quality of a government could then be assessed by measuring how well it fulfilled this purpose. But in fact liberty was only one among a cluster of goods. The British, it was true, had been peculiarly fortunate in discovering ways to create and maintain a broad range of liberties for themselves. But such good fortune did not eliminate the need to seek the other ideals as well. The support of true religion, the protection of property, national defense, the promotion of prosperity, undistorted justice, social tranquillity—all these vied with liberty as goods that a wise administration should pursue.[43] Indeed, they did more than just compete with liberty for attention. All, in truth, were at least partly inconsistent with the potential claims of liberty. The protection afforded the Church of England infringed to some extent upon the freedom of Protestant dissenters and considerably upon the freedom of Roman Catholics. The protection offered to property imposed limits on the freedom of nonowners. The need to provide for the national defense allowed the government to conscript sailors. The policies adopted for promoting prosperity entailed governmental prohibitions on various aspiring merchants. The procedures of justice involved the detention and often the punishment of subjects.

42. A partial exception is *Humble Address* 20.

43. The list is drawn from discussions of the purposes of government found in various Court Whig tracts. It is notable that the defense of property, though often mentioned, is rarely a prominent consideration in Court Whig writings. Of course, only those mesmerized by the figure of Locke or by scholars who make Whigs out to be apologists for bourgeois acquisitiveness will be surprised by this comparative inattention.

And the preservation of tranquillity rested upon the capacity of the government to restrain, coerce, and incarcerate through both law and physical force. When the topic they were addressing permitted pronouncements of a general sort, most Court Whig writers recognized the multi-faceted nature of government's responsibility. They often summed it up under a rubric that, naturally enough in a Latinate age, enjoyed wide circulation: *Salus populi suprema lex*.[44] It was a frustratingly vague prescription but not without use as a guide for conduct. The Patriots who contended daily with the ministers also held the well-being of the people to be the highest law. But the two camps disagreed on the substance of *salus*. To the Court Whigs the term was not equivalent to "liberty" pure and simple. Liberty constituted but a part of *salus populi*, and being only a part it could not make absolute demands. Thus the claims of liberty were bounded; proper liberty was a restrained liberty.

How were the claims of these various goods to be adjudicated? What means existed to weigh the partially incompatible demands of property, defense, tranquillity, and liberty? How was *salus populi* to be interpreted in concrete situations? The Court Whig answer to these questions was unequivocal. The constitution provided procedures for enacting and implementing decisions, but the nation must look to the ministry for wise proposals antecedent to such decisions. It was the ministry that initiated all proposals for altering "Laws and Usages," and its members, one Court Whig pamphleteer urged, "must be allowed to be the best Judges of their various Tendencies, and best capable of distinguishing their good or ill Effects." The ministry made the balanced constitution work. It was—though no one (so far as I know) said it outright—the balancing mechanism. Several writers came close to making this role explicit. The author of a tract from the year of the excise crisis assumed that the ministry's function was to assure that "the great *Machine of Government* moves *exact* and *easy*." William Arnall spoke of the ministry as a body that proposed and attempted actions, and in analyzing the constitution he positioned the ministry at least inferentially between the countervailing forces of crown and Parliament. Early in the

44. Squire, *Letter to a Tory Friend*.

next decade an anonymous author, speaking more concretely, ascribed to the ministry the duty of keeping the House of Commons steady and settled so that business might be smoothly transacted.[45] Each writer saw the ministry as the body that brought crown and Parliament into adequate resonance. And within the model of a balanced constitution, that vision was in effect to see the ministry as the balancing force.

The explanation for the difficulty Court Whig writers had in articulating this ministerial function was rooted in the procedure by which men became ministers: they were selected by the king. Chosen by the crown (in a manner in which the House of Commons entirely and the House of Lords largely were not), the ministers were considered an aspect of the crown. They even called themselves "the king's servants." Being an aspect of the crown, they were theoretically not free to serve as a balancing agency between the crown and the houses of Parliament. Since the crown had for some time been synonymous with the executive force in the constitution, it posed no difficulty for Court Whigs that since the days of William III de facto direction of affairs had been shifting powerfully away from the incumbent monarch to the ministers. Whoever in fact did the directing, whether monarch or minister, such direction was conceived of as the crown operating in its executive capacity. Thus it was possible to fit the ministry as an executive cabinet easily into the constitutional thinking of the age. And it was also easy for the opposition to attack it on the similarly traditional grounds that the king was being badly advised. What the Court Whigs could not quite come to was an acknowledgment that the ministers were not just advising the king—that they were in fact, as noted, directing him. Lord Hardwicke's famous conversation with George II, cited earlier, turned precisely on this point. George spoke accurately when he said he was being forced; Hardwicke knew that there was much merit to the king's lament but preferred to stick with older—and not entirely inappropriate—categories. Yet because Court Whigs could not articulate the truth about what ministries were doing, a tension persisted in their writings throughout the Court Whig period between reasonably accurate descriptions of what ministries really did and irrelevant analy-

45. *Humble Address*, 28; *Conduct of the Ministry Compared*, 5; [Arnall], *Opposition No Proof; Second Letter to a Member of Parliament*, 62–63.

ses of how the constitution was functioning. To this same inability analytically to separate the ministry from the crown may be ascribed the difficulties noted earlier in giving any precision to the concept of balance. Although very visible, the ministry was unknown to theory. And though making the judgments that brought the recognized elements of the constitution into balance, the ministry, because it appeared to be one of those elements, was theoretically disabled from accomplishing what it in fact did.

What in fact *did* it do? The Court Whig answer to this question was couched in general terms. It served both monarch and nation. Comprised of able men, alert to the interests of the kingdom and in tune with the mood of its political classes, the ministry had the task of determining which measures would be good for the kingdom and, if good, whether they could be enacted. Court Whig ministers were outspoken friends of the prerogative. What in theory was the king's was in practice theirs. But they did not speak as if they regarded the prerogative as a royal possession to be snatched from its owner. They tended instead to view the prerogative not as the personal property of the monarch but as a trust held by the crown for the people. Since Court Whigs cast themselves as friends of these people, they saw no threat to liberty in a strong and active prerogative. The king, its executant, was under the control of a ministry whose adherence to Whiggery guaranteed the effective and public-spirited exercise of its power. The Court Whigs were unembarrassed by the consolidation of governmental authority which occurred during their years of office through the suppression of the Scottish secretariat, the enactment of theatrical licensing, the (temporary) diminution of the power of the court of common council in London, the resistance against demands for both a more powerful militia and greater colonial autonomy, and the continued disallowance of convocation. In recommending and securing these measures the Court Whig ministers were simply fulfilling their duty to provide decisive, firm, and fair leadership to the kingdom. It was decisive by virtue of the ministerial command of the prerogative, firm by virtue of the status and wealth of the ministers, and fair by virtue of their Court Whiggery.

The activities of the ministry required the application of prudential judgment, and it was characteristic of prudential judgment—as the ministry's behavior in 1733, 1739, and 1748 dramatically demonstrated—that its conclusions might alter as the situation shifted. A tract from 1756 distinguished between "principles" and "conditions." A wise government kept certain fundamental principles always in mind, but the precise method of their application would vary in accordance with differing conditions.[46] Carried far enough, such reasoning could seem to justify ministerial indecisiveness. But Court Whigs held irrelevant Lord Chesterfield's assertion that the government had no fixed design. "It is very strange that he did not see that the *Variation* of Councils is a thing incident to the *State* of our *Affairs*, and *inseparable* from the *Form* of our *Constitution*." The chief constraint that Court Whigs saw operating upon a ministry's capacity to choose as it wished was its need to propose only those measures that could secure both parliamentary and royal approval. If it should seek to impose its will upon an unwilling legislature or monarch, it would soon find itself dismissed. Thus, the Court Whigs asserted, no ministry could behave in a manner disadvantageous to the kingdom. And if any single minister sought to abuse his trust, he would be isolated and driven from office. "Was it ever known," asked an apologist for Walpole, "that the People pursued a wicked M—r in vain?"[47] The most famous Roman exponent of prudential judgment, Cicero, had long ago provided a prescription for good government that all Court Whigs would accept: "Homines ad Deos nulla re propius accedunt, quàm salutem Hominibus dando."[48]

Seeing themselves and their ministry as sober, intelligent, and prudential, and believing the actions of the ministry to have been—with few exceptions—widely popular, the Court Whigs were finally unwilling to allow the opposition uncontestedly to appropriate for themselves the terms "Patriot" and "Country" with all their favorable implications. "True Patriotism," wrote one Court Whig in criticism of the opposi-

46. *Occasional Patriot*, 20–21; compare [Horace Walpole], *Rise and Fall*, 58.
47. *The Resignation Discussed* (London, 1748), 48; [Gordon], *Appeal*, 14; *Patriot and the Minister*, 46.
48. Epigraph to *A Defense of the Measures of the Present Administration. Being an Impartial Answer to What Has Been Objected Against It* (London, 1731).

tion's factionalism, "like true Religion, is a peaceable Principle." "The real Patriot," argued another, against the pretensions of the opposition, "will always keep his Integrity, and will never, for the sake of being in Power, or any other Consideration, no, not of Liberty or Life itself, dear as they are to some People, do any Thing that he knows is contrary to the true Good of his Country." That formulation included the conventional Court Whig subordination of liberty to *salus populi.* Yet another Court Whig writer employed lamely jogging doggerel to make the same point:

> Many there are, in weighty Trusts of State,
> Patriots of Right, who all base actions hate;
> Who neither King, nor Subject would betray
> Though Pow'r and Gold, a Gift before them lay.

Meanwhile, various Court Whig writers thought it odd that the so-called "Country" members often did not hold seats beyond the metropolis and that the term "Country" as a political designation should be denied men who loved their homeland. Francis Osborne argued that the Court *was* the Country. "The Court Interest is the Country Interest," he declared, and "there is not an Interest in the Kingdom carrying on against the Court, but what is an Interest against the Country."[49] That formulation included the conventional Court Whig contention that only the Court Whigs were true to the constitution.

The capstone of all Court Whig argumentation was the assertion that the kingdom had never been so well governed. Such a view incorporated the contention that liberty was secure. "No period of Time can be instanced, when LIBERTY hath been more amply exercised and enjoyed, than at the present Hour." With such pronouncements the Court Whigs met the chief thrust of opposition argument. But their position affirmed much more than simply the ministry's fidelity to freedom. From among several possible extended statements one will suffice to exemplify the range of the Court Whig claim.[50]

49. *Second Letter to a Member of Parliament,* 11; *A Dissertation on Patriotism: shewing, the use of those two great Qualifications of a Patriot, Integrity and Courage* (London, 1735), iv; *The Happy Government: or, The Constitution of Great Britain* (London, 1734); *Complete View,* 26; [Arnall], *Opposition No Proof,* 18; *London Journal,* April 20, 1734.
50. *Difference Computed,* 39; *Address to the Freeholders of Great Britain,* 34–35.

For do we not, if view'd with *Impartial Eye*, see our *Religion*, *Laws*, *Liberty*, and *Property*, *safe and secure*, under the mild and prudent *Administration* of our present most *Gracious Sovereign*? We can reflect back with infinite Pleasure and Satisfaction, that *no Invasion of Property*, *no Interruption of Justice*, *no extending the Prerogative*, no not in any *one Instance contrary to Law*, has been *attempted during his Reign*: But Liberty, Peace, Plenty, and a Flourishing Trade, are the *good Things* of which we may boast.

All the major Court Whig themes are here recapitulated—the devotion to a cluster of goods, the elevation of prudence, the reverence to the king, the adherence to legality. But in a broader perspective Cicero had already described a good administration. Not surprisingly, the Roman giant was invoked to support the Court Whigs.[51]

Omnino qui Reipublicae praefuturi sunt duo *Platonis* Praecepta teneant; unum, ut Utilitatem Civium sic tueantur ut, quaecuque agunt, ad eam referant, obliti Commodorum suorum; alterum, ut totum Corpus Reipublicae curent, ne, dum Partem aliquam tuentur, Reliquas deserant.

The Court Whigs saw themselves as faithful disciples of just such Ciceronian prudence.

51. *Letter to William Pulteney.* The quotation is from Cicero's *De officiis. On Duties*, trans. Harry G. Edinger (New York, 1974), I, 85.

Chapter VIII

The Ciceronian Vision

I

Although Court Whiggery took varied forms, a common disposition toward the task of government underlay this diversity. To define this disposition negatively it can be stated that Court Whigs were not Catonic. There was no way they could be. The Cato that the oppositionists of the age found serviceable was too suspicious of power to countenance its exercise by authority, too excited in his warnings to allow moderate solutions, and too inflexible in his posture to tolerate compromise. He was a symbol suitable to an hour of crisis, when the enemy was perfidious, when half-way measures were but pathmarks on the road to ruin, and when resistance to tyranny had become the overriding duty of the citizen. Cato breathed fire and defiance. He represented unflinching commitment to a cause. He was the zealot, the ideologue, the true believer. But Court Whigs believed that this attitude could not sustain governance. What was called for in a state characterized by a plurality of interests and a not insignificant element of popular participation was an attitude of toleration and flexibility. Ruler and ruled had to be willing to acknowledge that compromise might often be appropriate, that complex problems did not allow simple solutions, and that one might dissent from another's view without thereby demonstrating one's own iniquity. Thus almost from the moment Walpole's administration took form and found itself assailed by the Country Whiggery of *Cato's Letters*, the Court Whigs sought to deprive the opposition of the utility of their Roman symbol.

Two alternative programs suggested themselves. By the first the Whigs would try to make Cato their own; by the second they would seek to discredit him entirely. Initially the program of appropriating Cato was dominant. As soon as the government purchased control of the London *Journal* it sent out a signal over Hoadly's pseudonym "Britannicus." The author denounced those mischief-makers who encouraged men to carry their opposition to "Extremes"; he attributed their venom to "Resentment and Anger"; he accused them of failing to be constructive. The following week "Britannicus" gave greater focus to his previous remarks with the comment that a stern look and shoddy clothes did not suffice to make a Cato. Within another six weeks the writer had brought Cato completely within the Court Whig fold: "Who can help, indeed, lamenting the hard fate of CATO?—To see his *Name* made Use of to propagate Principles, which were those of his greatest Adversary." The hero of republican Rome was being tamed. Others turned to variations on the theme. A governmental writer of 1731, for example, lauded Addison's drama but added that "*Cato* itself has increased the Evils of the present Time, how many Poetasters have since then infested the World with wild Notions of Liberty and Patriotism! What strange romantick Whims have they had of Freedom, and Independence from Power." As late as 1741 Cato was hailed by a ministerial writer as one who preferred to pursue the true interests of his people even when such a course threatened him with unpopularity. The intention of such writers was manifestly to accept the luster of Cato's name while denying legitimacy to opposition efforts to invoke it.[1]

But this program had the flaw of publicizing a figure who was more readily assimilable in opposition attacks than in governmental defenses. Thus other Court Whigs turned to the bolder strategy of defaming the hero himself. One pamphleteer, perhaps Matthew Tindal, denounced Cato as unrealistic and hence demagogic. Cato, he noted, had defended Brutus although Brutus had been faithless to his friend and had, through his dreadful act, only brought on war. Another writer reminded readers in monarchical Britain that Cato had been a repub-

1. London *Journal*, September 15, 22, November 10, 1722; *Universal Spectator and Weekly Journal*, April 10, 1731, quoted in Loftis, *Politics of Drama*, 82; *Letter to a Member of Parliament*, 57.

lican. The Roman was guilty of making Brutus "the true Pattern and Model of exact Virtue. . . . With Cato and his Party it is plain, a *King* and a *Tyrant* are equivalent Names." Still another denounced Cato's encouragement to ingratitude. Even the London *Journal*, not notably hostile to Cato in Francis Osborne's day, found fault. Cato, it declared, fell short of the ranks of the fullest heroes because he "wanted *Fortitude* or *Resolution* of Soul, to *bear the present State of Things*," and because he displayed "rather a *sullen Stubbornness*, and high Pride of Heart, than *true Greatness* and *Love of Virtue*."[2]

It is patently true that the Cato against whom these writings were directed was the pseudonymous figure whose epistles so irritated Walpole. But it is important to realize that they were aimed more deeply at the world view associated with the name of Cato—at the Catonic vision. For only if this were so can we make sense of the strategy employed by Cato's opponents. The name "Cato" aggregated three separate historical personae: the Censor (234–149 B.C.), who defended integrity in the age of the Scipiones Africani and unweariedly thundered his terse monition about Carthage; the martyr at Utica (95–46 B.C.), who spoke through Addison as well as a host of classical encomiasts; and the political letter writer (1721–1724), who bedeviled Walpole. Since all three were understood to represent the same attitude— were in fact but three modulations of the same image of a zealot—an attack on one was an attack on all. Thus the letter writer was wounded when a critic found the Utican's opposition to Caesar inconsistent with his odd support for the still more wicked Pompey. Thus too it mattered not that a double confusion appeared in the title of one ministerialist pamphlet, *The Censor Censur'd: or, Cato turned Catiline*. For even though history was violated by making the Censor and Catiline contemporaries, and polemics were misconstrued by equating the letter writer with the Censor rather than with the man who died at Utica, the pamphlet was successful.[3] Indeed, the confusions enhanced its power. The foe of the ministry was not a man of flesh and bone but an

2. [Tindal(?)], *Defense*, 5, 30; *Cato's Principles*, 12, 17; *The Censor Censur'd: or, Cato turned Catiline* (London, 1722), 22; London *Journal*, July 1, 1732.

3. *Poplicola's Supplement to Cato's Letter, concerning Popularity* (London, 1722), 37; *Censor Censur'd*.

attitude and perspective on politics. Three different Catos symbolized that attitude, and the vulnerability of one could be transformed into the vulnerability of all. The inclusive quality of the symbol, initially an asset for its adopters, soon became a liability.

But it was insufficient for the Court Whigs simply to discredit the Catonic vision. What was needed was an alternative perspective—an approach to politics identified with a figure who matched Cato's love of liberty and country, exceeded him in flexibility and tolerance, and boasted a keener eye for political reality. Such a figure was at hand. The most famous Roman republican of all, Marcus Tullius Cicero— "Tully" as the eighteenth century was wont to call him—possessed exactly the combination of qualities that the Court Whigs needed. At the height of his public career he supervised the successful defense of Rome against Catiline and his fellow conspirators. For this action he became the first to receive the honorary designation of *Pater Patriae*. His public career closed when his powerful denunciations of Mark Antony drove that incensed man to secure the murder of his accuser. Like his contemporary Cato Uticensis, Cicero had aligned himself with the *optimates*, seeking to preserve the old balanced constitution from what he believed to be the demagoguery of the *populares*. He fought for the rights of property and for what he termed *concordia ordinum*—a happy cooperation between the senators and knights of Roman society. For his stand he suffered at the hands of Clodius' band of gangsters, whose assault on Cicero exemplified what a mad and frenzied mob might do when won over by a vicious manipulator of passion. Admittedly Cicero's career posed occasional problems: he appeared, for example, to have submitted to the power of the triumvirs on terms far less honorable than Cato's. But of such problems advantage could still be made. They showed either that Cicero knew the need to change responses as external conditions changed or that the great too could err. Thus, depending on one's apologetic needs, Cicero could be held to be an example of realistic flexibility or a demonstration that a few inevitable errors were not sufficient cause to remove a minister from office. And in any event the problems were only a minor blemish in a career otherwise rich in achievement and example.

Nor was this all. Whereas Cato needed men like Addison to give him tongue for later generations, Cicero spoke for himself. He was simultaneously a man of affairs and a philosopher. Of his numerous writings three stood preeminent for the eighteenth century. One, the treatise on the republic, was lost, save for Scipio's dream and some occasional fragments transcribed by other ancient authors. It was thus honored in its absence.[4] De Legibus contained portions of Cicero's laws for the republic but was esteemed most for its analysis of the origin of law, and De Officiis prescribed a code of conduct for the good man. Cicero had taken upon himself the task of transmitting the ideas of the Greeks to the Romans, but in so doing he transformed a moral and political philosophy appropriate to the πόλις to the wider Roman world—a world that in turn bore clear resemblances to early Hanoverian England. His philosophy was grounded in the conviction that self-sufficiency was essential to the good life. In a world of unpredictable and sometimes turbulent change, each individual was taught to rely on himself. This view was Stoic, but Cicero, far from being wedded to the Stoa, was eclectic in his philosophical doctrine. He was disposed to eschew the simplistic answer. Political life was complex, he taught, and most dilemmas admitted of no total resolution. The best statesman was the man who exercised prudentia in his conduct of office—that is, the man who kept the goal of justice in mind in his deliberations, who avoided extremes in proposing or executing policy, and who could discriminate between the important and the trivial.[5] The last point underlay the substance of Cicero's most famous criticism of Cato. Too much an original Stoic, Cato had not learned the lessons taught by the Middle Stoa: that evil comes in degrees, and that one could distinguish between major and minor sins.[6] Thus, whereas Cato would adhere to the principles of the pure Stoic wise man—mutare sententiam turpe

4. The palimpsest carrying the bulk of what we know of De Republica was not discovered until 1820.

5. "Prudentia est rerum bonarum et malarum neutrarumque scientia." De Inventione, 2. 53. 160, in Marcus Tullius Cicero, M. Tulii Ciceronis Opera, ed. J. G. Baiter and C. L. Kayser (11 vols.; Leipzig, 1860–69), Vol. I, 103–208.

6. See especially the light but sharp assault in Pro Murena, 61, in Cicero, Ciceronis Opera, Vol. IV, 246–79. Cicero also described Cato as inflexible rather than wise: "unus est qui curet constantia magis et integritate quam, ut mihi videtur, consilio aut ingenio." Ad. Att., 1. 18. 7, in Cicero, Ciceronis Opera, Vol. X.

est—Cicero taught a more flexible wisdom that finally admonished the acceptance of reality. It was the sort of pragmatic wisdom Court Whigs wanted vaunted in the 1720s.[7]

De Officiis, the most widely read ethical treatise of the era, dealt with the various duties incumbent upon man. All educated Britons knew Tully's *Offices*, for it held the center of the classical curriculum at school and university. And knowing it, they were familiar with Cicero's characteristic stance.[8] Men, he asserted, were morally flawed. "Now, the men we live with are not perfect and ideally wise, but men who do very well, if there be found in them but the semblance of virtue." This condition followed from the nature of man's spirit, which in its essential activities was composed of two forces, the appetite and the reason. Appetite impelled man, while reason guided. In a moral man, Cicero wrote, "reason commands, appetite obeys." But such perfect coordination of the two forces did not always obtain, and when it failed, immorality ensued. The four classical virtues stood preeminent for man: wisdom, justice, courage, and temperance. Each involved the application of reason to the affairs of man, generally in such a manner as to control the directives of appetite or fear. Virtues were not to be cultivated in private or solely through contemplation; their proper arena was the public life. "For the whole glory of virtue is in activity," Tully wrote in a famous phrase. And he later made clear that this judgment required of the natural leaders of a community that they offer their services to the state. "But those whom nature endowed with the capacity for administering public affairs should put aside all hesitation, enter the race for public office, and take a hand in directing the government; for in no other way can a government be administered or

7. The discussion in this and the next two paragraphs is heavily indebted to the essays in T. A. Dorey, ed., *Cicero* (London, 1965), especially to A. E. Douglas, "Cicero the Philosopher," and H. H. Scullard, "The Political Career of a *Novus Homo*." See also Lily Ross Taylor, *Party Politics in the Age of Caesar* (Berkeley, 1949), and Ronald Syme, *The Roman Revolution* (Oxford, 1939).

8. Martin Lowther Clarke, *Classical Education in Britain, 1500–1900* (Cambridge, 1959), 51, 71; Paul Fussell, *The Rhetorical World of Augustan Humanism: Ethics and Imagery from Swift to Burke* (Oxford, 1965), 302. Locke recommended the Bible and the *Offices* as the primers for instruction in virtue. James L. Axtell (ed.), *The Educational Writings of John Locke* (Cambridge, 1968), 294.

greatness of spirit be made manifest."[9] In such a manner did Cicero move from presuppositions about human nature to the need for men with the capacity for and status of leadership to assume the reins of power.

Cicero's instruction on the proper way to administer power was congenial to Court Whigs. "It is the particular responsibility of the magistrate," he declared, "to realize that he represents the character of the state and that he ought to maintain its dignity and distinction, to preserve its laws, to define rights, to remember the things entrusted to his care." Moreover, Tully avoided the dogmatic. Specifically, he held that moral principles were not absolute—that conduct must conform to the requirements of the occasion and that in unusual instances even the most powerful of ethical commands might be properly ignored. "Many actions that naturally appear to be right actions," he wrote, "turn into wrong actions in certain circumstances." The basis for Tully's rejection of moral absolutism was his insistence on the legitimacy of consulting expediency—*utilitas*—when choosing actions. By expediency he did not mean crass self-interest. But the term entailed, if not reference to selfish needs, then at least reference to the constraints of reality. The futile gesture, the heroic but impotent stand, the destruction of self in a hopeless cause—all were actions that Cicero was reluctant to deem moral. His crowning ethical conclusion, the product of a lifetime of participation in public affairs and reflection thereon, easy to misunderstand and mock but neither tawdry nor stupid, was that expediency and morality coincided. "There can still be no doubt," he declared, "that advantageousness [*utilitas*] can never conflict with right conduct." In this manner the great republican elevated the realm of the expedient to the level of the ethical. The same fusion informed his celebrated dictum about public policy: "salus populi suprema lex esto." Through his life and writings Tully gave Court Whigs a splendid exemplification of the virtues of that style of thought appropriate to expediential thinking—the virtues, that is, of common sense, moderation, toleration,

9. Marcus Tullius Cicero, *De Officiis*, trans. Walter Miller (New York, 1928), 1. 46; 1. 101; 1. 19; 1. 72. In assessing the extracts from Cicero the reader should keep in mind A. E. Douglas' warning: "Cicero is the least quotable of all great writers." "Cicero the Philosopher," 159.

forebearance, and of the broad over the narrow perspective. The goal of a statesman, he once wrote in a famous but difficult phrase, was "cum dignitate otium."[10] Because educated Britons had learned their Tully while mastering their Latin—because *utilitas* and *prudentia* and *otium* resonated in their minds—Court Whigs knew that the impress of Cicero had helped give form to those British minds.[11]

What Court Whigs needed was an opportunity to arouse this latent pattern of political Ciceronianism, to breathe life into Tully's Latin forms and ideas, to give them a forcefulness and a pertinence that could not be denied. Laurence Echard had provided the age with its standard history of Rome and with a picture of Cicero that was widely accepted. Tully was "a Man, as Julius Caesar observes, that obtain'd a Laurel as much above all Triumphs, as the Enlargement of the Bounds of the Roman Wit, was above that of the Bounds of the Roman Empire." Such an interpretation, though adulatory, lost much usefulness for the Court Whigs by its focus on Cicero's literary achievements. The Court Whigs sought to shift attention to the politician. It helped their cause that Addison, the glorifier of Cato, was also a strong admirer of Cicero. In various numbers of the *Freeholder*, first published in the very shadow of the Fifteen and later republished, he spoke of the Roman with the deepest respect. Tully was, for Addison, the best versed of all Romans in the theory and practice of government. He was, more extravagantly, "the most consummate statesman of all antiquity." John Toland was another Whig admirer of the Roman. In *The State-Anatomy of Great Britain* of 1717 he likened the British constitution to Cicero's mixed constitution, and five years earlier, in *Cicero Illustratus*, he had advanced a proposal—never effected—to bring out an annotated edition of Tully's works so that the oft-quoted master might be more correctly

10. Cicero, *De Officiis*, 1. 124; 3. 95; 3. 11. Marcus Tullius Cicero, *De Legibus*, trans. Clinton Walker (New York, 1928), 3. 3. 8. *Pro Sestio*, in Cicero, *Ciceronis Opera*, Vol. V, 1–54. See Charles Wirszubski, "Cicero's *Cum Dignitate Otium*: A Reconsideration," *Journal of Roman Studies*, XLIV (1954), 1–13.

11. Thaddäus Zielinski, *Cicero im Wandel der Jahrhunderte* (Leipzig, 1908), in Chapters 16 and 17 treats Cicero's influence on religious thought in eighteenth-century Britain. Wilbur Samuel Howell, *Eighteenth-Century British Logic and Rhetoric* (Princeton, N.J., 1971), *passim*, argues for Cicero's massive and rich influence upon the rhetoric of the era. For both Zielinski and Howell the Roman's influence transcended political divisions.

understood. In 1722 efforts were made to promote this consummate statesmanship and shrewd constitutionalism as replacements for Cato's unyielding morality. In attacking the demagoguery of Cato Matthew Tindal appositely quoted Cicero on the need for realism. The author of *The Censor Censur'd* assailed the ingratitude of the Catonic parties and quoted Cicero to the effect that "we ought to lay aside all Animosity and Hatred, in Consideration of the Commonwealth and Public Utility."[12] The Ciceronian alternative was being shaped.

Then in late 1722 and early 1723 came the dual opportunity that the Court Whigs needed. Wicked conspiracy suddenly seemed to abound. Francis Atterbury, bishop of Rochester, was implicated in a Jacobite plot against George I, and Robert Walpole moved against him with the full force of the law—and then some. Atterbury retreated into exile. By his vigorous action, Walpole asserted, he had helped save the state from the conspirators. Almost simultaneously the government moved against the so-called Blacks—men who darkened their faces as disguises while engaged in poaching—by securing passage of what was called the Black Act. This notorious measure not only transformed many crimes against property into capital offenses but also permitted procedural shortcuts in prosecutions that in effect curtailed traditional liberties of defendants. Ministerial spokesmen justified the severity of the legislation by arguing that Blacks, under leadership of a shadowy "King John," constituted a conspiracy against property and the state.[13] To the educated of an age steeped in classical history the parallel between Atterbury or "John" and Catiline leapt quickly to mind. Each

12. Laurence Echard, *The Roman History from the Building of the City, to the Perfect Settlement of the Empire by Augustus Caesar* (London, 1695), 372. (In 1683 the very popular translation of Plutarch's *Lives* associated with Dryden had appeared.) Joseph Addison, *Freeholder*, nos. 29, 51, in Vol. IV of *The Works of the Right Honourable Joseph Addison*, ed. Richard Hurd (4 vols.; New York, 1811). John Toland, *The State-Anatomy of Great Britain* (London, 1717); [Tindal(?)], *Defense*; *Censor Censur'd*, 22. See also Günther Gawlick, "Cicero and the Enlightenment." *Studies on Voltaire and the Eighteenth Century*, XXV (1963), 657–82.

13. For details of the Atterbury plot, see G. V. Bennett, "Jacobitism and the Rise of Walpole," in *Historical Perspectives: Studies in English Thought and Society in honour of J. H. Plumb*, ed. Neil McKendrick (London, 1974). On the Black Act, see Thompson, *Whigs and Hunters*, and Pat Rogers, "The Waltham Blacks and the Black Act," *Historical Journal*, XVII (1974), 465–86.

conspirator had sought to undo the state; each had then found himself destroyed through quasi-legal procedures that the appropriate legislatures had legitimized for times of extraordinary danger. With these comparisons the Court Whig difficulty evaporated. Now they were not only able to present Cicero's ideas and actions as worthy of reverence; they were able to do even better—to dress up Walpole himself as Tully *redivivus*.

The effort to drape Walpole with the toga was an important element in the Court Whig campaign to replace Catonism with Ciceronianism. Benjamin Hoadly experimented with the conflation of the Briton and the Roman as early as November, 1722.[14] But the central contribution to the polemical transformation was the pamphlet *Clodius and Cicero*. Published in 1727 and almost certainly the work of William Arnall, Walpole's chief propagandist, the tract was designed to let even the dullest of readers understand that Tully and Sir Robert were simply variations on the same theme of patriotic and responsible statesmanship. All people in high office—simply by virtue of holding that trust—will have detractors. "No matter for their Innocence, or Sufficiency, or Usefulness, or any superior Qualifications or Talents; their Exaltation and Importance is Crime enough." Thus almost any positive action by a person in power would be seized upon by his enemies as a sign of his bad intentions. Precisely for this reason, the existence of complaints against a government was never in itself evidence of evil practices by that government. "Opposition to Power, is far from being a sure Proof of the Abuse of Power." For an example one needed only to look to Cicero. Even he, "the ablest Statesman and Orator in *Rome*, and her best Patriot," had had his critics, and preeminent among them was his former friend Clodius, who had supported the suppression of the Catilinarians but had later turned demagogue to accuse Cicero of shedding blood in that action. The charge was acknowledged to be true. But Cicero had sanctioned bloodletting only with the authorization of the Senate and at a critical moment for the state. "It was to suppress a Conspiracy"—that word rich in immediate overtones for a reader of the 1720s—"the most barbarous and sanguinary that ever threaten'd

14. London *Journal*, November 3, 1722.

Rome," that Cicero had authorized the deeds for which Clodius reproached him. Every reader conversant with recent political events would have understood how to translate the allegory: Clodius was Pulteney and Cicero was Walpole.

Arnall then turned from his classical parallels to propound some general truths. No society could exist, he wrote, without occasional difficulties for some of its citizens. "There are certain Evils and Inconveniences inseparable from Society, nay blended with the Nature of it, and often arising from the best Regulations which human Wisdom can invent, or human Fraility can bear." But carping was not merely irrelevant to the determination of whether wickedness really existed in government. It was actually harmful, since it tended to disaffect the less reflective citizens from their habitual attitude of obedience. To complain was to undermine. Thus in Britain to criticize the government while professing loyalty to it was finally unpatriotic. Those who complained of unavoidable evils—who sought to stir up popular indignation against grievances that were irremediable—were serving only the Pretender. However much they might deny the fact, they simply abetted conspiracy. But Cicero had known how to deal with conspiracies against the state, and so, the reader could infer, did Walpole. The pamphlet concluded with a Ciceronian view of the limits of power: "No Civil Institution was ever framed with such Exactness and Equality, as effectually to preclude all Publick Grievances and Corruption."[15]

The campaign to depict Walpole as a reincarnation of Tully continued for the next fifteen years. Sometimes the comparison was oblique or merely implicit. In 1729 the London *Journal* reminded its readers that in classical times neither the "Statesman" nor the "Philosopher"— only Tully qualified for such dual designation—curried to the mob. Later, after Francis Osborne retired from the journal and Ralph Freeman, another pseudonymous writer, assumed the role of chief political correspondent, the *Journal* regularly adverted to the great Roman. Meanwhile, in 1733 Sir Richard Steele's old creation, Sir Anthony Freeport, was restored to breath to try to talk sense into Timothy Squat, a gentleman of invincible ignorance, unbounded zeal, and in-

15. [Arnall], *Clodius.*

tense parochialism, who therefore paraded Cato as his hero. In this fashion the Catonic image was measured by Ciceronian standards and found wanting. More pointedly, Clodiuses and Catilines abounded in Court Whig pamphlets of the 1730s, a particularly memorable example of the latter being the identification of the "late" Caleb D'Anvers with the conspirator in *The Patriot at Full Length*. "As he lived, so he died, an Enemy to his King, to his Country, and to all good Men." Most readers could be presumed to know who had thwarted the plans of that malevolent traitor. Meanwhile, when it was necessary to give expression to a Walpolean rebuttal of opposition contentions, Tully was often pertinently quoted.

But indirection, implication, and apposite quotation, though useful, were clearly not deemed polemically sufficient, and so in various tracts of the era the identification of Walpole with Cicero was made far more explicit. The London *Journal* devoted three articles to an exploration of the parallel between the Catilinarian conspirators and the Patriots and concluded with the approving reminder that Cicero had pursued the former "with great *Rigour* and *Severity*." "What People," asked a Walpolean pamphlet, "would not repose Confidence in a Cicero, different from that which a *Catiline* would expect from them?" A Court Whig denunciation of faction concluded with the judgment that "we have our Catilines as well as Rome, and 'tis well we are so happy to have a *Cicero* to oppose them." The Court Whig poet Leonard Welsted styled Pope as "the Friend of Catiline, and Tully's Foe." A brief and encomiastic biography of the chief minister lauded him, with Burghley, as *Pater Patriae*. And in a poetic defense of Sir Robert's command the opposition was rebuked:

> Cease, Faction, cease
>   where-e'er the Hate succeeds,
> A Cicero's banish'd
>   or a Sydney bleeds.

A ministerial outline of modern British history, under the transparent disguise of Roman nomenclature, gave Walpole's role to "Tullius."[16]

16. London *Journal*, July 13, 1729 (compare issues of November 15, December 20, 1735, January 22, October 20, 1737, May 6, 1738); *Dialogue*; *The Patriot at Full Length; or, An Inscription for an Obelisk* (London, 1735), 1, 7; [John, Lord Hervey], *The Reply of a*

Meanwhile, in 1741 the eminent Johann Lorenz Natter struck a medal bearing Walpole on the obverse and Cicero on the reverse.[17] The thrust of the ministerial campaign was clear; a Ciceronian attitude toward politics was being extolled and a Ciceronian governor being created.

In 1741, with the publication of Conyers Middleton's *The History of the Life of Marcus Tullius Cicero*, the Court Whig conflation of Walpolean and Ciceronian images received a powerful and masterful new endorsement. Acclaimed as a leading scholar of the day, Middleton had devoted years to the biography. It was dedicated to Lord Hervey, the patron whom Middleton praised as statesman and scholar. The study likened the Roman republican constitution to eighteenth-century Britain's. It singled Cicero out from among his illustrious republican colleagues for his "pacific and civil character" and commended him as a ruler of the sort that was "most beneficial to mankind, whose sole ambition is, to support the laws, the rights and liberties of his citizens." Against those, such as Anthony Collins, who held that Cicero was a religious skeptic, Middleton argued for the more traditional and more politically useful view: Tully was, with his beliefs in a creating and sustaining God and the immortality of the soul, as close to orthodoxy as one born before the Christian dispensation could be. Middleton also defended Cicero's behavioral inconsistencies, arguing that although the wise man may adjust his conduct to considerations of violence and self-preservation, his goals will remain unchanged. The proper biographical approach was not to dwell on the apparent anomalies of a career but to seek the overriding consistencies that defined the totality of a life. In his pointed summary Middleton compared Cato to Tully. "If Cato's virtue seem more splendid in theory, Cicero's will be found superior in practice: the one was romantic, the other rational; the one drawn from the refinement of the schools, the other from nature, and social life; the one always unsuccessfull, often hurtfull; the other always

---

Member of Parliament to the Mayor of His Corporation (London, 1733); London *Journal*, March 1, 8, April 16, 1735; *Letter to William Pulteney*, 20; *Danger of Faction*, 25; *The Life of the Right Honourable Sir Robert Walpole* (London, 1731); *Essay on Faction*, 7; [Arnall], *Opposition No Proof*, 9; Leonard Welsted, "Dulness and Scandal" (1732); *Sense of an Englishman*, 42; *The History of the Modern Patriots* (London, 1732).

17. Lewis, ed., *Yale Edition of Horace Walpole's Correspondence*, XVI, 299–300.

beneficial, often salutary to the Republic." The dedication contained an ambiguous statement that could be read as an explicit identification of Cicero with Walpole. But even if that interpretation were incorrect and the historian did not link past and present in such an unblushingly heavy-handed manner, there was no doubt among readers that Middleton meant the glory with which he surrounded Tully to be conferred on Sir Robert as well.[18] In this manner did scholarship ratify what over a decade of Court Whig polemic had instilled.

But despite all that Arnall, Middleton, and a host of ministerial scribblers could say, the Catonists remained for a long time unmoved. Bolingbroke publicly gloried in the designation "Cato."[19] Because he and the many for whom he spoke remained deeply suspicious of all who exercised power, they were firm in their resolve to resist the blandishments of Walpole and his minions. Neither honeyed argument nor careful scholarship could budge them from their fixed conviction that liberty stood in peril. Walpole's malevolence seemed undeniable. The Patriots' task was therefore to keep their minds undiverted and to pierce the smokescreen of government propaganda with blazing shafts of Catonic truth. The *Craftsman* was the most penetrating searchlight, but others cast their beams as well. And their message—that a new and *ministerial* despotism threatened the kingdom—did not grow dull from repetition. Provocations occurred often enough to keep a Catonist on the alert. What the South Sea cover-up had triggered in 1721 was confirmed by Walpole's retention of power in 1727 and further sustained by the excise crisis of 1733. In each instance the minister had thrown off his mask, revealing for all both his wickedness and his cunning. It was precisely the recurring nature of this revelation that drove the Patriots as late as 1737 to turn a revival of Addison's *Cato* into a partisan celebration for Prince Frederick.

In the process of reaffirming their adherence to the Catonic vision

18. Conyers Middleton, *The History of the Life of Marcus Tullius Cicero* (3 vols.; London, 1742), especially I, vii and xxxiii–xl, III, 350–56.

19. Privately Bolingbroke thought Cicero the wiser statesman. Henry St. John, Viscount Bolingbroke, *The Works of the Late Right Honourable Henry St. John, Lord Viscount Bolingbroke*, ed. Dr. Goldsmith (8 vols.; London, 1809), IV, 217–19. But though he wrote this glowing encomium on Tully in 1736 he prohibited its publication until after his death. It appeared as "On the Spirit of Patriotism" in 1752. In 1736 such views were best

the Patriots resisted the Ciceronian strategy of the Court Whigs. They might not dispute the identification of the Roman with the Briton[20]— after all, to a Catonist Cicero was no mighty hero—but they certainly sought to make clear its implications. George Lyttelton penned *Observations on the Life of Cicero* in 1731 in an effort to deflate the Ciceronian image propagated by the ministry. The essay was reissued in 1733. Tully, he wrote, was wrongly linked with men like Cato, Brutus, and Catullus. Whereas these three had struggled manfully and unrelentingly for liberty, Cicero had pursued a more checkered course. Thus, though his writings rang gloriously through the centuries, they actually constituted an indictment of their author, whose conduct fell far short of the standards he preached.[21] Alexander Pope, in a poem published in 1733 under the title *The Impertinent, Or a Visit to the Court*, put this reply into the mouth of a figure who had been told that he should attend at court:

> Ah gentle Sir! you Courtiers so cajol us—
> But *Tully* has it, *Nunquam minus solus.*

Later, when his *Fourth Dunciad* savaged the intellectual sycophants of the ministry, Pope explained that among his targets were the "Ciceronis."[22] Henry Fielding used the parodic arena of *Shamela* to denounce

---

kept concealed. On Bolingbroke's pleasure at being likened to Cato, see Malcolm Kelsall, "Augustus and Pope," *Huntington Library Quarterly*, XXXIX (1976), 117–18.

20. But then again they might. See W. T. Laprade, *Public Opinion and Politics in Eighteenth Century England to the Fall of Walpole* (New York, 1936), 346.

21. [George Lyttelton], *Observations on the Life of Cicero* (London, 1733). On this tract see Addison Ward, "The Tory View of Roman History," *Studies in English Literature*, IV (1964), 430–31. Many of the same points had been made in 1721, apparently without any thought that "Cicero" might be Walpole, in letters no. 23 and 30 of Gordon and Trenchard, *Cato's Letters*, I, 165–77, 231–36. A similar evaluative distinction underlay Lord Bristol's private wish that the son of his own son, Lord Hervey, might learn "the Ciceronian eloquence of the father & (may I say) the true Catonian patriotism of his grandfather."

22. Alexander Pope, *Fourth Satire of Dr. John Donne*, in Aubrey Williams (ed.), *Poetry and Prose of Alexander Pope* (New York, 1969), 273, first published as *The Impertinent, Or a Visit to the Court*, lines 90–91; George Sherburn (ed.), *The Correspondence of Alexander Pope* (5 vols.; Oxford, 1956), IV, 377. Pope's opposition to Walpole is one of the two subjects of a distinguished study: Maynard Mack, *The Garden and the City: Retirement and Politics in the Later Poetry of Pope 1731–1743* (Toronto, 1969). Mack's organizing terms seem splendidly applicable to the present argument. He sees Pope to be represented by

Richardson's self-serving Pamela for her "Ciceronian eloquence." John Arbuthnot sketched out a petty and foul-mouthed Cicero to remind Court Whigs, wincing from partisan assault, that vituperation was a hoary staple of political abuse. He also pointed a wrier lesson by remarking that scolding helps those who accuse—he now had Court Whig apologists in mind—"because (according to Tully himself) the title of an accuser to his right of altercation is founded upon his own innocence of those crimes which he lays to the charge of his adversaries." Lord Bolingbroke also whittled away at the Ciceronian image, ascribing "cunning" to the Roman, assessing his view of history as meriting "ridicule," and focusing attention upon his overbearing self-regard. Aaron Hill relegated Tully to the camp of those who inadvertently destroyed Roman liberty. In 1738 Bolingbroke's friend Nathaniel Hooke published *The Roman History*. Dedicated to Pope and praised by Fielding, it depicted Cicero as a peculiarly inconsistent politician—sometimes brave and wise but often stupid or craven. Hooke dismissed Tully's death with the remark that he "had brought this ruin upon himself and his friends by his rash and cruel counsels." Middleton's panegyric of Cicero provoked *The Death of M-l-n in the Life of Cicero*, in which the scholar was indicted for plagiarism, lack of novelty, inaccurate translations, and a willful disguising of Tully's faults. It was these faults, the Patriot writer continued, that disqualified Cicero from a position of equality with "the rigid Virtue and dauntless Sincerity of *Cato* and *Brutus*." But Cicero was still a far greater man than Walpole, and it was not the least of Middleton's misjudgments that he sought to praise the Briton through the Roman and thereby in effect "to bring the *Roman* Consul *down* to a level with the *British* Prime Minister."[23]

the garden, Walpole by the city—an ancient and compelling antithesis. But consider: Cato the Censor was famed for his agricultural writings, Cato Uticensis was famed for his withdrawal (for that is what Mack means by "retirement"), and Cicero was preeminently an *urban* figure.

23. Dr. John Arbuthnot, "A Brief of Mr. John Ginglicutt's Treatise," in *The Life and Works of John Arbuthnot*, ed. George A. Aitken (Oxford, 1892), 382–91; Bolingbroke, *Letters on the Study of History*, in Kramnick (ed.), *Lord Bolingbroke*, especially 11–12; [Aaron Hill], *An Enquiry into the Merit of Assassination: with a View to the Character of Caesar* (London, 1738); Nathaniel Hooke, *The Roman History from the Building of Rome to the Ruin of the Commonwealth* (4 vols.; London, 1751–71), IV, 363 (Fielding's praise occurs at the end of Chapter IX of *Journey from this World to the Next*); *The Death of M-l-*

Not until 1742 did the Catonic vision shatter. What two decades of Court Whig argument had failed to achieve was wrought with surprising swiftness by Sir Robert Walpole's departure from office and the politics attendant upon it. Hitherto sustained in their faith by a vision of Walpole as an aspiring Caesar, Patriots had found no merit at all in the Court Whig argument. But after Sir Robert's resignation, though Court Whig attitudes and policies continued to prevail in the government, the Patriots found it increasingly difficult to persuade people and themselves that the Pelhams were conspirators against liberty. That the brothers liked power seemed indisputable. Still, they had not immediately secured it, and their exercise of it seemed less threatening than Walpole's glorying in it. And if Walpole's resignation deprived the Patriots of their choicest target, the behavior of opposition politicians in the wake of the great man's fall—their willingness to sacrifice principle for place—sapped spirit from those Patriots who remained in opposition. Although such betrayal of faith was thoroughly comprehendible in terms of a Catonic view of human nature, it seemed to most to confirm the realism that underlay a Ciceronian perspective. Thus the 1740s witnessed the rapid dissolution of Catonism as a perspective informing opposition rhetoric, and by late in the decade the Catonic vision was no longer useful even to opponents of the government.

Two symbolic pamphlets point to the ascendancy of Ciceronianism among the Patriots. In 1747 Lord Chesterfield, once a member of the opposition and now returning to it, resigned the seals. In his published apology he defended his action by quoting Cato—but with words in which the martyr addressed common-sensical advice to flawed and unheroic followers. Two years later an opposition pamphlet appeared, *The Examination of Principles*, which, while flaying the ministry, also condemned Cato for his "inflexibility." Meanwhile, the ranks of the opposition began to dwindle as ambitious politicians, abandoning Cato for Tully, saw no need any longer to stand apart from the court. George

---

n in the *Life of Cicero* (London, 1741), especially 16, 45. These arguments got aired again in [Colley Cibber], *The Character and Conduct of Cicero, considered from the History of His Life, by the Reverend Dr. Middleton* (London, 1747). On this entire campaign, see Ward, "The Tory View of Roman History."

Lyttelton underwent an accommodation to Court Whig thought in these years that permitted him to serve later as a Court Whig chancellor of the exchequer. In retirement he explained his conversion with this rebuke to the spirit of Cato: "Marcus Cato, I revere both your life and your death; but the last, permit me to tell you, did no good to your country; and the former would have done more, if you could have mitigated a little the sternness of your virtue. . . . A little practical virtue is of more use to society than the most sublime theory, or the best principles of government ill applied."[24] The man who defied the world from Utica was simply no longer serviceable. In the course of a few brief years, even in the minds of oppositionists, what had once been deemed unyielding resistance had been transformed into inflexibility. No terminological shift could more clearly have demonstrated the rejection by political writers of the stark Catonic vision and the adoption of its more luminous Ciceronian replacement.

By mid-century Cicero had become a spokesman for liberty and order to whom almost all political writers, whether ministerial or not, could repair.[25] Thus, when the Newcastle administration collapsed late in 1756, succeeded by the ministry of the erstwhile Patriot William Pitt, the change marked only the end of Court Whig ministries, not the end of Court Whig thinking. The ideas for which the Court Whigs had contended had in fact won. What Sir Lewis Namier has shown to be behaviorally true for the political classes of the 1750s was ideologically true as well: the struggles of the day were personal rather than partisan, fought within a consensus on fundamentals. Court Whig thinking by the 1750s had become the reigning pattern of political

24. [Philip Dormer Stanhope, Lord Chesterfield], *An Apology for a Late Resignation* (London, 1748); [John Perceval, Lord Egmont], *An Examination of the Principles, and an Inquiry into the Conduct of the Two B—rs* (London, 1749), 42; Lord Lyttelton, *Dialogues of the Dead* (Dublin, 1765), 68.

25. Compare Johnson, *Formation of English Neo-Classical Thought*, 103. There were, of course, exceptions. Addison Ward draws attention to William Guthrie and William Melmoth as two others who joined Cibber in trying to unmask Cicero. Theirs were, it appears to me, voices crying in the wilderness. See Ward, "The Tory View of Roman History." Much more representative were the views of William Warburton, *The Divine Legation of Moses Demonstrated* (3 vols.; London, 1766), III, *passim*, and Richard Cumberland, *The Banishment of Cicero* (London, 1761).

thought.[26] This hegemony was short-lived, however, as ascendant ideological quarrels lay just below the horizon. Within a few years they would rise to shatter the consensus and usher in the ideological turbulence of the 1760s and beyond. But if fleeting, the victory of Court Whiggery was nonetheless sweeping. David Hume, a close student of political affairs and moral philosophy, lamented at mid-century that "the Fame of Cicero flourishes at present; but that of Aristotle is utterly decay'd."[27]

Hans Baron, in his influential study *The Crisis of the Early Italian Renaissance*, explored the related theses that fifteenth-century Florence was imbued with "civic humanism" and that the emergence of this new phase of humanism—a phase to be distinguished from the earlier literary humanism—was a consequence of the recovery of the political Cicero. Although there are obvious similarities between the respective roles of the Florentine Cicero whom Baron examined and the Britannic Cicero whose career I have just traced, the argument advanced in the present study is not parallel to Baron's. Whereas in Florence Cicero was used to awaken educated men to their duty to serve actively in the political life of the nation—which is to say, Cicero was cited to *create* a spirit of civic humanism—in Britain this spirit already existed. From the middle of the seventeenth century on, British gentlemen had known of, and in general been receptive toward, such an obligation. Cicero's role in Britain was far more precise. He and his writings represented one of two competing modes of civic humanism available to Britons. Whereas Cato stood for rigor, fixed adherence to principle, and abiding suspicion of authority, Cicero assumed a more relaxed posture, representing a tolerance of compromise and a willingness to let leaders lead. Each Roman affirmed the value of liberty; each taught the need for the educated to accept political responsibility. But they differed in their strategies for protecting liberty and in the precepts they

26. This assertion conflicts with John Brewer's recent statement that Country Whig ideology triumphed with Pitt's accession to power. Because I define Court Whig thinking somewhat differently than he, the two views are not in total opposition to each other. But an important difference still exists: I think Pitt finally accepted Court Whig ideas for his years of office, and Brewer argues that he did not. See Brewer, *Party Ideology*, 53.

27. David Hume, *Philosophical Essays Concerning Human Understanding* ((London, 1748), 4.

would urge the educated to follow in exercising responsibility. Eighteenth-century Britons were asked to choose whichever form of civic
humanism they thought sounder. They adopted, as we have seen, Cicero's, preferring the temperate to the bracing variety.[28] To deny a central Ciceronian parallel between Florence and Britain is not to deny
that in some respects Florentine and British conditions were similar. In
each state the world of commerce was extensive, providing an environment in which liberty might be acclaimed; in each, recent events,
threatening governmental institutions, had aroused a keener devotion
for the constitution. But the lessons that Cicero taught the Florentines
were already known to the British. And the distinction that Cicero
taught Britain was over-refined for Florence.[29]

Of the five men treated at some length in this study all viewed politics from the adaptable Ciceronian perspective. They were, of course,
by disposition akin to Cicero, and this affinity helped define their distance from Cato. But they had additional links with Tully. Hervey
shared his healthy skepticism and his suspicion of the overly abstract.
Hoadly shared the Roman's love of disputation and the comforts. Herring shared his interest in establishing the grounds for the matrix of
duties within which all men must act. Squire shared his enthusiasm for
a classically balanced constitution as a bulwark of liberty. But the most
Ciceronian of all was Hardwicke. In background, in training, in tone,
and in assumptions about politics, Hardwicke stood at one with Tully.
Both were *novi homines*. Both immersed themselves in legal studies.
Both believed the law the keystone of social stability. Both were *optimates* confronted by the threat of the accession of the *populares*. Both
preached the wisdom of caution and prudence in political deliberations. And Hardwicke's principle of political conduct—"*Let us stand
upon ye ancient ways*"—might well have been Cicero's. To the attentive

28. Another formulation might take the following shape. The stark alternative to
Cicero in fifteenth-century Florence was Caesar. But since, in Britain, Caesar had been
defeated in 1688, the alternative to Cicero was less polar. Cato and Cicero were simply
two different symbols for alternative non-Caesarian regimes.
29. On the paragraph, see Hans Baron, "Cicero and the Roman Civic Spirit in the
Middle Ages and Early Renaissance," *Bulletin of the John Rylands Library*, XXII (1938),
72–97; and Hans Baron, *The Crisis of the Early Italian Renaissance: Civic Humanism and
Republican Liberty in an Age of Classicism and Tyranny* (2 vols; Princeton, N.J., 1955).

reader of Hardwicke's letters it comes as no surprise to find the lord chancellor telling his son in 1744 "otium divos rogo."[30]

II

The impact of Cicero has not yet been fully explored. In three important ways he was much more than merely a symbol and spokesman of a Court Whig sensibility. First, and most concretely, he was the advocate of certain specific policies that could be taken to mark sound governance. He thus reinforced the policy inclinations of Sir Robert Walpole and Henry Pelham. Second, and somewhat more generally, he was the exponent of certain essential political principles. In this guise he articulated the ground rules of that good governance which, Court Whigs believed, issued in wise policies. Finally, and most abstractly, he was the philosopher whose embracing ethical theory provided the most formidable legitimization for Court Whiggery. In this context he became nothing less than the chief metaphysician of the most discerning of the Court Whigs. Tully, in sum, spoke to all the needs of the Court Whigs. He espoused useful policies, advocated attractive principles, and seemed to comprehend all of these ideas within a compelling theory of obligation. He thus did far more than merely craft a sensibility essential to the well-running of a state. Metaphorically it is fair to suggest that with his words about policy and principle he helped to bring that sensibility to earth while with his ethical theory he helped affix it to heaven.

At the level of discrete policies Cicero was at one with the leading Court Whigs. The casual reader of Tully's works, though perhaps perplexed by his informal lines of thought, would have no difficulty envisioning him speaking his conclusions to the concerns of the eighteenth-century gentry. Cicero, for example, was a fervent and frequent defender of private property. "It is the basis of a state and city," he wrote, "that each man has free and undisturbed possession of his own property." Locke himself could have embraced that view.[31] Tully urged

30. British Museum, Add. MSS 35351, fol. 45. Middleton (in *Life of Cicero*, III, 358) quoted Cicero: "Moribus antiquis stat Res Romana virisque."
31. Cicero, *De Officiis*, 2. 78. The parallel to Locke is less close than the quotation suggests. Cicero grounded property theory in conventional rather than natural rights. See *ibid.*, 1. 21.

the country to keep a watchful eye on its finances: "Nothing else sup-
ports a government more strongly than its credit." Against those who
urged belligerence in the late 1720s and 1730s Walpole held out for
the maintenance of peace. Against others—including some Court
Whigs—who urged continued and even heightened war in the 1740s
Pelham argued for a cessation of hostilities. Cicero was on their side.
A paraphrase from 1737 cited Tully as asserting that "the Blessings of
Peace . . . were so extensive as to make even the *Houses* and *Fields*
glad." The commentator then asked: "shall we question the *Judgment* of
Cicero?"[32] Finally, the Court Whigs also approved of the Roman's rebuke to those who fomented factions within the state. "Men who take
care of one group of citizens but neglect another group introduce into
the state an extremely destructive circumstance, treason and discord.
The result is that some appear to be leaders of the people while others
appear to support the aristocrats, but there are few who lead the whole
populace."[33] Walpole, like Cicero, saw himself as either above the
struggle or else a champion of the constitutional party—that is, of the
party of the nation as a whole.

As a defender of principles of good governance Cicero was similarly
useful. It was vitally important to the entire campaign of Court Whig
polemic that Tully could be represented as a friend of liberty. If his
commitment to this cause had been in doubt, he could never have
been useful to the Court Whigs at any other point in their struggle
against an opposition that saw the enemies of liberty abounding. But
Cicero's proclamation rang clearly—almost Catonically: "men of great
spirit ought to pursue independence by every means." Thus he stood
with the foes of tyranny. But he also made the proper qualifications.
Liberty was not license. Indeed, it could subsist only in a structure of
laws. "We are slaves to the laws," Tully sweepingly declared, "in order
that we may be free."[34] With both of these views Court Whigs con-

32. Cicero, *De Officiis*, 2. 84; 1. 74; London *Journal*, January 22, 1737. The author is
paraphrasing *De Lege Agraria*, II. 9.
33. Cicero, *De Officiis*, 1. 85. Pat Rogers, "Swift and Bolingbroke on Faction," *Journal
of British Studies*, IX (1970), 74–75, sees Cicero as the starting point for eighteenth-century thought on faction and party.
34. Cicero, *De Officiis*, 1. 68; *Pro Cluentio*, 53, in Cicero, *Ciceronis Opera*, Vol. IV,
81–146.

curred: liberty was simultaneously precious and yet bounded. They approved too of his affirmation of the nonutopian nature of political life. His pungent distinction between "Romuli faece" and "Platonica πολιτεία"—between the worlds that mankind does and does not inhabit—provided the classical text for a number of Court Whig diatribes against utopian enemies.[35] By excoriating utopians and defending moderated liberty Cicero located himself in the political center that Court Whigs found so congenial. His enemies, like theirs, were extremists. Although not as clearly developed as Aristotle's, Tully's advocacy of moderation was celebrated. Middleton explained it briskly: "Cicero chose the middle way between the obstinacy of Cato, and the indolence of Atticus: he preferred always the readiest road to what was right, if it lay open to him; if not, took the next, that seemed likely to bring him to the same end; and in politics, as in morality, when he could not arrive at the true, contented himself with the probable."[36] Lord Hervey might have been uneasy with some of those terms, but the line of argument that Middleton applied to Tully was the same one that Hervey chose for Walpole.

Court Whigs also acceded to Cicero's principled elevation of the state. It was not, in his view, an artificial and derivative body but, on the contrary, was deemed the highest of earthly institutions. With Aristotle he saw the political association as the arena in which man might find fulfilment of his potentiality. The state thus merited devotion. In setting forth a hierarchy of obligations at the conclusion of the first book of De Officiis, Tully ranked duty owed the state second only to duty owed divinity: "first duties are owed to the immortal gods, second duties to the fatherland, third ones to the parents and so on down the list of the ones remaining." But duties were reciprocal. The fatherland in its turn was obliged to serve those who were subject to its rule in the manner that Court Whigs proposed Britain serve its own citizens—that is, by promoting what was for the general good. A state without law was no state at all, Tully argued. And laws, he declared, met a variety

35. Cicero, Ad. Att., 2. 1. 8. See, e.g., [Tindal(?)], Defense, 5. It would not have escaped the memory of many educated eighteenth-century readers that Cicero made this distinction explicitly to illustrate Cato's poor judgment.

36. Middleton, Life of Cicero, III, 363. See Cicero, De Officiis, 1. 93–94.

of needs. They helped create liberty—a point already noted. They promoted the safety of citizens and the tranquillity and happiness of life. They made existence honorable. Thus Cicero interpreted the purpose of the state in the same multi-faceted fashion that the Court Whigs did. It was Cicero, after all, who gave celebrity to the idea that *salus populi* constituted *suprema lex*.[37] It is no wonder then that ministerial pamphleteers worked so assiduously to promote a Ciceronian vision of political reality. When fully embraced, the Ciceronian principles fostered not only a spirit of cooperation toward the government but also an inclination to support the program of the Court Whigs.

The best way to come to an understanding of Cicero's philosophical contribution to Court Whiggery is to examine his thinking about the virtue of a balanced constitution. Educated Britons knew that this was the form of constitution Tully found most satisfactory. It did not matter that *De Republica* was undiscovered. Cicero's views were adequately expressed in his extant writings. In *De Legibus* he alluded to both the lost work and to his own preference when he wrote that "this is the balanced type of state which Scipio praises and most highly approves in the treatise to which I have referred." Later in his treatment he acclaimed the "balanced and harmonious constitution" as the finest kind. And a preserved fragment from the missing treatise added detail to the point: "I look upon that to be the best kind of Government, which consists of the Kingly, Aristocratical, and Popular Forms." It was therefore easy for Court Whig writers to invoke the authority of "the great and penetrating Cicero" when extolling constitutional balance.[38] Such invocation was not, it should be clear, essential for polemics. The value of a balanced constitution was perhaps the least controverted political principle of the era. In praising its soundness Cicero spoke for the opposition as well as the ministry. But in spelling out the grounds for his preference for constitutional equilibrium Cicero used a legiti-

37. Cicero, *De Officiis*, 1. 160; Cicero, *De Legibus*, 2. 5. 11–12; 3. 3. 8. Compare *De Legibus*, 3. 1. 2.

38. Cicero, *De Legibus*, 3. 5. 12; 3. 12. 28; Middleton, *Life of Cicero*, I, xxxiii; Williams, *Love of Our Constitution*, 6. Although faithful to Cicero's ideas, the "quotation" about mixed government does not appear in *De Republica*, the essay to which Williams ascribes it. It may be a conflation of several texts from the work that resemble it in a general way.

mizing theory that not all Britons would accept. This was the theory of natural law.

As a method of accounting for Britain's successful constitutional balance under Court Whig ministries natural law theory found itself in competition with two rival theories also propounded by ministerial writers—a primitive utilitarianism and a deracinated natural rights theory.[39] These latter two have received far more publicity than the natural law theory. Some scholars, for example, have argued that a crude utilitarianism, enunciated by Locke, provided the foundation for Court Whig defenses of the constitution under which Walpole and the Pelhams served. Other scholars have held that such defenses drew instead chiefly upon John Locke's version of natural rights. The reader will have noticed, however, that John Locke, whether in his utilitarian or in his natural rights guise, has scarcely dominated the various justifications examined in the foregoing chapters.[40] Court Whig writers cannot be so easily confined. Moreover, in the final analysis neither utilitarianism nor natural rights theory is remotely as effective a legitimization for a balanced form of constitution as is the philosophy of natural law. Thus the Court Whigs who embraced natural law teaching

39. John Dunn identified three traditions of thought that might (though this was not exactly his point) legitimize the Whig supremacy at this time. They are, respectively, the tradition of Locke, the "philosophical" tradition, and the "conservative" tradition. The latter two, however, have a grab-bag quality about them, and I think a better set of categories is the one I have here suggested. Hoadly represents pure Lockeanism. Hervey—imperfectly—represents the ideas of utility which underlie Dunn's philosophical tradition. Herring, Squire, and Hardwicke represent the natural law tradition, with Herring providing it with an Anglican—or, in Dunn's terms, a conservative—gloss, Squire seeking to synthesize it with the Gothic constitution and Harrington, and Hardwicke focusing upon the notion of an immemorial constitution. John Dunn, "The Politics of Locke in England and America in the Eighteenth Century," in *John Locke: Problems and Perspectives*, ed. John W. Yolton (Cambridge, 1969), 60–62.

40. For the Court Whigs as utilitarians, see Pocock, *Machiavellian Moment*, 458–87. For the Court Whigs as natural rightists, see Kramnick, *Bolingbroke and His Circle*, 111–36, and Forbes, *Hume's Philosophical Politics*, Chap. V. The contention that Locke was far from the most influential Whig thinker in the first half of the eighteenth century I now take to be proved. See Kenyon, *Revolution Principles*, 1–2; Dickinson, *Liberty and Property*, 10; Jeffrey M. Nelson, "Unlocking Locke's Legacy: A Comment," *Political Studies*, XXVI (1978), 101–108. I cannot, however, concur in Kenyon's judgment that Locke's theory of contract had received "almost universal acceptance by the mid-eighteenth century." *Revolution Principles*, 17.

made a wise choice: they found a surer defense of their constitutional preferences than their allies did. In sum, the Court Whigs were sharply divided over what line of constitutional legitimization to adopt, and the period under scrutiny increasingly appears to be the pivotal one for an understanding of the disengagement of a major branch of Whig thought from Locke. With caution, one can even see in the debate that occurred among Court Whigs in the years from 1720 to 1760 the foundations for the later divisions among Jeremy Bentham, Thomas Paine, and Edmund Burke—with Burke emerging as heir of the truest Ciceronian stream of Court Whig thought.

The fundamental assumption of utilitarian writers is that mankind wants happiness. Following the Hobbist convention which transforms the goals of human nature into objects of moral pursuit, utilitarians affirm that the good is equivalent to the pleasurable. Many refinements of this notion are possible, and when utilitarianism is applied to social theory it is necessary to define with some care what might constitute socially acceptable pleasure. But the link between goodness and pleasure cannot finally be severed: from the utilitarian perspective the virtue of an action is measured by the happiness it fosters. In his political views Locke was not fundamentally a utilitarian thinker, but when his psychological work is examined—and his *Essay Concerning Human Understanding* was far more important than his treatises on government for giving Locke his high reputation in the early eighteenth century— utilitarian considerations manifestly intrude. Most strikingly, his key definitions employ utilitarian terminology. "First, that which is properly good or bad," he wrote in the *Essay*, "is nothing but barely pleasure or pain." Human beings, he believed, in their voluntary actions seek to secure pleasure or avert pain.[41] A utilitarian constitutionalist would thus judge the quality of a constitution by the amount of pleasure its functioning engendered in those subject to its control. All efforts to quantify pleasure must inevitably provide only the most imprecise of yardsticks, and even in the eighteenth century there were utilitarian thinkers grappling with the problem of reconciling a society of volitional pleasure-seekers with the maintenance of public order. Of such ratiocination, however, Court Whig polemic gives us little evidence.

41. A. P. Brogan, "John Locke and Utilitarianism," *Ethics*, LXIX (1959), 79–93.

Still, insofar as a significant proportion of ministerial tracts stood firmly on the assertion that Court Whig regimes deserved support because they brought happiness to the people, it cannot be denied that a crude utilitarianism pervaded many of the less consequential Court Whig pamphlets.

Examples abound. Indeed, utilitarian motifs regularly appear in and sometimes exclusively control the tracts of the era. In 1722 the Walpole ministry was defended with the argument that the prosperity and freedom of the British made fault-finding incomprehensible. Seven years later a pamphlet identified Court Whig rule with financial affluence. Two years later the regime was justified by virtue of having made the nation happy, prosperous, free, and safe. A tract from the year of the excise crisis rebutted opposition attacks with the assertion that under Walpole liberty, property, and free religion were enjoyed by unprecedented numbers. A further two years later a writer rested his case on the belief that no earlier era could match the present in happiness. The argument appeared again in 1740: the incontrovertible facts of plenty, prosperity, and liberty were sufficient arguments for the administration. And this type of justification did not disappear with the resignation of Walpole. A blatant exercise in war propaganda dating from 1744 legitimized the Court Whig regime and its Protestant monarch by asserting unqualifiedly that the royal government pursued nothing but the happiness of the people. A similarly heavy-handed tract from 1753 credited Britain's prosperity in trade, manufacturing, and the professions to the Glorious Revolution and its Court Whig defenders.[42] These citations are, it must be understood, simply examples. The utilitarian justification for the Court Whig constitution was a recurring theme of the ministerial pamphlets. Political tracts are generally addressed to men of common understanding: the Court Whigs thought that their most immediately advantageous line of argument was to remind the readers of the general happiness of the political nation.

Lord Hervey was a singular and striking example of a Court Whig

---

42. [Tindal(?)], Defense; Letter from a Gentleman in the Country; [Yonge], Sedition; Some Observations upon a Paper, intituled, The List (London, 1733); Difference Computed; Daily Gazetteer (London), October 6, 1740; Advantages of the Hanoverian Succession; B—. G—., Advantages of the Revolution.

utilitarian. In his reflections on the Walpole administration one may see both the attractiveness of the utilitarian justification and yet its final insufficiency. His account of human nature makes clear his essential acceptance of utilitarian psychology. He acknowledged that altruistic behavior was not unusual, but he insisted that the principle that directed men in all their actions was the pursuit of pleasure, interest, or esteem. In the light of this view of humankind the function of the law was not so much the fostering of virtue as the prevention of conflict. To Hervey's own way of thinking the chief recommendation for the regime he lived under was that it had brought unparalleled happiness and prosperity to Britons. Indeed, he privately thought that the most effective refutation of the Patriot contrast between an iniquitous present and a golden past was simply to ask "for which age of our ancestors they would like to change the circumstances of the present?"[43] He wrote often and with vigor about the virtues of a balanced constitution, but what he was truly defending in his tracts was the way Sir Robert Walpole handled affairs. "Constitution," as noted earlier, seemed to have little meaning for him divorced from "administration." Hervey was, whether expressing preferences among classical writers or defending constitutional arrangements, a man primarily interested in the techniques of management, not the principles of governance. In fact, his utilitarianism was thoroughly irrelevant to any purported defense of a balanced constitution.

Hervey's dilemma is expressed by posing two questions. How would he be able to support the Walpole government if the kingdom suffered from poverty or discontent? Indeed, why then should he? If the measure of good governance is happiness, then the government that presides over an unhappy or a penurious people is ipso facto not a good one. Moreover, because the utilitarian rationale focuses on results, not principles, it provided no credible grounds for opposing an authoritarian regime that held sway over a prosperous people. The very next generation would witness the appearance on the continent of monarchs who, in essence, justified their absolutist claims on the grounds that the mounting prosperity of their kingdoms or of key elements in them gave warrant to the methods they adopted. Hervey was in no

43. Ilchester, *Hervey and His Friends*, 132, 242.

position to reject this kind of argument. Indeed, trustful of Walpole's intentions, he had unabashedly urged the elimination of various impediments to quick, vigorous, and none too fastidious governmental action that he saw as defects in the British constitution. That Hervey valued liberty and restraint need not be doubted. But he cherished them because in Britain they had been productive of material happiness—because they were means to ends. No regime and no scheme of government can be secure when their claims to validity rest on their continuing capacity to generate the material foundations of happiness. Cicero himself was cited by Court Whigs as warning that "pleasure while she seems to imitate virtue is the mother of all evil."[44] Utilitarianism, in brief, provided no protection against a truly benevolent despot.

For this reason some Court Whig thinkers sought refuge in theories of justification that issued in unchanging principles. The notion of immutability served here as the key. To men of more penetrating understanding a theory rooted in immutable principle was far preferable to the superficially attractive but fundamentally flaccid doctrine of utilitarianism. A Court Whig regime protected by such a theory would be proof against the vicissitudes of climate, trade, and war, for neither these nor any other misfortune could invalidate a constitution that conformed to proper timeless principles. And such a theory lay at hand, under the capacious and ancient rubric of natural rights. Such rights were believed by many to have been the inalienable freehold of mankind even before the creation of civil society. A proper constitution, it therefore followed, respected them. Thus it was that some who dreaded the infirmity of utilitarian resistance to authoritarianism turned to the political ideas of John Locke or Algernon Sidney. What the pleasure principle could not guarantee the theory of inalienable rights might still secure. In his second *Treatise of Government* Locke maintained that human beings had natural rights to life, liberty, and estate. Since the rights were natural—which is to say, since they were the possession of all human beings simply by virtue of their humanity— they could not legitimately be abrogated. Thus any regime that waged

44. Cicero, *De Legibus*, 1. 17. 47, as quoted (very loosely) in London *Journal*, January 3, 1736.

war on natural rights was, by that very action, demonstrating its ille-gitimacy. Locke had insisted that a proper government was one that ruled by the consent of the people. It had, he believed, originated in a primal contract, through which free individuals had united with each other to create a government for the express purpose of protecting natural rights. As long as the government remained faithful to that trust, it merited full support. But if it lost sight of that purpose or fell under the control of men bent upon using the power of government to pursue the goals of private greed, it lost its constitutional legitimacy. Once it was no longer legitimate, it invited some type of resistance. The attraction of a constitutional theory based on natural rights was that it contained an insurmountable obstacle to authoritarianism: the inalienable rights of human beings could not be trespassed upon.

Among the Court Whigs Benjamin Hoadly was a powerful represen-tative of this brand of ancient political wisdom.[45] More than that, he personified the precise shift from utilitarianism to natural rights theory, since for some purposes he was quite at home with utilitarian argu-ments. Like all Court Whigs he regularly suggested that people needed only to consult their own present comfortable circumstances to know that they lived under an easy regime. He also employed utilitarian ideas when he sought to justify the ministry's vigorous and none too punctili-ous handling of enemies: almost invariably it was "publick Happiness" that was served by the occasional governmental incursions upon civil rights. But at the core Hoadly was a libertarian. He recognized a poten-tial for the abuse of liberty in the frequent invocation of *raison d'état*. He also knew that in the last analysis utilitarian theory offered no se-cure haven to liberty. Thus when "Britannicus" described the true pa-triot he identified him as a person who "has a constant Regard to the Rights and Happiness of his Fellow-Subjects." It was a critical yoking: natural right was of equal standing with the pleasure principle. With Locke, Hoadly believed that all human beings had been endowed by God with certain natural and hence inalienable rights in the "State of

45. See also the frequently reissued *The Judgment of Whole Kingdoms and Nations, concerning the Rights, Power and Prerogative of Kings, and the Rights, Privileges and Properties of the People* (London, 1713), then believed to be a work of Lord Somers'; Hay, *Essay on Civil Government; Loyalty to Our King; Balance.*

Nature." In his writings he identified at least four—the Lockean trilogy of life, liberty, and estate, and the right to paternal authority which Locke also recognized. Again with Locke he held that these natural rights were in fact derived from the primal natural right, a "Right to Self-Preservation." These rights could not be effaced. They were products of nature itself, not of mere circumstance. When men first contracted together to form a government, they conveyed to certain rulers a carefully restricted power to exercise some of these rights. They consented, in short, to be governed, for only consent could give legitimacy to governance. But they did so in order that the social stability necessary to the observance of the remaining rights might be fostered. And they never surrendered their right to self-defense, even when it was deemed necessary to exercise that right against the very government they had created. As a churchman who knew the injunction about turning the other cheek, Hoadly was prepared to acknowledge that Christian subjects might sometimes appropriately recede from demanding rights to which they were entitled.[46] But no constitutional order could legitimately subsist that did not afford protection to the natural rights of life, liberty, and estate. Each individual held them; each could exercise them.

The Court Whig appeal to natural rights as a justification for the Court Whig constitution dealt satisfactorily with the flaw of the utilitarian justification. The regime no longer depended upon prosperity for its legitimization. But natural rights theory contained two liabilities of a different sort. One was essentially pragmatic, for an appeal to natural rights lay at the heart of much opposition criticism of the government, and in fact it seemed more appropriate there than in ministerial counterattacks.[47] It was the type of theory congenial to those who oppose

46. See Hoadly, *Works*, II, 22, 131, 132, 143–44, 169, 271, III, 7, 213, 285–88, 314–16.

47. See, for suggestive examples from three relevant decades, Gordon and Trenchard, *Cato's Letters*, II, 216–17; *Craftsman*, July 21, 1734; *Liberty and Right: or, An Essay, historical and political, on the constitution and administration of Great-Britain* (2 pts.; London, 1747). Bolingbroke himself, and Tories in general, were wary of natural rights theory. The viscount saw in it the same implications the Court Whigs did, and no more than they did he want the reign of disorder. Kramnick, *Bolingbroke and His Circle*, 45–48. But Caroline Robbins (*Eighteenth-Century Commonwealthman*, 5) identifies natural rights doctrine as the core of "Real Whig"—i.e., republican—thought.

the exercise of power, since it focused attention upon the misuse of power. Precisely for this reason, then, many Court Whigs found it a dangerous justification. Those entrusted with power invariably handle it in a manner that some find objectionable. For Court Whigs to couch their defenses in terms of natural rights—save when useful for deflecting opposition exaggerations and lies—was to concede to the opposition the advantage of choosing the terms of debate. The Court Whigs who invoked natural rights theory, though unquestionably believing that the ministerial record could bear scrutiny, were nevertheless yielding a tactical victory to their opponents. When the issue of rights preempts all other concerns in the public forum, those who wield authority will sooner or later be cast as oppressors. The second liability was more theoretical. The logical consequence, so it seemed, of a constitution based on the consent of the governed and designed to protect natural rights was the sovereignty of the representative legislature. Locke himself, though defending a balanced constitution, had often argued in this manner. And sometimes when he had not he had invoked the still more radical notion of a popular sovereignty lying behind even legislative sovereignty. To Court Whigs these were dreadful conceptions, vitiating all notions of equilibrium, introducing a new absolutism into government, and destroying the balanced constitution. Court Whigs had not retreated from a utilitarian theory that could muster no defense against a benevolent despot just so they could embrace a natural rights theory that in their view could produce but the flimsiest defense against mobocracy. Again Cicero was pertinently cited to reinforce the concern: if government should not overbear its citizens, neither should it "make them run into Licentiousness . . . by too great a Relaxation of Power." Something different from both was needed.[48] And Cicero was the most celebrated advocate of that missing solution.

The answer lay in the acceptance of the more traditional doctrine of

48. Locke, *The Second Treatise of Government*, Sections 149, 219, 222; Williams, *Love of Our Constitution*, 7. M. Seliger, *The Liberal Politics of John Locke* (London, 1968), 47–58, rightly notes that there is considerable congruence between utilitarian theory and natural rights theory. One congruence—noted by the Court Whigs—was that both lacked what the Court Whigs regarded as necessary constraints. My discussion of the doctrine of natural rights draws on the examination of its relationship to natural law

natural law. Locke, and Hoadly after him, had been right in seeking some immutable element by which to protect the state from the tyrant. But they had seized the wrong element. Instead of focusing upon natural rights they ought, so various thoughtful Court Whigs believed, to have focused upon the teaching that was anterior to natural rights—the classical doctrine that the moral and political world was governed by a natural law which was independent of human will but accessible to human reason. The most celebrated and influential exponent of this philosophy was Cicero.[49] It was, strictly speaking, not original with him or even with his Stoic teachers. But whereas earlier writers had invoked the notion of natural justice to provide a foundation for the ethical world, it was Tully who adapted the doctrine to the legal and political world. "Law" he defined as "the highest reason, implanted in Nature, which commands what ought to be done and forbids the opposite." Such a definition implied the existence of objective standards of right and wrong—standards inherent in the nature of mankind and social reality. "Right is based," Tully declared, "not upon men's opinions, but upon Nature." And it was given to man to know these standards. Man was distinguished from other animals by virtue of his reason. "Those creatures who have received the gift of reason from Nature have also received right reason and therefore they have also received the gift of law, which is right reason applied to command and prohibition."[50] Right reason—*recta ratio*—was the key. By using it mankind could discover the natural moral order and make conduct conform to it. A fragment from *De Republica* that Lactantius bequeathed

found in the preface of Leo Strauss, *The Political Philosophy of Hobbes: Its Basis and Its Genesis*, trans. Elsa M. Sinclair (Chicago, 1952).

49. Treated in Book III of *De Officiis* and more systematically in Book I of *De Legibus*. Keyes's translation in the widely used Loeb Classical Library edition (New York, 1928) is free in dealing with the ideas of nature and natural law. The Latin text should be consulted. Margaret C. Jacob, *The Newtonians and the English Revolution, 1689–1720* (Ithaca, N.Y., 1976), also sees natural law entering into Whig thought in the eighteenth century. Parallels between her work and the present study should not be pressed—subject matter, methods, and assumptions differ—but it is significant that what has caught Jacob's eye is the reception by defenders of the British status quo of a doctrine of natural law.

50. Cicero, *De Legibus*, 1. 6. 18; 1. 10. 28; 1. 12. 33. See Edward S. Corwin, *The 'Higher Law' Background of American Constitutional Law* (Ithaca, N.Y., 1955).

to the eighteenth century summarized Cicero's instruction about natural law:[51]

The true law, says he, is right reason, conformable to the nature of things; constant, eternal, diffused thro' all; which calls us to duty by commanding, deters us from sin by forbidding. . . . This cannot possibly be over-ruled by any other law; nor abrogated in the whole or in part . . . nor can there be one law at *Rome*, another at *Athens*; one now, another hereafter; but the same eternal immutable law, comprehends all nations, at all times, under one common Master and Governor of all, God.

Whereas a utilitarian constitutionalism glorified the capacity of the government to bring satisfactions, and a constitutionalism grounded in natural rights theory honored the right of the citizen to hold the government responsible for his freedom, the philosophy of natural law focused on *limits*. Neither government nor citizen could lawfully transgress them. For Cicero, as for his Court Whig emulators, it was important that constitutional theory legitimize the restraints that a sound constitutional order embodied—that it demarcate the permissible from the impermissible in such a fashion that everyone in the community was aware of the demarcation and subject to the restraints. In *De Legibus* he cautioned: "Not only must we inform [magistrates] of the limits of their administrative authority; we must also instruct the citizens as to the extent of their obligation to obey them."[52] The limits that natural law theory imposed on the government existed by virtue of the theory's insistence that good ends did not finally justify regular recourse to evil means. The limits it imposed on the citizens existed by virtue of its requirement that the good of the community supersede the good of the individual. Here was a constitutional teaching superbly consonant with doctrines of equilibrium. For it was through the mechanism of constitutional balance that a people might be able to enforce limits. A properly balanced constitution embodied the natural law—indeed, was its practical realization. For if natural law defined limits, it was a balanced constitution that institutionalized them. And a balanced constitution, as Court Whig and Patriot both proudly agreed, was what

51. Quoted in Middleton, *Life of Cicero*, III, 351–52.
52. Cicero, *De Legibus*, 3. 2. 5.

Britain possessed. There was still a cause for division among Court Whigs, however, for opinions varied on precisely how natural law had come to inform the constitution. Some writers, such as Herring, imputed the felicitous union to divine direction alone. Others, such as Squire, conferred a peculiar wisdom upon Britain's Germanic founders, to whom the great discovery could be attributed. And finally there were those, like Hardwicke, who saw in the common law the source and vehicle of transmission for Britain's peculiarly insightful understanding of the natural law.

That an Anglican divine should find natural law philosophy congenial was not surprising; Richard Hooker had made it a part of the conventional thinking of many eighteenth-century clergymen. Thus Herring, in interpreting the parable of the Good Samaritan, found his chief ground for approving of the traveler's actions in the fact that they were "in Obedience to the Law of Nature." Thus too his most frequent term of denunciation was "unnatural." It was a forceful epithet, for it implied much more than merely proceeding by ways not sanctioned by nature. To violate nature was, for Herring, to invite retribution. "Now Nature is a very stubborn Thing," he warned, "and, tho' kept down for a while, it is apt to recoil terribly upon the Man who warps it." Herring found it particularly alarming that some Britons, in fleeing despotism, had sought security in utilitarian or natural rights doctrine. "It is to be feared," he declared, "that while we have been guarding against a blind Obedience, there are those who have almost lost all Notion of one that is just and necessary." He upheld the Ciceronian idea that "the Public Good is the only End of Government," and he proceeded to define that "Good"—in Ciceronian or Aristotelian terms that the utilitarian or natural rights theorist would find unacceptable—as in chief measure "the Practice of distributive Justice, and proportioning Rewards, or Punishments, to the Merits, or Demerits, of Men."[53] In all these respects he took his bearings from his commitment to the natural law; and because the concept of law entails the concept of obligation, we may appreciate anew and now from a fresh perspective the intensity of Herring's devotion to duty and obedience.

53. Herring, *Seven Sermons*, 137, xxix, 60, 104, 83.

But how is natural law to be known? Herring saw two routes of access. For the reflective minority reason was the path, it being, Herring held, man's highest faculty. But few had the capacity to exercise it in the plenitude of its power and thereby to discern the "Dictates of Natural Reason." For the unreflective majority, therefore, the Gospel provided an alternative avenue to truth. Religion vouchsafed to all men in a clear and direct fashion what right reason through diligent application revealed to the wise few. Indeed, the preeminent role of the Christian religion, the archbishop argued, was to make preexisting moral truths clear even to those of clouded vision. The teachings of Jesus and his church—with the single exception of the doctrine of the Resurrection—were accessible to the religiously unlettered, for they were the teachings that reason itself could discover. But the faith made them universally acceded to. Human beings were made for society and government, Herring believed, and in that society they had designated duties. With Cicero, Herring held that the good and the useful were identical—that whether one consulted reason, faith, or experience, one would find the same solution commended. It was this identity of the injunctions of "religion" and the requirements of "policy" that provided Herring with his grounds for supporting the Court Whig constitution. Hooker had long ago demonstrated for Anglicans that Scripture did not impose or require a particular political order.[54] Thus Moses Lowman's effort to prove Georgian polity the analogue of Hebrew polity was politically unnecessary. Thus too Christian political writers were not required to embrace the theory of the divine right of kings or urge the creation of a hierocratic state. What God had conferred on Britain was something quite different from rule by either an all-powerful monarch or an omnipotent clergy. It was a balanced constitution, in which the monarch stood as protector of the true faith, but by which no element in the body politic could acquire inordinate power. Religion taught obedience to the powers that be. So did policy. The constitutional order that existed in Britain was, by simple virtue of its existence, legitimized: it was God's work. And being God's work, it

54. Richard Hooker, *Of the Laws of Ecclesiastical Polity: An Abridged Edition*, eds. A. S. McGrade and Brian Vickers (New York, 1975), Book I, Chap. 10.

conferred all that God thought good for man. This constitutional order was defined by law. And, as Herring put it, itemizing those goods, "there is Reason, and Spirit, and Liberty in Law." Herring's entire teaching was therefore imbued with natural law doctrine; and the balanced British constitution was informed by natural law because providential decree had made it so.[55]

With wider historical knowledge than Herring—and, I will suggest, less piety—Samuel Squire was not satisfied with invoking God as the immediate source of the constitution's happy reception of natural law. That it sprang originally from the Creator was, of course, not to be denied. But Squire saw it as embodied in and thus mediated through the Anglo-Saxon constitution—that ancient balanced polity of the German people, brought to Britain in the fifth and sixth centuries of the Christian era and ever since the frame of British political life. This incorporation of natural law meant that the Anglo-Saxon constitution emphasized obligations over rights: "there is very little mentioned [in Anglo-Saxon laws] but of duty of one man to another . . . ye rule of right & law of nature were y^r guides in y^s respect." Men were endowed with a sense of "natural equity" but not all men had used it as wisely as the British—to build a society in which "God and Nature" worked together to command consideration of others. For the guidance of that society people resorted to their "natural reason" and to custom. And a central rule of good governance that the "plainest principle of nature or common sense" gave to men was the requirement that all citizens should be consulted on public matters that affected them. Thus for Squire the natural law forbade arbitrary government. In assailing the doctrine of the divine right of kings he invoked the traditional unity of what reason, experience, and Scripture taught: indeed, he proclaimed such a doctrine "contrary to the voice of nature, disagreeable to the dictates of right reason, repugnant to the antient constitution, and entirely unsupported by the writings of the evangelists and apostles." In justifying the Glorious Revolution he declared that "necessity and self-preservation are the great laws of nature." Squire even tried to make the neo-Harringtonian strand in his thought submit

55. Herring, *Seven Sermons*, 11, 14, 25, 36, 58–60, 105–106, 222.

to natural law when he declared the natural agrarian of Anglo-Saxon England to be an "ancient law of nature."[56]

That last argument was rather unpersuasive, and in fact neo-Harringtonian sociology and Ciceronian prudence could coexist only uneasily in Squire's thinking. Because Squire relied so extensively on Harrington it can scarcely be maintained that his constitutionalism was founded exclusively on natural law doctrine. But he stands as another example of a Court Whig writer who sought to build his constitutional apologia on the firm ground of immutable principle. And he did so even when, as a mature historian, he had shaken off his belief in the unyielding permanence of Anglo-Saxon institutions and recognized that Britain's past was marked by flux. To hew to this revised view of the constitution in a thoroughly persuasive manner it would have been necessary for Squire to be more sure-footed than was his wont. In fact, he stumbled. When he emphasized the time-controlled nature of the regime he found himself led into historicist bogs, unable to disguise the tendency of historicism to dissolve the validity of such transhistorical truths as natural law made claim to embody. But when, contrariwise, he emphasized the timeless character of the natural law that underlay his history, he found himself forced to minimize the facts of historical change, even though so much evidence bore testimony to the existence of such change. Thus, though Squire adopted the useful notion that the timeless element in the British constitution was the principle of balance, he chose to defend this principle not by consistent appeal to natural law, even though he was equipped to do so, but by appeal to Harrington. In this manner the tension between ancient prudence and modern sociology dogged Squire to the end. It took another Court Whig to develop a natural law interpretation of the British constitution that was faithful at once to the fact of change and the need for permanent values.

Lord Hardwicke was the man who advanced this more serviceable view of how the natural law could be related to constitutional equilibrium. Although his conception of the constitution bore some superfi-

56. Squire, handwritten notes bound in British Museum copy; Squire, *Enquiry* (1745), 53; Squire, *Enquiry* (1753), 60; Squire, *Historical Essay* (1748), 34, 38; [Squire], *Letter to a Tory Friend*; [Squire], *Remarks*, 27.

cial similarities to Squire's, it was in fact a radically different proposition. Squire appealed to an Anglo-Saxon constitution, the product of a particular era in English history; Hardwicke appealed rather to an immemorial constitution, ever changing and superbly flexible. Squire could confidently identify concrete institutions upheld by the constitution and identify too some of the men who helped shape them; Hardwicke preferred to speak of the tendencies of the constitution and presupposed a founding without founders—indeed, a perpetual, never-ending founding.[57] Following Coke, he believed that legal precedent embodied natural law. Distinguished from all other animals by virtue of his ability to reason, man used this capacity of "natural reason" to arrive at laws that could be deemed just. These laws comprised the core of the common law. As conditions changed, so too would the laws, for altered situations might well require altered terms of justice. But whatever the substantive content of common law at any given time, this content was rendered legitimate by the natural law that lay behind it.[58]

It has already been remarked that Hardwicke invoked many different models of balance when discussing the constitution. We may now understand why he was so imprecise in his usage. For him balance was not the mechanical contrivance that Squire saw—that elegant but conventional tripartite construction of king, Lords, and Commons. Instead it was a contention between two dynamic principles—the democratical and the prerogative. It was moreover a contention fought at several levels, for balance was needed not only at Westminster but also in the law courts, the quarter sessions, and the army. In this struggle neither principle could win. Whatever the arena, each principle was checked by customs and institutions thrown up by its adversary; and

57. This concept of the constitution is illuminatingly examined in Pocock, *The Ancient Constitution*. See too his important article, "Burke and the Ancient Constitution—A Problem in the History of Ideas," *Historical Journal*, III (1960), 125–43. Dickinson, *Liberty and Property*, 140–41, neglects to differentiate between an immemorial constitution and the Anglo-Saxon constitution, conflating them under the rubric of "ancient constitution."

58. Yorke, *Life of Hardwicke*, II, 427. Henry de Bracton and Sir Edward Coke had held similar views. And Hardwicke was well acquainted with the writings of England's great legists.

though these customs and institutions might alter over time, the capacity of each principle to sustain itself remained intact. Such customs and institutions, born unnoticed and unmarked, were the products of "natural reason." They were, that is, part and parcel of the common wisdom that in Britain went by the name of the common law. They emerged when needed as concrete responses to concrete difficulties and, in proving serviceable, proved themselves wise. But since "natural reason" was itself the means by which natural law was apprehended, the product of "natural reason"—common law—was undergirded by the natural law. In this fashion natural law could be seen as the justification for and source of balance in Britain's honored constitution. And for this reason Hardwicke was prepared to follow Coke in declaring that common law—because it was grounded in natural law—was superior even to positive law and was a standard by which to void statutes that contravened it.

But this analysis poses a new problem. Hardwicke achieved his central position in the history of English jurisprudence as the consolidator of equity. Equity had developed in England over the centuries as a corrective to injustices wrought by the common law. By presiding over and thereby regularizing the operations of equity through the court of chancery, Hardwicke obviously accepted the view that equity might supersede the common law. But if he accepted that principle, how can one assert that he saw the common law as the embodiment of natural law? The answer is simple and revealing. The theory behind equity was that principles of natural justice ought to be honored. The occasion for its invocation was the unusual circumstance in which the common law, ordinarily consonant with natural justice, issued in a legally correct but manifestly unfair judgment. Since the common law spoke in directives designed to cover entire categories of actions and was thus framed in general terms whereas human situations were both complex and diverse in nature, occasionally situations arose in which a fidelity to the letter of the law threatened to violate the sense of natural justice. In such instances, when invited, the lord chancellor might intervene, exercising, as it was said, his conscience. Hardwicke never believed that he was thereby empowered to ignore the common law. "This court is a court of conscience," he admitted, but he went on to argue that a remedy issuing from conscience was "discretionary on certain grounds, and not arbitrary, but governed by rules of equity." Elsewhere he provided a terser formulation: "aequitas sequitur legem." This line of reasoning constituted an acknowledgment that common law was not perfect, but it did not constitute an attack on natural law itself. If the common law was in certain peculiar instances deficient, it was in those instances simply not a vehicle for natural law. It was precisely because of instances of this sort, where common law failed to conform to natural law, that equity had developed.[59] For in equity the conscience that operated was a conscience that, without arrogance or a misplaced conviction in the penetration of its own insight, strove through tutored "natural reason" to arrive at justice. Reason, in sum, remained the source of true law. It was conventionally expressed in the common law. It was occasionally expressed in equity. But however expressed, its discernment assured the existence and vitality of the natural law foundation of English jurisprudence.

Hardwicke was less confident than Squire (or Cicero) that any and every human being, simply by applying his mind, could arrive at the truths of natural law. Like Herring, he believed that most people needed instructional aid. Whereas the archbishop emphasized the role of the church and its trained clerics in supplying such aid, the chancellor focused on the role of the common law and its own trained expositors. But both men—and Squire too—had the same purpose in mind: to make objective justice cognizable to the British and operative in their political life. For a just society, they held, could tolerate neither tyranny nor mobocracy. Faithful to the philosophy of natural law, such a society created restraints rather than powers. The natural law was thus the only truly adequate weapon against those Patriots who glorified royal power and those who would magnify parliamentary power, but also against those allies who recklessly embraced utilitarianism or took comfort in natural rights theory. Just as he taught an attitude appropriate to the age, advocated some policies its leaders found congenial, and preached principles that informed its political

59. Yorke, *Life of Hardwicke*, I, 103–104, II, 427, 428, 442; Holdsworth, *History of the English Law*, XII, 259, 262.

thought, Cicero also proposed a constitutional and moral philosophy that handled its most fundamental problem.[60]

III

More however must be said. If adherence to the philosophy of natural law finally gave the Court Whigs a secure foundation for their defense of the concept of a balanced constitution, it would seem to have consorted uneasily with their reiterated insistence on the doctrine of sovereignty. Natural law established the boundaries beyond which the power of the state was not to go; sovereignty implied that all states had unlimited power. In fact, however, the tension between the two was more apparent than real, for the theories were not addressing themselves to the same aspects of the political order. The doctrine that in all political bodies there was a locus of ultimate authority was taken by Court Whigs to be a statement of fact. It was believed to describe the way the international system of political entities operated. Sovereignty existed: every state possessed it. The philosophical position that the structure of human reality set limits to what state authority ought to do was on the other hand a moral teaching. It declared what Court Whigs believed to be a truth about that ethical world that all mankind lived in. Natural law existed: every state should observe it. The doctrine of sovereignty, in sum, was a descriptive theory, the philosophy of natural law a prescriptive one. Sovereignty taught that, for states, all things were possible; natural law, accepting sovereignty, taught that nevertheless not all things were permitted.

It should be recalled that the Court Whigs had decided to stress the importance of sovereignty because they had felt the need to defend themselves against Patriot accusations that the government was wielding too much power. All governments, they had retorted, have unlimited power; what is important is how they exercise that power. To explicate that point the Court Whigs had insisted that the crucial distinction was whether a government was arbitrary or lawful, and that

60. Kenyon treats Court Whiggery with undue harshness when he asserts that it underwent a "moral breakdown" after 1715. He may disapprove of what it taught, but he should beware of mistaking a shift in vision for a loss of vision or of confusing alteration with decay. He seems, in truth, an inhabitant of the brilliant but fevered world of the *Dunciad*—a redoubt of Catonism. Kenyon, *Revolution Principles*, 177.

so long as it was lawful—and Britain's was—the sovereign authority of the state was exercised to the end of serving rather than crushing the people. It was not difficult to link this teaching that lawfulness prevented oppression with the collateral teaching that natural law forbade oppression. Natural law was discoverable by right reason, and in Britain—at least in Squire's, Herring's, and Hardwicke's view—the common law was a distillation of "natural reason." The conflation of right reason and natural reason was irresistible and led, in Hardwicke's formulation, to the conviction that Britain's constitutional order was a product of natural reason—that it embodied agencies which, cognizant of immutable moral directives, prevented the state from behaving oppressively. It was this complex of ideas, in which common law was seen as an emanation of the same reason that discovered natural law, that enabled Court Whigs to visualize the lawful government that allowed sovereignty to serve the people as that moral government which observed the injunctions of natural law.

This gradual acceptance of a philosophy of natural law to account for British governmental practice became the touchstone by which the Court Whigs determined whether to accept or reject other discrete theories which, in the political heat of the day, they sometimes found themselves promoting. One such theory was the teaching that law was simply the will of those who held authority. Adherents of this theory of positive law were never numerous among Court Whigs, for it was a doctrine more congenial to those who sought to undo constitutional equilibrium and enhance the power of the Commons. But some were influential. Bishop Hoadly, it will be recalled, adumbrated a conjunction of contractualism and positive law. It was not until the decade of the 1730s, however, that Francis Osborne, writing in the London *Journal*, gave this teaching its fullest Court Whig exposition. The conjunction provided a splendid basis for allowing Court Whigs to retain their affection for the notion that all governmental power took its origin in the people while simultaneously maintaining that the directives of a government were virtually irresistible. All government, Osborne taught, rested on consent. Only by consent could one person acquire command over another. But once that command was conveyed, the commanders had a full authority, hedged only by their obligation to remain faithful to the constitution. Their authority to legislate was unchecked; their legislative will was the definition of law. On these points Osborne could be quite explicit. "In a Word, the Rights of the *People*, are the Rights of the *Governed*, not the Rights of the *Governors*; nor have they any *Right*, *Power*, or *Authority*, while the Laws are observed, over the *Executive* or *Legislative* Power of the Kingdom." The legislature, he wrote on another occasion, "must *judge*, what *Laws* are best for us."[61] The teaching was manifestly attractive. It rooted governmental power in the governed, but it freed the hands of government to act in whatever manner it saw fit, provided only that it observed the procedural requirements of the constitution. The theory was also, however, at odds with the philosophy of natural law. It is probably no coincidence that as Court Whiggery accepted the implications of natural law it abandoned an advocacy of positive law such as one finds in Osborne's essays.

Some Court Whig writers were very quick to see the incompatibility of the doctrines of natural law and positive law. They saw too that Cicero himself had addressed the issue. In 1728, over the nom de plume "Philalethes," the London *Journal* ran an essay in which it declared that "no *Positive Laws* can be made to the Injury of, or contrary to, the Law of Nature." If a legislature presumed to enact a measure that contravened the dictates of natural law, such a measure would have no force. Appeal was made to Cicero. "If, says Tully, *Right* was made by the *Resolution* of the *People*, by the *Decrees* of *Princes*, by the *Determinations* of *Judges*, it might be Right to *Thieve*, Right to commit *Adultery*, Right to forge *Wills*, supposing that these Things should happen to be approv'd by the Votes or Ordinance of any People." Another journalist, writing as "Publicola," advanced the same point more compactly: "Law does not *make* but *declare*, Right and Wrong." It is more

---

61. London *Journal*, June 2, September 1, and May 26, 1733. Samuel Squire, in *Letter to a Tory Friend*, advanced a variation on this argument. Jeffrey Nelson has recently suggested that this line of thought characterized "mainstream" Whig thinking in the Court Whig era. The evidence suggests that Nelson is in error. But he would appear to be correct in seeing American loyalists as disciples of Court Whig thinking; the element in that thought that they seized upon, however, was balance. "Ideology in Search of a Context: Eighteenth-Century British Political Thought and the Loyalists of the American Revolution," *Historical Journal*, XX (1977), 741–49.

significant, however, that even Francis Osborne, the foremost spokesman for the positive theory of law among regular Court Whig writers, was himself wont to acknowledge the hegemony of natural law. In 1730 he stated that "the great *Law of Nature*, or *Reason* of Things . . . is *Fundamental* to all *other Laws*" and that "all Things must submit to *that Law*, but *That* to Nothing." In 1732 he wrote of "this *Law of Nature*, by which all *other Laws* must be *tried*, and to which they must all *submit*"; and to underline his point he quoted Cicero's condemnation of the rape of Lucretia as a deed that would have been criminal even had there been no statute declaring it so. In 1735, in the very act of resigning his pen, he affirmed what "Publicola" and countless earlier natural lawyers had believed: "Law can *declare* and *enforce* what is Right, but *not constitute Right*."[62] Court Whiggery thus rejected the theory of positive law. Whatever its short-term utility, the theory was compelled to yield to the implications of natural law philosophy.

If the acceptance of natural law obliged Court Whigs to abandon whatever inclination they may have had to adopt the theory of positive law, it was more hospitable to two other political theories which sometimes found expression in their writings. One of these theories, the notion of prescription, has been examined as an aspect of the thinking of Lord Hardwicke. But he was not alone in employing it. A Court Whig pamphlet of the late 1740s, for example, in pronouncing upon the Glorious Revolution, noted that even if it had been an event illegal in itself, the passage of time since 1688–1689 had given legitimacy to the order it had created—indeed, as much legitimacy as the Roman order possessed when, in the days of Nero, Scripture commanded subjection to higher powers. For obvious reasons this prescriptive defense of the Glorious Revolution increased in plausibility as the temporal distance of the commentator from the event lengthened. Another pamphlet, in legitimizing popular participation in legislative activity, declared that the right had existed since "time immemorial." Denominating rights established in this manner as "*prescriptive* Rights, or Usages *immemorial*," the author noted that "the Want of such authentic Monuments [as would ordain such rights] does not invalidate, or call

62. London *Journal*, March 9, 1727/28, December 14, 1728 (quoting *De Legibus*, 1. 16. 42.); London *Journal*, December 19, 1730, April 8, 1732, June 28, 1735.

[them] in question."[63] Natural law doctrine could readily assimilate this theory of prescription. Under the presumption that usages of ancient origin proved their value by their persistence, Court Whiggery comprehended prescriptive rights among those rights that their forefathers, through consulting natural reason, had deemed appropriate or necessary. In such a manner the line from the late Court Whigs to Edmund Burke may be drawn, and it turns out to be far more direct than is sometimes believed.

The other Court Whig theory which the doctrine of natural law was able to assimilate was the widely advanced view that necessity legitimized the Glorious Revolution. As Locke's contractual theory of legitimization became either embarrassing or cumbersome, Court Whigs turned in growing numbers to the view that the necessitous situation of 1688—the extraordinary nature of the times—had in itself justified actions that, narrowly speaking, were illegal. Francis Osborne noted that those actions might not bear a scrupulous judicial scrutiny, but, he added, "'tis no Matter whether this was done in a strict *Legislative* Way, or out of a *Legislative* Way." Edward Bentham, already cited as a defender of the notion of prescriptive rights, gave his endorsement to Osborne's interpretation. The actions taken by Britain in 1688 and 1689 were, he acknowledged, "new and unprecedented." "But," he added, "so was the Occasion." Standing laws, he explained, were designed for the common course of affairs. When emergencies arose, standing laws wisely fell silent. "It is sufficient therefore if the Conduct of our Ancestors in the Revolution was warranted by the general Reason of the Case." Clearly such warrant existed in 1688: "few Revolutions in Government have been founded on a more apparent Necessity." Samuel Squire meanwhile lent the support of scholarship to this doctrine of necessity.[64] At first glance this justification by necessity—a

63. Bentham, *Letter*, 23–24; *Political Magnet*, 7–8.

64. London *Journal*, April 8, 1732; Bentham, *Letter*, 17; Squire, *Historical Essay*, 91. It is instructive to compare the respective roles that the Glorious Revolution played in Whig thought of the first and second postrevolutionary generations. For most of the Whigs investigated by Kenyon in *Revolution Principles*—the immediate postrevolutionary generation—political and constitutional thinking was rooted in the events of 1688–89: it was designed to explicate them. For most of the Court Whigs of Walpole's day the revolution, though the most important circumstance of modern British history, was no

theory scarcely distinguishable from the view that the end justifies the means—seems starkly at variance with the insistence of natural lawyers that limits exist on what is permissible. But an accommodation between the two was possible. The advocates of the view that necessity legitimized the actions of 1688–1689 carefully delimited the area of application of their teaching to truly extraordinary situations. It was not, therefore, a view susceptible to frequent invocation. The exponents of the theory of natural law on the other hand had no difficulty in acknowledging—for Cicero himself had done so—that in extraordinary situations the ordinary laws no longer bound. What was appropriate on such unusual occasions was for prudential men to exercise authority and to consult the abiding interests of the people involved. Thus the two theories converged: the view that necessity sufficed to legitimize the Glorious Revolution was a specific citation of a more general theory, approved by the defenders of natural law, that in the extraordinary situation ordinary rules lost their force.

In a wide variety of ways therefore the Ciceronian impress rested upon maturing Court Whig thought. Ciceronian thinking compelled Court Whigs to abandon the doctrines that could not be assimilated to natural law philosophy, but it offered a reinforced plausibility to doctrines that could be made to conform to the flexible demands of the natural law. It would be a patent exaggeration to attribute all the themes, thrusts, and inclinations of Court Whig thinking to the great Roman republican. It was the Patriot opposition that chose the precise topics that were discussed in the political forums during the Court Whig era, and it was therefore the opposition that set the agenda for the public debate. But Cicero provided a philosophy and focus to which ministerial writers could repair—and to which, with the passage of the years, in increasing numbers they did repair. It is thus not an exaggeration to say that Cicero was the single most important theorizing influence on the greatest of the ministerial apologists of the years between 1725 and 1755. In this respect one may call the age Ciceronian.

---

longer the Glorious Revelation. Court Whigs fitted it into their views, easily or uneasily as the case may be, but they did not treat it as determinative of philosophy—and indeed many, following the lead of the managers of 1710, spoke of it as an anomaly.

Bibliography of Works Cited

Primary Sources

Manuscript Collections

British Museum
  Add. MSS 4318
  Add. MSS 5831
  Add. MSS 32690–32953
  Add. MSS 35351–36182
University of Nottingham Library
  Pw V 120
  Pw V 121

Pamphlets, Broadsheets, and Sermons

An Address to the Freeholders of Great Britain, in Favour of our Constitution. London: J. Roberts, 1734.
An Address to the Freeholders of the County of Oxford, on the Subject of the Present Election. London: n.p., 1753.
An Address to the People of Great Britain; occasioned by the Republication of the Craftsmen [sic]. London: J. Peele, 1731.
The Advantages of the Hanoverian Succession. London: M. Cooper, 1744.
The Anti-Craftsman: being an Answer to the Craftsman Extraordinary. London: J. Brindley, 1729.
An Apology for Government According to Law. London: J. Roberts, 1735.
An Apology for the Conduct of the Present Administration. London: n.p., 1744.
An Appeal to the Nation: or, The Case of the Present Prime Minister of Great-Britain truly stated. London: J. Jolliffe, 1731.

[Arnall, William.] *Clodius and Cicero.* London: J. Peele, 1727.

———. *A Letter to a Freeholder, on the late reduction of the land tax to one shilling in the pound.* London: J. Peele, 1732.

———. *Observations on a Pamphlet.* London: J. Roberts, 1731.

———. *Opposition No Proof of Patriotism.* London: J. Roberts, 1735.

B—, G—. *The Advantages of the Revolution.* London: n.p., 1753.

The Balance: or the Merits of Whig and Tory, Exactly weigh'd and fairly determin'd. London: n.p., 1753.

Bentham, Edward. *A Letter to a Young Gentleman of Oxford.* London: S. Birt, 1749.

The Case of the Opposition Stated, between the Craftsman and the People. London: J. Roberts, 1731.

The Case re-stated. London: M. Cooper, 1748(?).

The Case Truly Stated; or the Merits of Both Parties Fully Considered. London: n.p., n.d.

Cato's Dream. Dublin: n.p., 1723.

Cato's Letter to the Bishop of Rochester. London: n.p., 1723.

Cato's Principles of Self-Preservation and Publick Liberty. London: n.p., 1722.

The Censor Censur'd: or, Cato turned Catiline. London: n.p., 1722.

Chesterfield, Philip Dormer Stanhope, Earl of. *An Apology for a Late Resignation.* London: John Freeman, 1748.

A Church of England-man's Reasons for taking the Oaths to His Present Majesty King George. London: J. Peele, 1723.

[Cibber, Colley.] *The Character and Conduct of Cicero, considered from the History of His Life, by the Reverend Dr. Middleton.* London: n.p., 1747.

The Citizen's Procession, or, The Smugler's [sic] Success and the Patriot's Disappointment. London: A. Dodd, 1733.

Clarke, Alured. *A Sermon preached . . . January XXXI, 1731.* London: n.p., 1731.

A Coalition of Patriots Delineated, Or, A Just Display of the Union of Jacobites, Malecontents, Republicans. London: T. Cooper, 1735.

A Complete View of the Present Politicks of Great-Britain. London: T. Cooper, 1743.

The Conduct of the Late Administration with regard to Foreign Affairs, from 1722 to 1742. Dublin: G. Faulkner, 1742.

The Conduct of the Ministry Compared with Its Consequences: or an Im-

partial View of the Present State of Affairs. London: J. Crichley, 1733.

The Conduct of the Ministry impartially examined. London: S. Bladon, 1756.

The Conduct of the Two B—rs Vindicated. London: M. Cooper, 1749.

A Continuation of the Plain Reasoner. London: M. Cooper, 1745.

The Country Correspondent. Being, a Letter from a Country Gentleman to a Friend in Town. London: T. Cooper, 1739.

The Craftsman's Doctrine and Practice of the Liberty of the Press. London: n.p., 1732.

The Crafts of the Craftsmen. London: J. Roberts, 1736.

The Criterion of the Reason and Necessity of the Present War. London: n.p., 1745.

Croxall, Samuel. *A Sermon preach'd . . . January XXX, 1729.* London: n.p., 1729.

The Danger of Faction to a Free People. London: n.p., 1732.

The Danger to Civil Liberty from an Independent Army. Being a Short Argument Against Giving Military Officers Commissions for Life. London: n.p., 1734(?).

[Davenant, Charles.] *The True Picture of a Modern Whig set forth in a Dialogue between Mr. Whiglove and Mr. Double.* London: n.p., 1701.

The Death of M–l–n in the Life of Cicero. London: E. Nutt, 1741.

A Defense of the Measures of the Present Administration. Being an Impartial Answer to What Has Been Objected Against It. London: J. Peele, 1731.

[Defoe, Daniel?] *The Wickedness of a Disregard to Oaths; and the Pernicious Consequences of it to Religion and Government.* London: n.p., 1723.

A Dialogue between Sir Anthony Freeport and Timothy Squat, esquire, on the Subject of Excises. London: J. Roberts, 1733.

The Difference Computed, in a Brief History of Arbitrary Power. London: J. Roberts, 1735.

A Dissertation on Patriotism: shewing, the use of those two great Qualifications of a Patriot, Integrity and Courage. London: J. Roberts, 1735.

[Egmont, John Perceval, Earl of (1711–70).] *An Examination of the Principles, and an Inquiry into the Conduct of the Two B—rs.* London: A. Price, 1749.

———. *Faction Detected by the Evidence of Facts.* London: J. Roberts, 1743.

[Egmont, John Perceval, Earl of (1683–1748).] *The Thoughts of an Impartial Man upon the Present Temper of the Nation.* London: n.p., 1733.

An Enquiry into the Danger of Multiplying Incapacities on the Gentlemen of England to sit in Parliament. London: J. Roberts, 1739.

An Enquiry into the Present State of Our Domestick Affairs. London: T. Cooper, 1742.

An Essay on Faction. London: n.p., 1733.

An Essay upon Publick Credit, in a Letter to a Friend. London: H. Carpenter, 1748.

An Excellent Sermon in Defense of Passive-Obedience and Non-Resistance. London: J. Dormer, 1733.

A Final Answer to the Treasonable Invectives of the Craftsman. London: T. Cooper, 1734.

The Freeholder's Alarm to His Brethren; or, the Fate of Britain Determin'd by the Ensuing Election. London: J. Roberts, 1734.

A Full and True Account of the Strange and Miraculous Conversion of All the Tories in Great Britain; by the Preaching of Caleb D'Anvers, prophet and apostle to these nations. London: J. Roberts, 1734.

Gibson, Edmund. *The Lord Bishop of London's Third Caveat Against Sedition.* London: n.p., 1731.

[Gordon, Thomas.] *An Appeal to the Unprejudiced, concerning the present discontents occasioned by the late convention with Spain.* London: T. Cooper, 1739.

―――. *The character of an independent Whig.* London: J. Roberts, 1719.

The Happy Government: or, The Constitution of Great Britain. London: n.p., 1734.

Hay, William. *An Essay on Civil Government.* London: R. Gosling, 1728.

Hayter, Thomas. *A Sermon Preached . . . June 11, 1746.* London: n.p., 1746.

―――. *A Sermon Preach'd . . . January 30, 1749–50.* London: n.p., 1750.

[Hervey, John, baron.] *Ancient and Modern Liberty Stated and Compared.* London: J. Roberts, 1734.

―――. *An Answer to the Country Parson's Plea against the Quakers Tythe-Bill.* London: J. Roberts, 1736(?).

―――. *The Conduct of the Opposition and the Tendency of Modern Pa-*

triotism. London: R. Fleming, 1734.

———. *Farther Observations on the Writings of the Craftsman*. London: J. Roberts, 1730.

———. *A Letter to the Author of Common Sense; or The Englishman's Journal, of Saturday, April 16*. London: T. Cooper, 1737.

———. *A Letter to the Craftsman on the Game of Chess, &c*. London: J. Peele, 1733.

———. *Miscellaneous Thoughts on the Present Posture both of Our Foreign and Domestic Affairs*. London: J. Roberts, 1742.

———. *Observations on the Writings of the Craftsman*. London: J. Roberts, 1730.

———. *The Question Stated with Regard to Our Army in Flanders*. London: J. Roberts, 1743.

———. *The Reply of a Member of Parliament to the Mayor of His Corporation*. London: J. Roberts, 1733.

———. *Sequel of a Pamphlet intitled Observations on the Writings of the Craftsman*. London: J. Roberts, 1730.

[Hill, Aaron.] *An Enquiry into the Merit of Assassination: with a View to the Character of Caesar*. London: T. Cooper, 1738.

An Historical View of the Principles, Characters, Persons, &c. of the Political Writers in Great Britain. London: n.p., 1740.

The History of the Modern Patriots. London: n.p., 1732.

A History of the Rise, Progress, and Tendency of Patriotism . . . With a Curious Dissertation on the Diseases and Cures of Patriots. London: W. Owen, 1747.

A Hue and Cry after Part of a Pack of Hounds, which broke out of their Kennel in Westminster. London: F. Style, 1739.

An Humble Address to the People of England. Being, a demonstration that a land-tax is more prejudicial to trade and liberty, than an inland duty on wine and tobacco. London: T. Cooper, 1733.

The Judgment of Whole Kingdoms and Nations, concerning the Rights, Power and Prerogative of Kings, and the Rights, Privileges and Properties of the People. London: n.p., 1713.

The Landed Interest Consider'd: being serious advice to gentlemen, yeomen, farmers, and others, concerned in the ensuing election. London: J. Roberts, 1733.

Lavington, George. *A Sermon preached . . . May 29, 1747*. London: J. & P. Knapton, 1747.

A Letter from a Gentleman in the Country to Sir R— W—. London: R.

Walker, 1729.

A Letter from a Gentleman in Worcestershire to a Member of Parliament in London. London: n.p., 1727.

A Letter from a Merchant of London to a Member of Parliament. London: A. Dodd, 1733.

A Letter to a Member of Parliament. Concerning the Present State of Affairs at Home and Abroad. London: T. Cooper, 1740.

A Letter to Mr. P—, in which the Controversy betwixt the Friends of the Present Administration and Him is fairly stated. London: J. Crichley, 1731.

A Letter to William Pulteney, esq, concerning the administration of affairs in Great Britain. London: J. Roberts, 1733.

Liberty and Right: or, An Essay, historical and political, on the constitution and administration of Great-Britain. Two parts. London: J. Robinson, 1747.

The Life of the Right Honourable Sir Robert Walpole. London: n.p., 1731.

Loyalty to Our King. London: M. Cooper, 1745.

[Lyttelton, George, Baron.] A Letter to the Tories. London: n.p., 1747.

———. A Modest Apology for My Own Conduct. London: M. Cooper, 1748.

———. Observations on the Life of Cicero. London: n.p., 1733.

Mason, John. Subjection to the Higher Powers . . . a sermon preach'd . . . November 5, 1740. London: R. Hett, 1741.

Mr. Addison turn'd Tory: or, The Scene Inverted. London: J. Baker, 1713.

A Modest and Impartial Reply to a Pamphlet Lately Published. London: n.p., 1749(?).

[Morris, Corbyn.] A Letter from a Bystander to a Member of Parliament. London: J. Roberts, 1742.

The Necessity of Lowering Interest and Continuing Taxes, demonstrated. London: E. Coxton, 1750.

Observations upon Cato, a Tragedy. London: n.p., 1713.

The Occasional Patriot. London: n.p., 1756.

The Ordinary of Newgate's Account of the Parentage, Birth, Education, Strange Life and Behaviour, of Caleb D'Anvers, esq. London: T. Cooper, 1734.

Parker, William. A Sermon preached . . . January 31, 1757. London: n.p., 1757.

Party Spirit in Time of Publick Danger, considered. London: T. Waller, 1756.

The Patriot and the Minister Review'd. London: n.p., 1743.

The Patriot at Full Length; or, An inscription for an obelisk. London: T. Cooper, 1735.

Plain Matter of Fact; or, Whiggism the Bulwark of the Kingdoms. London: J. Roberts, 1742.

The Political Magnet: Or, An Essay in defence of the late revolution. London: W. Sandby, 1745.

Poplicola's Supplement to Cato's Letter, concerning Popularity. London: n.p., 1722.

The Popularity of Modern Patriotism. London: n.p., 1731.

Potter, John. *A Sermon Preach'd at the Coronation of King George II.* London: n.p., 1727.

The Present Measures prov'd to be the Only Means of Securing the Balance of Power in Europe, as Well as the Liberty and Independency of Great-Britain. London: n.p., 1743.

The Proper Reply of a Member of Parliament. London: n.p., 1733.

Remarks on the Craftsman's Vindication of His Two Honble Patrons. London: J. Peele, 1731.

Remarks on the R-p-n of the H— of C—ns to the K-g; and His M-y's A-f-r. London: A. Moore, 1728.

The Resignation Discussed. London: J. Roberts, 1748.

A Review of the Controversy. London: n.p., 1734.

A Second Letter to a Member of Parliament Concerning the Present State of Affairs. London: T. Cooper, 1741.

The Sense of an Englishman on the Pretended Coalition of Parties, and on the Merits of the Whig Interest. London: n.p., 1734.

A Serious Address to the Electors of Great-Britain on the present Election. London: C. Corbett, 1747.

A Serious Address to the Freeholders of Great Britain. London: n.p., 1734.

A Serious Remonstrance to the Publick. In regard to the many bold uncommon insults and reflections lately publish'd against the government. London: J. Roberts, 1740.

Sherlock, Thomas. *A Caution Against Speaking Evil of Our Governors and of One Another.* London: J. Roberts, 1733.

———. *A Sermon preach'd before the Queen.* London: n.p., 1735.

Smedley, Jonathon. *A Discourse Concerning the Love of Our Country.* London: R. Baldwin, 1716.

Some Observations upon a Paper, intituled, The List. London: J. Peele, 1733.

Some Remarks upon a Late Pamphlet, entituled, An Humble Address to the Knights, Citizens, and Burgesses in the Ensuing Parliament. London: T. Cooper, 1735.

Some Thoughts upon a Bill for General Naturalization: addressed to those of all denominations who act upon Whig-principles. London: M. Cooper, 1751.

[Squire, Samuel.] *Letter to a Tory Friend on the Present Critical Situation of Our Affairs.* London: n.p., 1746.

————. *A Letter to John Trot-Plaid, author of the Jacobite Journal, on Mr. Carte's History. By Duncan MacCarte, a Highlander.* London: n.p., 1748.

————. *Remarks on Mr. Carte's Specimen of His General History of England.* London: n.p., 1748.

[Steele, Richard.] *A Comparison between Cato and Caesar.* London: n.p., 1713.

Theobald, Lewis. *The Life and Character of Marcus Portius Cato Uticensis.* London: Bernard Lintott, 1713.

[Tindal, Matthew?] *A Defense of Our Present Happy Establishment; and the Administration Vindicated.* London: J. Roberts, 1722.

A Vindication of the Conduct of the Ministry. London: J. Roberts, 1734.

A Vindication of the Honour and Privileges of the Commons of Great-Britain. London: J. Roberts, 1740.

[Walpole, Horace, Baron.] *The Interest of Great Britain Steadily Pursued.* London: J. Roberts, 1743.

————. *The Rise and Fall of the Late Projected Excise, impartially consider'd.* London: J. Peele, 1733.

[Walpole, Sir Robert.] *Observations upon the Treaty between the Crowns of Great-Britain, France, and Spain.* London: n.p., 1729.

————. *Some Considerations concerning the Public Funds, the Public Revenues, and Annual Supplies.* London: J. Roberts, 1735.

————. *Some General Considerations concerning the Alteration and Improvement of Publick Revenues.* London: J. Roberts, 1733.

Williams, Philip. *The Love of Our Constitution in Church and State . . . A Sermon preach'd . . . 11th of June 1738.* Cambridge: W. Thurlbourne, 1738.

Wingfield, Thomas. *The Mischiefs of Unreasonable Opposition to Government. A Sermon preach'd . . . January the 30th, 1748–9*. London: J. Clarke, 1749.

A Word in Season to the Old Whigs. London: n.p., 1754.

[Yonge, Sir William.] *Sedition and Defamation display'd: in a Letter to the Author of the Craftsman*. London: J. Roberts, 1731.

Young, Edward. *An Apology for Princes . . . January the 30th, 1728/9*. London: T. Worrall, 1729.

Collected Contemporary Works

Arbuthnot, John. *The Life and Work of John Arbuthnot*. Edited by George A. Aitken. Oxford: Clarendon Press, 1892.

Bolingbroke, Henry St. John, Viscount. *The Works of Lord Bolingbroke*. 4 vols. Philadelphia: Carey and Hart, 1841.

———. *The Works of the Late Right Honourable Henry St. John, Lord Viscount Bolingbroke*. Edited by Dr. Goldsmith. 8 vols. London: J. Johnson, 1809.

Gordon, Thomas, and John Trenchard. *Cato's Letters; or, Essays on Liberty, Civil and Religious, and other important Subjects*. 2 vols. Originally published in 1733. New York: Russell and Russell, 1969.

Herring, Thomas. *Seven Sermons on Public Occasions by the Most Reverend Dr. Thomas Herring, Late Lord Archbishop of Canterbury*. London: n.p., 1763.

Hoadly, Benjamin. *Sixteen Sermons, formerly presented, now collected into one volume*. London: J. and P. Knapton, 1754.

———. *Twenty Sermons*. London: J. Knapton, 1755.

———. *Works*. Edited by John Hoadly. 3 vols. London: W. Bowyer and J. Nichols, 1773.

Pearce, Zachary. *Sermons on Several Subjects*. 4 vols. London: J. Derby, 1778.

Robertson, J. Logie, ed. *The Complete Poetical Works of James Thomson*. London: Henry Frowde, 1908.

Sherlock, Thomas. *Several Discourses preached at the Temple Church*. Vol. IV. London: J. Whiston and B. White, 1758.

Squire, Samuel. *Works*. 4 vols. London: n.p., 1741–63. This is a special "made-up collection" in the British Museum.

Published Correspondence

Garnett, R. "Correspondence of Archbishop Herring and Lord Hardwicke during the Rebellion of 1745." *English Historical Review*, XIX (1904), 528–50, 719–42.

Letters between Lord Hervey and Dr. Middleton concerning the Roman Senate. London: W. Strahan, 1778.

Letters from the Late Most Reverend Dr. Thomas Herring, Lord Archbishop of Canterbury, to William Duncombe, Esq; deceased, from the Year 1728 to 1757. London: J. Johnson, 1777.

Letters to and from the Rev. Philip Doddridge, D.D. Edited by Thomas Stedman. Shrewsbury, U.K.: J. and W. Eddowes, 1790.

Lewis, W. S. *et al.*, eds. *The Yale Edition of Horace Walpole's Correspondence*. 42 vols. New Haven, Conn.: Yale University Press, 1937–80.

Lord Hervey and His Friends, 1726–38. Edited by Giles Stephen Holland Fox-Strangways, earl of Ilchester. London: Murray, 1950.

Pope, Alexander. *The Correspondence of Alexander Pope*. Edited by George Sherburn. 5 vols. Oxford: Clarendon Press, 1956.

Scholarly Works from the Period

Birch, Thomas. *The Life of the Most Reverend Dr. John Tillotson, Lord Archbishop of Canterbury*. London: J. & R. Tonson, 1752.

Blackwell, Thomas. *Memoirs of the Court of Augustus*. 3 vols. Edinburgh: A. Millar, 1753–63.

Bolingbroke, Henry St. John, Viscount. *Letters on the Study and Use of History*. Printed in *Lord Bolingbroke: Historical Writings*. Edited by Isaac Kramnick. Chicago: University of Chicago Press, 1972.

Burnet, Gilbert. *History of His Own Time*. Edited by Thomas Burnet. 2 vols. London: T. Ward, 1724–34.

Clarendon, Edward Hyde, Earl of. *The History of the Rebellion and Civil Wars in England, begun in the Year 1641*. 3 vols. Oxford: printed at the Theatre, 1717.

Courteville, Raphael. *Memoirs of the Life and Administration of William Cecil, Baron Burleigh*. London: T. Cooper, 1738.

Cowper, William, Earl. *An Impartial History of Parties*. Printed in John, Lord Campbell. *Lives of the Lord Chancellors and the Keepers of the Great Seal of England*. Vol. IV. Philadelphia: Blanchard and Lea, 1846.

Echard, Laurence. *The History of the Revolution and the Establishment of England in the Year 1688*. London: J. Tonson, 1725.
———. *The Roman History from the Building of the City, to the Perfect Settlement of the Empire by Augustus Caesar*. London: M. Gillyflower, 1695.
Gordon, Thomas. *The Works of Tacitus*. 2 vols. London: T. Woodward and J. Peele, 1728–31.
Hooke, Nathaniel. *The Roman History from the Building of Rome to the Ruin of the Commonwealth*. 4 vols. London: James Bettenham, 1751–71.
Hume, David. *Philosophical Essays Concerning Human Understanding*. London: David Millar, 1748.
Larrey, Isaac de. *Histoire d'Angleterre, d'Ecosse, et d'Irlande*. 4 vols. Rotterdam: R. Leers, 1697–1713.
Lowman, Moses. *A Dissertation on the Civil Government of the Hebrews*. London: J. Noon, 1740.
Middleton, Conyers. *The History of the Life of Marcus Tullius Cicero*. 3 vols. London: W. Innys, 1742.
Oldmixon, John. *The Critical History of England, Ecclesiastical and Civil*. 2 vols. London: C. Rivington, 1724–30.
Rapin-Thoyras, Paul de. *A Dissertation on the Whigs and Tories*. Printed in his *The History of England*. Vol. II. London: J. Harrison, 1789.
St. Amand, George. *An Historical Essay on the Legislative Power of England*. London: T. Woodward, 1725.
Squire, Samuel. *An Enquiry into the Foundation of the English Constitution*. London: C. Bathurst, 1745.
———. *Historical Essay upon the Balance of Civil Power in England*. London: M. Cooper, 1748.
Warburton, William. *The Divine Legation of Moses Demonstrated*. Vol. III. London: Fletcher Gyles, 1766.

Memoirs from the Period

Cibber, Colley. *An Apology for the Life of Colley Cibber*. Edited by B. R. S. Fone. Ann Arbor: University of Michigan Press, 1965.
Hervey, John, Baron. *Memoirs of the Reign of George the Second, from His Accession to the Death of Queen Caroline*. Edited by John Wilson Croker. 2 vols. Philadelphia: Blanchard and Lea, 1848.

————. *Some Materials Towards Memoirs of the Reign of King George II*. Edited by Romney Sedgwick. 3 vols. London: W. Kimber, 1931.

Newspapers and Periodicals

Craftsman (London), 1726–40.
Daily Gazetteer (London), 1735–48.
Freeholder, nos. 1–55. Printed in *The Works of the Right Honourable Joseph Addison*. Edited by Richard Hurd. Vol. IV. New York: William Durrell, 1811.
London Journal, 1721–38.

Influential Older Works

Barker, Ernest, trans. and ed. *The Politics of Aristotle*. Oxford: Oxford University Press, 1973.
Bloom, Allan, trans. and ed. *The Republic of Plato*. New York: Basic Books, 1968.
Cicero, Marcus Tullius. *De Officiis*. Translated by Walter Miller. New York: G. P. Putnam's Sons, 1928.
————. *De Officiis/On Duties*. Translated by Harry G. Edinger. New York: Bobbs-Merrill, 1974.
————. *De Re Publica, De Legibus*. Translated by Clinton Walker Keyes. Loeb Classical Library. New York: G. P. Putnam's Sons, 1928.
————. *M. Tulii Ciceronis Opera*. Edited by J. G. Baiter and C. L. Kayser. 11 vols. Leipzig: Bernhard Tauchnitz, 1860–69.
de Bracton, Henry. *Bracton De Legibus et Consuetudinibus Angliae*. Edited by George E. Woodbine. 3 vols. New York: Yale University Press, 1915–42.
Harrington, James. *The Commonwealth of Oceana*. Edited by Henry Morley. London: Routledge, 1887.
Hobbes, Thomas. *Leviathan*. Edited by Michael Oakeshott. London: Macmillan, 1970.
Hooker, Richard. *Of the Laws of Ecclesiastical Polity: An Abridged Edition*. Edited by A. S. McGrade and Brian Vickers. New York: St. Martin's, 1975.
Locke, John. *The Educational Writings of John Locke*. Edited by James L. Axtell. Cambridge: Cambridge University Press, 1968.

————. *Two Treatises of Government.* Edited by Peter Laslett. Cambridge: Cambridge University Press, 1960.

Machiavelli, Niccolo. *The Prince and the Discourses.* Edited by Max Lerner. New York: Random House, 1950.

[Tyrrell, James.] *Patriarcha Non Monarcha.* London: n.p., 1681.

Works with Extensive Manuscript Material

Coxe, William. *Memoirs of the Administration of the Right Honourable Henry Pelham.* 2 vols. London: Longman et al., 1829.

————. *Memoirs of the Life and Administration of Sir Robert Walpole, Earl of Orford.* 3 vols. London: T. Caddell, Jr., and W. Davies, 1798.

Yorke, Philip C. *The Life and Correspondence of Philip Yorke, Earl of Hardwicke, Lord High Chancellor of Great Britain.* 3 vols. Cambridge: Cambridge University Press, 1913.

Miscellaneous

Addison, Joseph. *Cato, a Tragedy.* London: J. Tonson, 1713.

Cibber, Colley. *Caesar in Egypt.* London: John Watts, 1725.

Cobbett's Parliamentary History of England. Vols. IX–XIV. London: T. C. Hansard, 1811–13.

Cumberland, Richard. *The Banishment of Cicero.* London: J. Walter, 1761.

Lyttelton, George, Baron. *Dialogues of the Dead.* Dublin: Oliver Nelson and John Exshaw, 1765.

Ollard, S. L., and P. C. Walker, eds. *Archbishop Herring's Visitation Returns, 1743.* The Yorkshire Archaeological Society. Record Series. Vols. LXXI–LXXIX. Wakefield, U.K.: n.p., 1928–31.

Pope, Alexander. *Poetry and Prose of Alexander Pope.* Edited by Aubrey Williams. New York: Houghton Mifflin, 1969.

————. *The Twickenham Edition of the Poems of Alexander Pope.* Edited by John Butt et al. 10 vols. New Haven, Conn.: Yale University Press, 1942–67.

Swift, Jonathan. *Gulliver's Travels; an account of the four voyages into several remote nations of the world.* New York: Heritage, 1940.

Toland, John. *The State-Anatomy of Great Britain.* 8th edition. London: J. Philips, 1717.

Secondary Sources

Books

Atherton, Herbert M. *Political Prints in the Age of Hogarth: A Study of the Ideographic Representation of Politics.* Oxford: Clarendon Press, 1974.

Bailyn, Bernard. *The Ideological Origins of the American Revolution.* Cambridge, Mass.: Belknap Press, 1967.

Baron, Hans. *The Crisis of the Early Italian Renaissance: Civic Humanism and Republican Liberty in an Age of Classicism and Tyranny.* 2 vols. Princeton, N.J.: Princeton University Press, 1955.

Bennett, G. V. *The Tory Crisis in Church and State, 1688–1730: The Career of Francis Atterbury, Bishop of Rochester.* Oxford: Clarendon Press, 1976.

Blitzer, Charles. *An Immortal Commonwealth: The Political Thought of James Harrington.* New Haven, Conn.: Yale University Press, 1960.

Brewer, John. *Party Ideology and Popular Politics at the Accession of George III.* Cambridge: Cambridge University Press, 1976.

Browning, Reed. *The Duke of Newcastle.* New Haven, Conn.: Yale University Press, 1975.

Carswell, John. *The South Sea Bubble.* Stanford, Ca.: Stanford University Press, 1960.

Clarke, Martin Lowther. *Classical Education in Britain, 1500–1900.* Cambridge: University Press, 1959.

Corwin, Edward S. *The 'Higher Law' Background of American Constitutional Law.* Ithaca, N.Y.: Great Seal Books, 1955.

Cruickshanks, Eveline. *Political Untouchables: The Tories and the '45.* New York: Holmes and Meier, 1979.

Dickinson, H. T. *Bolingbroke.* London: Constable, 1970.

————. *Liberty and Property: Political Ideology in Eighteenth-Century Britain.* London: Weidenfeld and Nicolson, 1977.

————. *Walpole and the Whig Supremacy.* London: English Universities Press, 1973.

Dickinson [Rastall], William. *Antiquities Historical, Architectural, Chorographical, and Itinerary, in Nottinghamshire and the Adjacent Counties.* Newark, U.K.: Holt and Hage, 1801.

Dickson, P. G. M. *The Financial Revolution in England: A Study in the Development of Public Credit 1688–1756.* London: Macmillan, 1967.

Dorey, T. A., ed. *Cicero*. London: Routledge and Paul, 1965.

Foord, Archibald S. *His Majesty's Opposition, 1714–1830*. Oxford: Clarendon Press, 1964.

Forbes, Duncan. *Hume's Philosophical Politics*. Cambridge: Cambridge University Press, 1975.

Fritz, Paul S. *The English Ministers and Jacobitism between the Rebellions of 1715 and 1745*. Toronto: University of Toronto Press, 1975.

Fussell, Paul. *The Rhetorical World of Augustan Humanism: Ethics and Imagery from Swift to Burke*. Oxford: Clarendon Press, 1965.

Goldgar, Bertrand A. *Walpole and the Wits: The Relation of Politics to Literature, 1722–1742*. Lincoln, Neb.: University of Nebraska Press, 1976.

Gwyn, William B. *The Meaning of the Separation of Powers: An Analysis of the Doctrine from Its Origin to the Adoption of the United States Constitution*. New Orleans: Tulane University, 1965.

Halsband, Robert. *Lord Hervey: Eighteenth-Century Courtier*. Oxford: Oxford University Press, 1974.

Hearnshaw, F. J. C., ed. *The Social and Political Ideas of Some English Thinkers of the Augustan Age, A.D. 1650–1750*. London: G. G. Harrap, 1928.

Hill, B. W. *The Growth of Parliamentary Parties 1689–1742*. London: Allen & Unwin, 1976.

Holdsworth, Sir William. *A History of English Law*. Vol. XII. London: Eyre Methuen, 1938.

Holmes, Geoffrey. *British Politics in the Age of Anne*. New York: Macmillan, 1967.

————. *The Trial of Doctor Sacheverell*. London: Eyre Methuen, 1973.

Howell, Wilbur Samuel. *Eighteenth-Century British Logic and Rhetoric*. Princeton, N.J.: Princeton University Press, 1971.

Jacob, Margaret C. *The Newtonians and the English Revolution, 1689–1720*. Ithaca, N.Y.: Cornell University Press, 1976.

Johnson, James William. *The Formation of English Neo-Classical Thought*. Princeton, N.J.: Princeton University Press, 1967.

Kenyon, J. P. *Revolution Principles: The Politics of Party 1689–1720*. Cambridge: Cambridge University Press, 1977.

Kramnick, Isaac. *Bolingbroke and His Circle: The Politics of Nostalgia in the Age of Walpole*. Cambridge, Mass.: Harvard University Press, 1968.

Langford, Paul. *The Excise Crisis: Society and Politics in the Age of Wal-*

pole. Oxford: Clarendon Press, 1975.

Laprade, W. T. *Public Opinion and Politics in Eighteenth Century England to the Fall of Walpole*. New York: Macmillan, 1936.

Loftis, John. *The Politics of Drama in Augustan England*. Oxford: Clarendon Press, 1963.

Mack, Maynard. *The Garden and the City: Retirement and Politics in the Later Poetry of Pope 1731–1743*. Toronto: University of Toronto Press, 1969.

McKillop, A. D. *The Background of Thomson's "Liberty."* Houston: Rice Institute, 1951.

Mansfield, Harvey C., Jr. *Statesmanship and Party Government: A Study of Burke and Bolingbroke*. Chicago: University of Chicago Press, 1965.

Nichols, John. *Illustrations of the Literary History of the Eighteenth Century*. 6 vols. London: Nichols, Son, and Bentley, 1817–31.

————. *Literary Anecdotes of the Eighteenth Century*. 9 vols. London: Nichols, Son, and Bentley, 1812–15.

Plumb, J. H. *Sir Robert Walpole*. 2 vols. Boston: Houghton Mifflin, 1956, 1961.

Pocock, J. G. A. *The Ancient Constitution and the Feudal Law*. Cambridge: Cambridge University Press, 1957.

————. *The Machiavellian Moment: Florentine Political Thought and the Atlantic Republican Tradition*. Princeton, N.J.: Princeton University Press, 1975.

Realey, Charles Bechdolt. *The Early Opposition to Sir Robert Walpole, 1720–1727*. Lawrence: University of Kansas Press, 1931.

Robbins, Caroline. *The Eighteenth-Century Commonwealthman: Studies in the Transmission, Development, and Circumstances of English Liberal Thought from the Restoration of Charles II until the War with the Thirteen Colonies*. Cambridge, Mass.: Harvard University Press, 1959.

Rowden, Aldred W. *The Primates of the Four Georges*. London: J. Murray, 1916.

Rubini, Dennis. *Court and Country, 1688–1702*. London: Hart-Davis, 1968.

Schochet, Gordon J. *Patriarchalism in Political Thought: The Authoritarian Family and Political Speculations and Attitudes, Especially in Seventeenth-Century England*. New York: Basic Books, 1975.

Schwoerer, Lois G. *"No Standing Armies!" The Antiarmy Ideology in Seventeenth-Century England*. Baltimore: Johns Hopkins University

Press. 1974.

Sedgwick, Romney, ed. *The History of Parliament: The House of Commons 1715–1754*. 2 vols. New York: Oxford University Press, 1970.

Seliger, M. *The Liberal Politics of John Locke*. London: Allen & Unwin, 1968.

Stephen, Sir Leslie. *History of English Thought in the Eighteenth Century*. 2 vols. New York: G. P. Putnam's Sons, 1962.

Straka, Gerald M. *Anglican Reaction to the Revolution of 1688*. Madison: University of Wisconsin Press, 1962.

Strauss, Leo. *The Political Philosophy of Hobbes: Its Basis and Its Genesis*. Translated by Elsa M. Sinclair. Chicago: University of Chicago Press, 1952.

Syme, Ronald. *The Roman Revolution*. Oxford: Clarendon Press, 1939.

———. *Tacitus*. 2 vols. Oxford: Clarendon Press, 1958.

Taylor, Lily Ross. *Party Politics in the Age of Caesar*. Berkeley: University of California Press, 1949.

Thompson, E. P. *Whigs and Hunters: The Origin of the Black Act*. New York: Pantheon, 1975.

Vile, M. J. C. *Constitutionalism and the Separation of Powers*. Oxford: Clarendon Press, 1967.

Weston, Corinne Comstock. *English Constitutional Theory and the House of Lords 1556–1832*. New York: AMS, 1965.

Whitman, Anne *et al.*, eds. *Statesmen, Scholars and Merchants: Essays in Eighteenth-Century History Presented to Dame Lucy Sutherland*. Oxford: Clarendon Press, 1973.

Wilkes, John. *A Whig in Power: The Political Career of Henry Pelham*. Evanson, Ill.: Northwestern University Press, 1964.

Zagorin, Perez. *The Court and the Country: The Beginning of the English Revolution*. New York: Atheneum, 1969.

Zielinski, Thaddäus. *Cicero im Wandel der Jahrhunderte*. Leipzig: B. G. Teubner, 1908.

Articles

Balsdon, J. P. V. D. "Cicero the Man." In *Cicero*, edited by T. A. Dorey. London: Routledge and Kegan Paul, 1965.

Baron, Hans. "Cicero and the Roman Civic Spirit in the Middle Ages and Early Renaissance." *Bulletin of the John Rylands Library*, XXII (1938), 72–97.

Bennett, G. V. "Jacobitism and the Rise of Walpole." In *Historical Perspectives: Studies in English Thought and Society in honour of J. H. Plumb*, edited by Neil McKendrick. London: Europa, 1974.

Boulton, James T. "Arbitrary Power: An Eighteenth-Century Obsession." *Studies in Burke and His Time*, IX (1968), 905–26.

Brogan, A. P. "John Locke and Utilitarianism." *Ethics*, LXIX (1959), 79–93.

Browning, Reed. "Samuel Squire: Pamphleteering Churchman." *Eighteenth-Century Life*, V (1978), 12–20.

Burke, P. "Tacitism." In *Tacitus*, edited by T. A. Dorey. New York: Basic Books, 1969.

Burns, J. H. "Bolingbroke and the Concept of Constitutional Government." *Political Studies*, X (1962), 264–76.

Butterfield, Herbert. "Some Reflections on the Early Years of George III's Reign." *Journal of British Studies*, IV (1965), 78–101.

Clark, J. C. D. "The Decline of Party, 1740–1760." *English Historical Review*, XCIII (1978), 499–527.

Colley, Linda J. "The Loyal Brotherhood and the Cocoa Tree: The London Organization of the Tory Party, 1727–1760." *Historical Journal*, XX (1977), 77–95.

Dickinson, H. T. "Benjamin Hoadly, 1676–1761: Unorthodox Bishop." *History Today*, XXV (1975), 348–55.

———. "The Eighteenth Century Debate on the 'Glorious Revolution'." *History*, LXI (1976), 28–45.

Dunn, John. "The Politics of Locke in England and America in the Eighteenth Century." In *John Locke: Problems and Perspectives*, edited by John W. Yolton. Cambridge: Cambridge University Press, 1969.

Earl, D. W. L. "Procrustean Feudalism: An Interpretative Dilemma in English Historical Narration, 1700–1725." *Historical Journal*, XIX (1976), 33–51.

Gawlick, Günther. "Cicero and the Enlightenment." *Studies on Voltaire and the Eighteenth Century*, XXV (1963), 657–82.

Goldsmith, M. M. "Faction Detected: Ideological Consequences of Robert Walpole's Decline and Fall." *History*, LXIV (1979), 1–19.

———. "Public Virtue and Private Vices: Bernard Mandeville and English Political Ideologies in the Early Eighteenth Century." *Eighteenth-Century Studies*, IX (1976), 477–510.

Hay, Douglas. "Property, Authority and the Criminal Law." In *Albion's Fatal Tree: Crime and Society in Eighteenth-Century England*, edited by

Douglas Hay *et al.* New York: Pantheon, 1975.

Hill, B. W. "Executive Monarchy and the Challenge of Parties, 1689–1832: Two Concepts of Government and Two Historiographical Interpretations." *Historical Journal*, XIII (1970), 379–401.

Johnson, James William. "The Meaning of Augustan." *Journal of the History of Ideas*, XIX (1951), 507–22.

Kelsall, Malcolm. "Augustus and Pope." *Huntington Library Quarterly*, XXXIX (1976), 117–18.

———. "The Meaning of Addison's *Cato*." *Review of English Studies*, New Series, XVII (1966), 149–62.

Kenyon, J. P. "The Revolution of 1688: Resistance and Contract." In *Historical Perspectives: Studies in English Thought and Society in Honour of J. H. Plumb*, edited by Neil McKendrick. London: Europa, 1974.

Kramnick, Issac. "Augustan Politics and English Historiography: The Debate on the English Past, 1730–35." *History and Theory*, VI (1967), 33–56.

Nelson, Jeffrey M. "Ideology in Search of a Context: Eighteenth-Century British Political Thought and the Loyalists of the American Revolution." *Historical Journal*, XX (1977), 741–49.

———. "Unlocking Locke's Legacy: A Comment." *Political Studies*, XXVI (1978), 101–108.

Paglia, Camille A. "Lord Hervey and Pope." *Eighteenth-Century Studies*, VI (1973), 348–71.

Pargellis, Stanley. "The Theory of Balanced Government." In *The Constitution Reconsidered*, edited by Conyers Read. New York: Columbia University Press, 1938.

Pocock, J. G. A. "Burke and the Ancient Constitution—A Problem in the History of Ideas." *Historical Journal*, III (1960), 125–43.

———. "Machiavelli, Harrington, and English Political Ideologies in the Eighteenth Century." *William and Mary Quarterly*, 3rd ser., XXII (1965), 549–83.

Rogers, Pat. "Swift and Bolingbroke on Faction." *Journal of British Studies*, IX (1970), 71–101.

———. "The Waltham Blacks and the Black Act." *Historical Journal*, XVII (1974), 465–86.

Scullard, H. H. "The Political Career of a *Novus Homo*." In *Cicero*, edited by T. A. Dorey. London: Routledge and Paul, 1965.

Skinner, Quentin. "The Principles and Practice of Opposition: The Case of Bolingbroke versus Walpole." In *Historical Perspectives: Stud-*

ies in English Thought and Society in Honour of J. H. Plumb, edited by
Neil McKendrick. London: Europa, 1974.

Ward, Addison. "The Tory View of Roman History." *Studies in English Literature,* IV (1964), 413–56.

Wirszubski, Charles. "Cicero's *Cum Dignitate Otium*: A Reconsideration." *Journal of Roman Studies,* XLIV (1954), 1–13.

Index